MODELING AND SIMULATION BASED SYSTEMS ENGINEERING

Theory and Practice

MODELING AND SIMULATION BASED SYSTEMS ENGINEERING

Theory and Practice

Editors

Lin Zhang
Beihang University, China

Chun Zhao
Beijing Information Science and Technology University, China

World Scientific

NEW JERSEY · LONDON · SINGAPORE · BEIJING · SHANGHAI · HONG KONG · TAIPEI · CHENNAI · TOKYO

Published by

World Scientific Publishing Co. Pte. Ltd.

5 Toh Tuck Link, Singapore 596224

USA office: 27 Warren Street, Suite 401-402, Hackensack, NJ 07601

UK office: 57 Shelton Street, Covent Garden, London WC2H 9HE

British Library Cataloguing-in-Publication Data
A catalogue record for this book is available from the British Library.

MODELING AND SIMULATION BASED SYSTEMS ENGINEERING
Theory and Practice

ISBN 978-981-126-017-9 (hardcover)
ISBN 978-981-126-018-6 (ebook for institutions)
ISBN 978-981-126-019-3 (ebook for individuals)

For any available supplementary material, please visit
https://www.worldscientific.com/worldscibooks/10.1142/12960#t=suppl

Typeset by Stallion Press
Email: enquiries@stallionpress.com

Preface

Model-based Systems Engineering (MBSE) is considered the most important means to achieve innovative design and development of complex products or systems. It emphasizes the role and value of the model and fully embodies the model thinking. MBSE promotes the document-based communication mode in traditional systems engineering to the model-based communication mode, which significantly improves the efficiency of large-scale collaboration between participants and minimizes the ambiguity, misunderstanding and even errors that may occur in communications.

However, for the development of a complex system, getting through the obstacles in personnel communications is not the whole of modeling. How to make full use of formalized models to quickly verify and optimize the system performances, so as to realize the digitalization and intellectualization of the whole process of system R&D, which really brings the maximum value of the model into play.

In recently years, the modeling and simulation (M&S) community has proposed the concept of Modeling and Simulation based Systems Engineering (MSBSE), which deeply integrates M&S technologies into MBSE, making the model in MBSE simulatable, to realize the maximum value of MBSE. MSBSE can break through the time and space constraints, realize repeated trial and error in virtual space, and make the manufacturing or construction of complex products or systems in the real world succeed at one time, which is also consistent with the idea of digital engineering.

The colleagues in the M&S community have started to take actions and make conscious efforts for this work. Many achievements in M&S will provide strong support and references for the research and application of MSBSE, but so far, a complete system of MSBSE technology, including the language, methodology and software tools, has not been established.

This book collects some valuable thoughts and related work on MSBSE from esteemed scholars and researchers, hoping to attract more researchers and practitioners' interest and attention, and provide a basis and reference for the formation of MSBSE technology system.

Editors

Lin Zhang
School of Automation Science and Electrical Engineering
Beihang University, Beijing, P. R. China
zhanglin@buaa.edu.cn

Chun Zhao
School of Computer Science
Beijing Information Science & Technology University
Beijing, P. R. China
zhaochun@bistu.edu.cn

Contents

Chapter 1

Introduction

Lin Zhang[*,‡] and Chun Zhao[†,§]

School of Automation Science and Electrical Engineering
Beihang University, Beijing, P. R. China
†*School of Computer Science*
Beijing Information Science & Technology University
Beijing, P. R. China
‡*zhanglin@buaa.edu.cn*
§*zhaochun@bistu.edu.cn*

A model is an abstract and formalized expression of an object to study and embodies high intelligence of human beings in understanding the world.[1] The importance of models has been paid more and more attention in all walks of life. MBSE (Model-based Systems Engineering) emphasizes the application of models in systems engineering,[2,3] which aims to support activities including requirements, design, analysis, verification and validation in the life cycle of a system by transforming document-based interactions into model-based collaborations, which can significantly improve the efficiency of system development. But this is not enough to overcome the limitations of physical integration and testing in the traditional systems engineering, so as to completely realize the digitalization of the design and development process of a complex product or system. Modeling & simulation (M&S) technology plays an increasingly important role in the design and development of complex products or systems, which can provide a powerful support to solve this problem.

M&S-based Systems Engineering (MSBSE) is the extension of MBSE, which enhances the value of MBSE and the ability of digitally evaluating and optimizing the whole system through comprehensive applications of M&S technology,[4] to help system engineers find errors in system design as early as possible and reduce the cost and shorten the time of system development to the maximum.

MSBSE mainly involves three research domains, they are model engineering, that is, theories and technologies for the whole lifecycle of a model, e.g. construction, management, evaluation and use;[1] languages, methodology and software tools of MSBSE; theories and technologies of M&S for systems engineering. They are also foundations to support digital engineering. For the MSBSE to support the design and development of complex products or systems, there are many challenges,[5] such as:

(1) construction of models: One of the main problems for model construction of a complex system is the lack of unified modeling standards for different domains and mechanisms to guarantee the credibility and quality of models, resulting in a lack of authority in the construction of models at the source and a large number of legacy models are difficult to be integrated.

(2) use of models: The overall system, subsystem, single component/discipline models are difficult to coordinate, and the physical and information systems are difficult to be optimized correlatedly. The model's integratability and reusability are poor, and it is difficult to inherit and evolve the model at different stage of the system's life cycle.

(3) evaluation of models: There is no effective means to evaluate a collaborative and large-scale model and the integrated model of white box, gray box and black box models, which make it difficult to guarantee the credibility of the model and evaluate the simulation results accurately.

(4) management of models: The model management is not systematic, and there is a lack of platforms to support centralized management of decentralized model resources and on-demand use of model resources, which makes it difficult to efficiently share and reuse models.

(5) integrated multidisciplinary modeling and simulation of the whole system: The current methodology based on system modeling languages (such as SysML) have to use other languages or tools (such as Modelica, Simulink, etc.) to achieve the whole system modeling and simulation validation, which makes it difficult to ensure the consistency and traceability of the whole system model parameters.

(6) MSBSE technology system: MSBSE deeply integrates simulation technology, as a result, the MBSE needs to expanded and improved in terms of language, methodology and software tools to form a complete methodology and technology system of MSBSE.

In recent years, researchers have made many valuable achievements in response to the above challenges. This book systematically introduces the most recent advances in theory and practice of MSBSE, which will give substantive guidance to researchers and engineers for their further research and applications and can also help graduate students to study and understand MSBSE.

Chapter 2 discusses the problem of using M&S and AI to enable complex adaptive systems engineering. In the authors opinion, systems engineering needs to evolve to build fast-fielded, resilient, and adaptive systems that leverage positive reinforcement feedback loops with multiple experimental and real-world information sources. The very basis of systems engineering must evolve from today's development paradigms to a future that leverages modeling, simulation, and artificial intelligence to drastically improve the capability and agility for developing new systems.

Chapter 3 gives a review of DEVS (Discrete Event System Specification) in the context of MBSE. The DEVS formalism was developed to constitute a well-founded computational basis for systems theory-based modeling and simulation. DEVS will play an important role in developing the methodology of modeling and simulation based systems engineering. In this chapter, envisioned applications of DEVS methodology to MBSE is discussed. Some example case studies are given.

Chapter 4 introduces a hybrid system modeling framework, XDEVS. XDEVS expands the concept of states in DEVS. The continuous state is introduced in XDEVS, which enhances the ability to model hybrid systems. A simulation engine is developed to drive the XDEVS model safely and efficiently. XDEVS can clearly express the structure of the model and reduce the burden on modelers. XDEVS has been incorporated into the compiler and simulation engine of X language that will be introduced in the next chapter.

Chapter 5 introduces an integrated modeling and simulation language (X Language) to support MSBSE. The X language makes up for the defect that current MBSE modeling languages cannot directly carry out simulation validation. Based on the XDEVS and the design concept of existing modeling languages such as SysML and Modelica, X language can uniformly describe the system-level architecture and physical behavior models as a whole. On this basis, models can be simulated directly to support system validation. X language has two modeling forms, namely graphics and text, and can be converted to each other. Compiler and simulation engine are developed to enable X language to support the simulation of continuous, discrete event, hybrid and agent models.

Chapter 6 proposes a modeling method of algorithm-hardware based on the X language. In this method, X language is used to build the algorithm-hardware models according to the characteristics of hardware algorithms. Then the X language models are converted to the Very-High-Speed Integrated Circuit Hardware Description Language (VHDL). A model of Kalman filter is built with the proposed method. The feasibility of modeling method of algorithm-hardware based on X language is verified.

Chapter 7 proposes a data-driven modeling method with reverse process. Based on the partial least squares (PLS) algorithm and the gray relational analysis (GRA) method, the analysis method of the performance related factors, the extraction method of characteristic variables, and the performance modeling method are studied. The effectiveness of the proposed modeling methods is verified with a case study of an industrial steam turbine.

Chapter 8 develops a real-time model integration approach for global CPS (cyber-physical systems) modeling by reusing developed submodels. A constrained directed graph of submodels is constructed by reverse matching. Submodel properties, including co-simulation distance between submodel nodes, reuse benefit and simulation performance of model nodes, are satisfied. The proposed method is applied to a typical model integrated computing scenario containing multiple model-integration solutions.

Chapter 9 introduces the concept of model maturity. How to build a high-quality model is the first consideration in MBSE or MSBSE. The authors introduce the model maturity to track the status of a model during its life cycle, especially in the use and management phases, which will be an important supplement to the evaluation of model quality. A framework of index system for model maturity evaluation is established. A hierarchical evaluation method based on qualitative and quantitative analysis (HEQQ) for model maturity is proposed. A case study is used to validate the feasibility and effectiveness of the proposed method.

Chapter 10 proposes a task-based collaborative method for an FPGA-based edge computing system to support the collaboration among FPGA-based edge nodes, edge nodes, and the cloud. Authors build four basic behaviors, analyzes the critical attributes of each behavior, and summarizes the task model suitable for FPGA-based edge nodes. Tasks with specific functions can be created by modifying different attributes of model nodes. The model and the task-based collaborative method are verified by simulation experiments.

Chapter 11 proposes a hybrid intelligent dynamic modeling approach to estimate the surface temperature of hypersonic vehicles (HVs) with the combination of mechanism equations, test data and intelligent modeling technology. A simplified model based on a mechanism equation and experimental formulas is presented for predicting or simulating transient heat conduction procedure efficiently, while a case-based reasoning (CBR) algorithm is developed to estimate two uncertain coefficients in the simplified model. A support vector regression (SVR)-based model is developed to compensate the modeling error. Simulations experiments demonstrate the effectiveness of the proposed approach.

Chapter 12 introduces a product development platform based on M&S technologies to realize the agility, collaboration and visualization of alloy material development process. In this platform, the whole-process simulation module builds multi-level simulation models based on metallurgical mechanisms. The design knowledge management module represents the multi-source heterogeneous material design knowledge through ontology model. The data-driven modeling module applies machine learning algorithms to mine the relationships between product mechanical properties, material components, and process parameters. Application in actual steel mills shows that the platform can improve the efficiency of product design process.

Chapter 13 focuses on the validation of models with uncertainties. A new method is proposed to validate the dynamic responses of the models over the time domain through introducing the discrete Chebyshev polynomials and area metric. For each time series, the orthogonal expansion coefficients are extracted by representing the time series with the discrete orthogonal polynomials. Then, the area metric and the u-pooling metric are employed to validate all the uncorrelated coefficients at a single validation site and multiple validation sites respectively, and the final validation result is obtained by summarizing the metric values. The feasibility and effectiveness of the proposed method are demonstrated through the example of the terminal guidance stage of a flight vehicle.

Chapter 14 proposes a mixed reality simulation evaluation method to realize the real-time ergonomic evaluation of the digital human body followed by a real person, and support multi-scheme comparison and rapid iteration in the early stage of civil aircraft design. Authors take the civil aircraft cockpit as an example, and establish the cockpit physical environment and the corresponding virtual cockpit environment based on the virtual-real matching technology. Experimental results show that the proposed method can effectively improve the evaluation accuracy of cockpit design.

References

1. L. Zhang, Y.W. Shen, X.S. Zhang, *et al.* The model engineering for complex system simulation, Proceedings of the I3M Multiconference, SEPTEMBER 10-12, 2014, Bordeaux, France.
2. A. W. Wymore. Model-Based Systems Engineering. Series on Systems Engineering, Vol. 3., CRC Press, 1993, Boca Raton, FL.
3. J. A. Estefan. Survey of Model-Based Systems Engineering (MBSE) Methodologies. International Council on Systems Engineering, 2008, San Diego, CA.
4. D. Gianni, A. D'Ambrogio, A. Tolk. Modeling and Simulation-Based Systems Engineering Handbook, Taylors & Francis Group, 2014.
5. L. Zhang, K.Y. Wang, Y.J. Laili, *et al.* Modeling & Simulation based System of Systems Engineering (in Chinese), Journal of System Simulation, July 2021.

Chapter 2

Using modeling and simulation and artificial intelligence to improve complex adaptive systems engineering

Andreas Tolk[*,§], Philip Barry[†,¶] and Steven C. Doskey[‡,∥]

*The MITRE Corporation, 1001 Research Park Blvd #220
Charlottesville, VA 22911, USA

†George Mason University, 4400 University Dr, Fairfax
VA 22030, USA

‡The MITRE Corporation, 7525 Colshire Dr, McLean
VA 22102, USA

§atolk@mitre.org
¶pbarry@gmu.edu
∥sdoskey@mitre.org

Abstract

Designing components that provide required functionality and recommending architectures allowing for their composition are recognized objectives of systems engineering. Design ensures that constituent components work together and provide their requisite functionality. Architectures, as frameworks, encapsulate these components into a system, or systems of systems, to reach a common goal. Traditionally, design and architecture were mostly static as systems were architected and designed early in the systems engineering lifecycle and held constant through development and operation. Over the recent decades, the concept of complex adaptive systems has become common place in several domains, such as the Internet of Things, Industry 4.0, or Cyber Physical Systems. These complex adaptive systems, unlike their predecessors, are no longer static but can evolve throughout development and adapt during the operations phase. Further, each component can be adaptive, quickly changing, updated, and reconfigured throughout the systems engineering lifecycle. As such, design is no longer a phase, but a continuum across the lifecycle, e.g., a continuous process. The dynamics are true for architecture, as it has evolved into a flexible framework that is not only used to bring components together, but to ensure that data are aligned, and processes are harmonized when components are selected and arranged to fulfil new tasks throughout the systems operation. This positions operating as the third leg of systems engineering, leading to the three categories of:

(1) Designing (pivoting to digital engineering and digital twins to ensure functional performance);

(2) Architecting (including executable architectures that evolve to ensure operational effectiveness); and

---

*Corresponding author.

(3) Operating (allowing composition, reconfiguration, adaptation to ensure operational agility).

Such an enhanced view on systems engineering can only be reached by extending systems engineering to include tools developed in collaboration with complexity science, artificial intelligence, and modeling and simulation. Complexity science will allow us to understand the system as a whole, including functionality emerging from relations between components when they are composed into accidental collectives or purposeful ensembles. Artificial intelligence will provide the means needed to identify endogenous or exogenous requirements for self-modification and self-organization of components, the computational creativity needed to compose such self-modified components into new systems, and the reasoning capability to select the most feasible composition. Finally, modeling and simulation will provide the foundation for conceptualization, exploration of the possibility space, and execution, from digital twins within executable architectures to trade-off support even under deep uncertainty.

1. Introduction

Designing components that provide the required functionality and recommending architectures to enable their composition has been a traditional objective of systems engineering (SE). Design practices evolved to ensure that constituent components work together and provide their requisite functionality. Architectures, as frameworks, described how these components could be integrated into a system or system of systems. Typically, design and architecture were mostly statically developed early in the SE life cycle and held constant through development and operation.

This began to change as complex adaptive systems (CASs) became commonplace in domains such as the Internet of Things, Industry 4.0, and Cyber Physical Systems. CASs, unlike their predecessors, are not static but can evolve throughout the development and adapt during the operations phase. Each component can quickly change, be updated, and be reconfigured throughout the system's engineering life cycle. As a result, design is no longer a discrete phase at the beginning of the life cycle but a continuum across the lifecycle. The same dynamics hold for architecture. Modern architecture is a flexible framework that is used not only to bring components together but also to ensure that data continue to be aligned. This allows processes to be harmonized, thus allowing the selection and arrangement of agile components to fulfil new tasks throughout the system's operation.

The recognition of the continuous nature of architecture and design has led to three categories of SE activities:

(1) **Designing**, with a focus on ensuring functional performance of the engineered system.
(2) **Architecting**, with a focus on ensuring operational effectiveness by providing integration guides for system components and increasingly for systems into portfolios or systems of systems.
(3) **Operating**, with a focus on ensuring operational agility through reconfiguration and high-performance interoperability.

The ability to continually change the landscape of design and architecture can only be achieved by extending the SE with tools developed in collaboration with complexity science, artificial intelligence (AI), and modeling and simulation (M&S). Complexity science can facilitate a holistic understanding of the system, including functionality emerging from relations between components when they are composed into accidental collectives or purposeful ensembles (an ensemble is a designed composition, a collective is a composition that emerged). AI provides the means needed to identify endogenous or exogenous requirements for self-modification and self-organization of components, the computational creativity needed to compose such self-modified components into new systems, and the reasoning capability to select the most feasible composition. Finally, M&S can provide the foundation for conceptualization, exploration of the possibility space, and execution.

The M&S-based SE (MSBSE) is a logical venue for this chapter which proposes a common way forward. Our proposed solution is neither meant to take away from the accomplishments of any focused partial solution in the various fields, nor as it was intended to criticize shortfalls of current SE approaches. Our proposed solution extends the idea of MSBSE as it was featured in a handbook by Gianni et al.,[1] mainly from the perspective of simulation experts. The focus of this paper is improving SE, so the focus is on engineered systems. To better place the contributions into a broader context, this paper will first present the changing landscape of systems that required the change of SE as well. It then will extend the view even further to complexity science before looking at the contributions that AI and simulation can provide before bringing the components together into a new solution. The notion of digital twins will be important in this context, but the use will be expended beyond its current understanding, making it a central piece of the common way forward.

2. The Changing Landscape of Systems

According to Sillitto et al.[2]

> a **system** is an *arrangement of parts or elements that together exhibit behavior or meaning that the individual constituents do not.* More specifically, an **engineered system** is a *system designed or adapted to interact with an anticipated operational environment to achieve one or more intended purposes while complying with applicable constraints.*

A system has clear borders with the environment it interacts with, and users of the system are usually seen as part of this environment. Buede and Miller suggest the definition of external systems that interact with the system of interest across their borders, providing and receiving inputs. Additional input can be received from the context.[3] In contrast to the external systems, this context does not receive inputs from the system. In traditional SE, understanding the system's border is one of the most important tasks when designing the system.

Aside from having a clear delimitation, the traditional view also assumes that systems are designed, are built, and then operate within their design parameters. There is the option of implementing changes during maintenance, but these changes are typically minimal. While a component may be replaced by a newer generation, the principle set of functions a system provides to its users and the interfaces to external systems remains static and well defined.

These views have changed considering the increasing use of information technology (IT) and the dependence of systems on IT support. While mechanical components are relatively hard to replace, changing the firmware or software of a supporting computer element or adding additional computational functionality is easier. System functionality can easily be adapted to generate alternative desired behaviors. Software can be updated and even replaced on the fly.

The increasing reliance on IT has also resulted in the blurring of what were once clear borders. While the physical structure of mechanical components clearly identifies where one component ends and another one begins, the borders of IT components are often more logical than physical. For example, the information stored in a distributed database can be physically distributed over many supporting and participating IT components that are not part of the system itself. The borders between the components as well as the borders between systems have become fluid, particularly with the pervasiveness of cloud and fog computing.

At the same time, a new form of collaboration between systems has become possible. IT allowed a group of systems to solve problems together more easily by using standardized communication protocols. Different systems that had previously been used to conduct different tasks now had to be interwoven in a deliberate and *a priori* fashion to solve a common problem. With standardized protocols for communication at the physical, syntactic, and semantic levels, it has become possible to create such interwoven groups on the fly from subsystems that were never intended to provide the aggregate capability.

Creating interwoven groups on the fly is an illustration of system of systems. A System of Systems is made up of components, which are systems themselves. Individual systems are composed to reach a common objective, but each system has its own independent function as well. Maier[4] observes that the participating systems are operationally and managerially independent, requiring operational control and management for their original purpose. They may be geographically distributed, and the systems may evolve by themselves. However, as the functions are interconnected to provide a new set of capabilities which are needed to reach the common objective, the systems are no longer entirely independent from an aggregate system view. Furthermore, the interplay between the individual systems can result in emergent behavior at the system of systems level that can neither be accomplished by any of the individual systems nor be explained by analyzing the individual systems themselves. These emergent behaviors can happen by design or they can be unintended.

Almost in parallel with the rise of logically based systems of systems, individual systems have become much more adaptive. Adaptive systems observe their situated environment and decide on their actions based on their rule sets. In addition to using the situation to trigger actions, they also observe the results of their actions and assess whether the actions are having the desired effect. Architects and software engineers are now creating software based on observing the intended and unintended effects of decisions, applying learning algorithms as used for software agents, as examples in recent publications show.[5] The results are systems that are complex, adaptive, intelligent, and often even autonomous, as discussed among others by Mittal and Tolk.[6] Our focus in the reminder of this paper will be on systems that are complex and adaptive, including options for self-configuration, self-modification, and self-organizations.

3. The Changing Landscape of Systems Engineering

While some system designs adhere to older design paradigms, many systems (or composable services) have fluid borders and evolving requirements throughout their life cycle. Traditional SE assumes that a system has a defined life cycle, evolves over many versions, and is eventually retired. While this approach may be valid for some systems, a newer model of a system has emerged in which the need for new services to be delivered by the system arises quickly and then diminishes. In fact, a system can be a collection of *ad hoc* services. The natural consequence is that the idea of a system as a well-defined and deterministic collection of components needs to be revised.

The practice of SE has been evolving over many years to provide a methodology for building ever more complicated systems as shown in Fig. 1.[7] The foundation of this approach has been a well-defined set of discrete steps with associated activities. While organized and labeled differently, forms of the following activities can be found in most system development models.

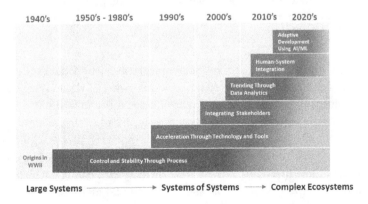

Fig. 1.   Systems engineering evolution.

- **Concept Development** — A set of activities that are carried out early in the system's engineering life cycle to collect and prioritize operational needs and challenges, develop alternative concepts to meet the needs, and select a preferred concept as the basis for subsequent system or capability development and implementation.[8]
- **Requirements Engineering** — The process of defining, documenting, and maintaining system needs as formal requirements in the engineering design process.[9]
- **System Architecture** — The conceptual model defines the structure, behavior, and additional views of a system. An architecture description is a formal description and representation of a system, organized in a way that supports reasoning about the structures and behaviors of the system.[10]
- **System Design and Development** — System design is the process of defining the components, modules, interfaces, and data for a system to satisfy specified requirements. System development is the process of creating or altering systems, along with the processes, practices, models, and methodologies used to develop them.[8]
- **System Integration** — The process of bringing together the component subsystems into one system (an aggregation of subsystems cooperating so that the system can deliver the overarching functionality) and ensuring that the subsystems function together as a system and in IT as the process of linking together different computing systems and software applications physically or functionally to act as a coordinated whole.[11]
- **Test and Evaluation** — The process by which a system or components are compared against requirements and specifications through testing. The results are evaluated to assess progress of design, performance, supportability, and more. Developmental test and evaluation (DT&E) is an engineering tool used to reduce risk throughout the acquisition cycle. Operational test and evaluation (OT&E) is the actual or simulated employment, by typical users, of a system under realistic operational conditions.
- **Transition Operation and Maintenance** — The point in a system's life cycle when it moves from the development phase to the manufacturing, fielding, or sustainment phase.[8]

Beginning with the introduction of the spiral model by Boehm in 1986, it has been generally acknowledged that trying to conduct any of the major activities in a system's engineering development cycle once is generally unrealistic due to changing requirements and technology. The dynamic nature of environmental factors and the unstructured nature of the systems being developed required a significant evolution in methodologies and tools for SE in the future. They also led to agile methods designed to maximize speed and flexibility in dealing with change, which was particularly important for large systems of systems which had many necessary concurrent systems that were evolving. Furthermore, as the scope of developed systems became ever larger, it became impossible for engineers to fully understand the status of the system development effort at a given checkpoint.

The recognition of the inadequacy of traditional engineering methodologies led to the development of the scaled agile framework (SAFe), which is based on the four tenets of continuous exploration, continuous integration, continuous deployment, and release on demand. Typically, this is done in a series of iterations that are designed to deliver increments of capability. Each of these iterations is done in a relatively short time, often in a matter of days. The traditional SE activities are still done, just with much less formal documentation and by functional increments as opposed to working on the entire system all at once. The continuous-development–continuous-integration nature of SAFe integrates well with the DevOps methodology, which aligns software development and IT operations to shorten system development time and to reduce integration and deployment risk.[11]

Complementing the advances in methodologies, digital tools have become prevalent, flexible, and useful in designing large-scale systems. To avoid the trap of many different proprietary languages and methodologies built around digital tools, model-based systems engineering (MBSE) allows for system definitions to be developed in an agreed upon language, such as the Systems Modeling Language (SysML) — and graphical representation. The MBSE development approach places models at the center of system development activity. MBSE has proven to be a valuable tool in documenting and analyzing the design and development of complex systems.

Use of MBSE has become standard practice for formalizing the use of models in requirement elicitation, trade studies, design, analysis, and verification and validation (V&V) activities throughout a system's life cycle. MBSE provides greater rigor and effectiveness in the development of complex systems; it detects and corrects defects early and can be used to manage complexity, maintain consistency, and assure traceability during system development. MBSE also facilitates the concurrent execution of life cycle activities and potentially accelerating system development.

MBSE differs from model-based engineering (MBE). While MBSE still focuses on a particular system under development using models, MBE looks at systems in their context and portfolio. To this end, MBE models are predominantly "system relationship models" and are useful for showing relationships among system functions, requirements, developers, and users. MBE uses digital models to represent systems and services in concept, design, development, tests, and operations. Digital twins are a form of MBE in which a physical twin is connected to a virtual twin through sensors so that the digital twin contains all the information that can be used to monitor and improve the physical counterpart in real time and through longitudinal analysis of data.

Both MBSE and MBE are contained in digital engineering (DE), an integrated digital approach that uses authoritative sources of system data and models as a continuum across disciplines to support life cycle activities from concept to disposal.

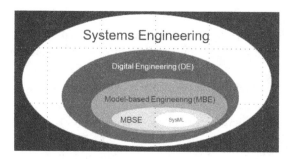

Fig. 2.   Model relationships.

DE incorporates the creation of computer readable models to represent all aspects of the system and to support all the activities for the design, development, manufacture, and operation of the system throughout its life cycle. These computer models share a common data scheme so that in effect a digital thread integrates diverse stakeholders across the life of a service. Figure 2 illustrates the relationships between MBSE, MBE, DE, and SE. They also address the often criticized ambiguity of SysML, as ambiguities must be resolved in the process of building such computer models, using well-defined and verifiable steps leading from the SysML specification to an executable model, like the early ideas of Mittal,[12] although not applying simulation-specific formalisms.

The move to DE and knowledge sharing across portfolios and platforms has been accelerated by cloud-based platforms that provision and manage custom SE collaboration environments. These environments allow SE teams developing CASs to quickly generate new environments, archive, and restore old environments, accommodate development threads, perform multiple types of testing in parallel, and perform V&V efforts.

4. Complexity Science, AI, and M&S Methods to Address the New Challenges

DE and its components of MBE and MBSE provide the tools to address some of the challenges in the emerging landscape of the new class of systems discussed above. However, these tools are not sufficient to move SE to the next level to intentionally design and operate CASs. To do that, SE will need to integrate, adopt, and develop tools and techniques from complexity theory, AI, and M&S.

4.1. *Complexity science*

Complex systems theory's lineage traces back to the 1950s ideas on cybernetics, like Norbert Wiener's[39] work on cybernetics mathematics and W. Ross Ashby's[40] publication on cybernetics of mind. They also are rooted deeply in system science, which traces back even further.

4.1.1. *Complexity science definitions*

Two of the leaders in complexity research are the Santa Fe Institute and the New England Complex Systems Institute. The Santa Fe Institute observes the following.

> Complexity arises in any system in which many agents interact and adapt to one another and their environments.... As individual agents interact and adapt within these systems, evolutionary processes and often surprising "emergent" behaviors arise at the macro level. Complexity science attempts to find common mechanisms that lead to complexity in nominally distinct physical, biological, social, and technological systems.[13]

The New England Complex Systems Institute's use of the term is similar.

> Complex systems is a new field of science studying how parts of a system give rise to the collective behaviors of the system and how the system interacts with its environment.... The field of complex systems cuts across all traditional disciplines of science, as well as engineering, management, and medicine. It focuses on certain questions about parts, wholes, and relationships.[14]

Understanding complexity and emergent behavior is essential when considering design options, testing requirements, and the definition of acceptable operational envelopes. As systems become larger and the borders between a system and its environment become blurry, emergent behavior is likely to develop. Traditional SE, while recognizing the need to identify and measure emergent behavior, does not have the tools to model and explore emergence.

4.1.2. *The rise of complex systems*

Complex systems and complexity science began with linear approximations of relations between system components that were predictable and easy to engineer. This simple approach showed great utility as even nonlinear relations could be approximated using linear relations if the predictions were relatively short term and short distance related. Furthermore, the systems being designed could be understood through first principles and reductionism; by understanding the components, the system could be understood as well. The system behavior is congruent with the developers' design; engineering and governing the system are simple tasks.

As systems became more complicated, it became apparent that the behavior of groups of components was nonlinear. Consequently, linear approximations were no longer adequate. This was particularly stark as the time and scope of the system operations were extended. While complicated systems can still be *partially* understood using the principles of reductionism, it is becoming necessary to look at the system holistically as well. Information was carried not only by the components but also often by its nonlinear relations between components. Behavior was still predictable, but increasingly sophisticated tools were needed to be able to understand, engineer, and govern systems. Among others, the work of Holland[15,16] provides a wider view of complex adaptive systems as they are observed in nature, in social systems, but also in engineering. It is the latter group of engineered systems that is in the focus of this paper, although research results from other systems are often helpful.

Complex systems constitute a new class of systems which are distinct from complicated systems and which cannot be understood by reductionism. Complicated systems, while composed of many components, are principally predictable, whereas complex systems generally are not. Complex systems' behaviors, while not predictable, may be explainable using holistic and systemic complex system science methods. It has become necessary to leverage advances in the scientific understanding of complexity to better evaluate the effects of emergence and to provide the capability to construct and engineer complex systems.

4.1.3. *Emergence and collective behavior*

Emergence is not solely a characteristic of a system but more a relationship between an observer, the models he uses to explain things, and his observations. If an observation does not match the expectation based on the model, it is a surprise, an "emerging" property.[17] But if a property is surprising, it is often the result of the experience of the observer. As Rouse observes, what is surprising for a layman or novice may be immediately obvious to an expert.[18]

Emergent properties can only be explained once observed, which presents a challenge for SE. The challenge for systems engineers is to understand and, preferably, model likely emergence before the system is operational and, ideally, even before it is built. If emergence is positive, systems engineers want to take advantage of it, harness it, and preferably be able to make it happen again. However, if the emergence is negative, steps may be taken to avoid it. In any case, detecting, understanding, and managing emergence is a common goal.

4.2. *Artificial intelligence*

In the discussion so far, it has been asserted that the scale of systems and the fluid nature of their architectural, design, and implementation components make it difficult if not impossible to use traditional SE tools to understand those components and their complex interactions. AI may provide the means to address these challenges. AI can be used to identify endogenous or exogenous requirements for self-modification and self-organization of components, the computational creativity needed to compose such self-modified components into new systems, and the reasoning capability to select the most feasible composition.

Consider how systems engineers conceptualize a system's capability with a general set of requirements or system needs. There are often a myriad of ways of defining a system to satisfy them, which constitutes a combinatorial optimization problem. Consequently, there are also numerous possible compositions for architecting, designing, and operating a system. This problem can be viewed as an exploration of the multidimensional space to find optimal configurations, where the parameters of the space describe the architecture, the design, or the operational parameters. Typically, the number of possible compositions will be quite large. So, to make the design space exploration feasible, the challenge is to generate sufficiently many compositions to effectively explore the domain space while focusing on the feasible, not the merely possible.

This problem becomes more challenging as the components under consideration may be dynamic; an exact accounting of the availability of a given component in the future may be impossible due to changing environmental conditions. This increases the risk for a successful architecture or design, as the individual behaviors of components may be unknown, particularly if some components have been developed outside of the enterprise. Further, as discussed above, the interactions between the components may lead to unanticipated emergent effects.

The sheer combinatorial and stochastic behavior of complex systems requires additional tools and approaches to ensure predictable and acceptable functionality. MBSE has provided a digital foundation to enable the computational exploration and evaluation. AI can provide a mechanism to create potential architectures, evaluate them in a simulation environment, and recommend specific architectures and designs as well as derived architecture and design tenets.

4.2.1. *Combinational, exploratory, and transformational creativity*

AI can provide an approach to explore the possible set of feasible designs and identify the desirable ones. To enable this, SE will need to borrow from computational creativity. Boden[19] suggests that there are several forms of computational creativity. The first is a combinational creativity which works by creating links between ideas that were previously not directly linked. In the context of the current discussion, combinational creativity can be envisioned as an application of AI that pools from a set of existing components and combines them in a way that is new but consistent with loosely defined domain constraints. To avoid the combinatorial explosion that random connections can make, AI must be cognizant of relevant constraints but technically and environmentally informed to identify feasible connections. A type of combinational creativity known as similarity-driven combinational creativity suggests the use of templated knowledge and analogical reasoning that may reduce the combinatorial explosion and enable AI to quickly dismiss nonsensical combinations.

Exploratory creativity as defined by Boden[19] is based on a common understanding or theory of the domain. The domain space is both specified as well as constrained such that structures created will fit the rules. The rule set which defines and constrains the domain space is often implicit. To profitably explore the space and generate acceptable architectures and designs, AI must have a computationally meaningful understanding of both what these rules and constraints are and how to apply them. This differs from combinational creativity, which has a much looser set of rules and may result in unfeasible architectures and designs. Exploratory creativity can be enabled by the models, and the knowledge encapsulated in MBSE is then realized in simulation, which will be discussed later.

Transformational creativity is perhaps the most intriguing and challenging type of computational creativity as it relaxes or even removes some of the constraints described above. In essence, AI can engage in a form of counterfactual reasoning. Pearl[20] describes counterfactual reasoning as a three-step process. First, explain the past given current evidence. Second, modify one of the factors in the past situation. Third, predict the future, given the understanding of the past and the introduction of the new condition.

In the context of transformational creativity, AIs will use an existing model or may even create a model of a possible architecture and then evaluate it. As part of the modeling effort, AI will create a causal dependency model to explain primary factors in the architecture and their likely instantiations, given the established architectural and design guidance. In the spirit of counterfactual reasoning, AI would investigate what would happen if the constraint set were to change. The analysis process would take the form of the creation of a simulation with alternate constraints, and the subsequent model runs. This approach is described in more detail in Sec. 4.3. While intriguing, transformational creativity remains an elusive goal, as agreed upon implementations of counterfactual reasoning are an area of active research.

4.2.2. *Evaluation*

As Linus Pauling famously said, "The way to get good ideas is to get lots of ideas and throw the bad ones away." Even with the active recognition of the constraint space and the domain's associated rules, it is entirely likely that there is a very real potential for generating many possible combinations of architectures, designs, and implementations. Evaluating each of these possible combinations of components in any meaningful way is likely unfeasible due to the computational cost and the large number of parameters.

AI provides an alternate approach to this brute force evaluation. One can view the problem of identifying viable designs, architectures, and implementations as a search for an optimum through a $m \times n$ dimensional space, where m is the number of components and n is the number of connections between these components. $m \times n$ can be represented as a directed graph where n represents any transmittal of matter, information, or energy between two components. Evaluating the population of directed graphs becomes an exercise in determining the maximum utility of a given design on a multi-dimensional surface that represents the operational environment. The utility calculations can be based on evaluating the results of specific models and simulations that instantiate the directed graphs against one or more measures of effectiveness in a simulated environment.

The search of large combinatorial spaces is a classic AI problem. In general, there are two types of searches: Uninformed and informed.[21] Uninformed searches have no extra information available to them. A uniformed search attempts to determine the path that is promising and will likely not use any mechanism for optimization. Typically, an uninformed search employs techniques such as breadth-first search, depth-first search, iterative deepening, and bi-directional search.

An informed search, on the other hand, has additional information that would aid in identifying the best candidates. As an example, consider a genetic algorithm that searches the $m \times n$ space and evaluates how well the configurations do in simulation space. Additional information is provided to reward sub-designs that have been successful in the past and penalize the sub-designs that have been proven to be ineffective in the form of a reward function with the genetic algorithm. The reward function would provide additional information to potentially accelerate the search as well as look for an optimal solution.

4.3. *Modeling and simulation*

Simulation is widely recognized as a computational tool that helps generate numerical insights into the dynamics of a modeled system. However, it is the model behind the simulation that provides the real epistemological value. Modeling is the task-driven simplification and abstraction of what we know about the system of interest, resulting in a conceptualization that becomes not only the foundation of our implementation but also the model used to explain things, as mentioned in Sec. 4.1.2. Modeling is a systemic part of SE and the essence of capturing our knowledge.

Simulations have too often been developed in a parallel effort, in which software engineers were trusted with the conceptualization task as part of the simulation development. Instead, the conceptualization should be not only well aligned but, optimally, also derived directly from the SE work.[22] SE has started to move in this direction with the increased use of DE and digital twins.[23] As DE becomes prolific, simulation has the potential to become an executable body of knowledge.

Integrating the artifacts of DE in all phases of the system life cycle into a realistic testbed is the logical next step, as the digital twin-like artifacts can take on the role of an agent, so that early testing of the system concepts becomes feasible. Examples are the testing of rule sets for autonomous systems before testing them in real-world settings, including scenarios that are too dangerous or too expensive, or the testing of systems' performance within the portfolio, even if none of the systems is implemented yet. Agent-based approaches are a proven tool in the study of complex systems; they can provide insights into interacting components and stakeholders, as frequently seen at the Santa Fe Institute and the New England Complex Systems Institute.

Another aspect of simulation is that it provides approximations for complex system descriptions that have no closed analytic solution. While the application of statistical methods often leads to sufficient results, statistical methods assume that the random variables are independent and identically distributed. By applying the central limit theorem, simulationists often assume that the variables under examination are normally distributed. However, complex systems likely will not follow such constraints. With many diverse components with strong interdependencies, closed analytic solutions are very challenging and not representative of the actual phenomenology. This is particularly acute when the system is adaptive and constantly changing.

The systems under discussion are complex, consisting of a number of components, and possibly changing their configuration dynamically. Consequently, an accurate model of the system under development, as well as the current and future environments of operation, is essential for analysis. This analysis is perpetual, meaning that throughout the development phases and into operation, there is a continual analysis of both the current technical path and the set of possibilities as balanced against a set of measures of effectiveness.

As alluded to above, deciding how to configure and run simulations is nontrivial. While evolutionary algorithms or some other optimization will identify a set of architectures or designs, it is still necessary to design the experiment to explore ranges of parameters, runtimes for simulations, and the behaviors of the other entities within the simulation. Consequently, the simulation environment as well as the process of setting up and running the simulations must evolve with both the external environment as it changes; they must also evolve into an environment with higher fidelity as the design becomes more detailed.

AI can be used to identify the necessary changes in the simulation environment as well as the design of the experiment. AI can take the form of a knowledge-based forecasting agent that will partner with the systems engineers to present results of simulation-based forecasting, accepting changes to both the simulation as well as the analysis of the results, and continue to home in on better forecasting. AI can be used for the continual integration of the simulation environment and the system being developed to ensure tight coupling of the virtual and real systems to ensure accurate simulation results.

As the methodology becomes better defined, many models will perform better than a single model. James Surowiecki wrote *The Wisdom of the Crowds* (2005),[24] where he pointed out that many evaluators, even if they are relatively unskilled, will do better than one or a few. As there are so many variables in both the design as well as the environment, exploring counterfactuals with one simulation rapidly becomes intractable. Using a "wisdom of the crowds" approach, where many simulations are concurrently run for a given perpetual forecast and the results are aggregated, is likely to produce a better result. Knowledge-based AI agents can assist SE in designing the experiments, evaluating the specific results, and then aggregating across the simulation results for a composite forecast.

Of particular interest in forecasting the potential for "black swan" events, Taleb[25] defined a black swan event as having three characteristics:

- It is an outlier, as it lies outside the realm of regular expectations, because nothing in the past can convincingly point to its possibility.
- It carries an extreme 'impact'.
- Despite its outlier status, human nature makes us concoct explanations for its occurrence after the fact, making it explainable and predictable.

Perpetual forecasting with many agents and many simulations, with thoughtful design of experiments, and potential counterfactual reasoning can provide a data-driven approach to identify problem areas early. Intelligent agents can, as before, structure the simulation runs and aggregate the data, highlight potential black swans, and propose possible architectural or design changes to reduce the risk.

5. Bringing Designing, Architecting, and Operating Together

5.1. *A new systems engineering approach*

The first steps to tie the different aspects of SE, complexity science, AI, and M&S together into a conceptually aligned framework to support complex adaptive SE have been defined and are currently being applied. The use of M&S methods in support of CASs has been the topic of several tracks in recent simulation conferences as well as in several publications (see Ref. 6). The advantages of using synthetic situated environments to provide development and test support for CASs has been shown to have great promise.

Similarly, the use of digital twin technology has been recognized widely. Madni and Sievers[26] show how the use of digital twins in parallel to the application of their physical twins is advantageous for agile adjustments and recommendation of operations and even for preventive maintenance. However, although they recommend a tight alignment of the digital twin with the model-based tool and other SE tools, they mainly focus on collecting real-life data (such as performance, health, and maintenance) collected by the physical twin as the basis for their insights. Figure 3 illustrates the current state of the art in digital twin use. As seen in the figure, the digital twin is placed inside of the well-known V of SE, is developed in the course of design and architecture, and is then used for optimization, as discussed by Madni and Sievers,[26] once the physical system is in operation.

The evolution of SE for complex adaptive SE builds on and extends these approaches. First, it is essential that SE tools not only have to be aligned with the digital twin but also be the source from which the physical systems are built and the digital twin is created. A specification sufficient to build a system should also be sufficient to define its digital counterpart. Second, not only is the digital twin constructed in parallel and then used to more effectively exploit real-world data to optimize the operation but also the digital twin becomes the centerpiece of the new design-architect-operate principle, as each insight is used to revisit the development cycle again.

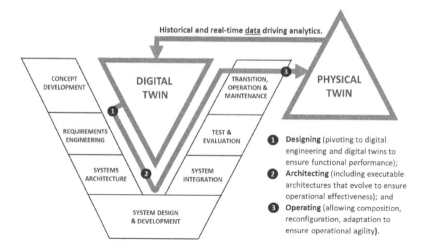

Fig. 3.   State-of-the-art view on digital twin applications.

In the design, architecting, and implementation of complex systems, it is frequently necessary to adapt the initial concepts, integrate new requirements, and change the system architecture. To support this, the third extension embeds the digital twin into a synthetic situated environment, in the same way that it is used for M&S support of complex systems, such as described by Mittal and Tolk.[6] The digital twin no longer merely represents the system; it becomes an agent in the context of its operational environment. The environment is instantiated using the real-world data, historical as well as currently observed by the physical system, but also subjecting the digital twin to unobserved but nonetheless possible situations. This allows for the use of complexity science methods to understand the system, as well as the system in its context, better. In addition, as all data are available, it also allows the identified AI methods to evaluate and analyze alternative configurations, new components, and even improvements to the architecture by allowing a quicker reconfiguration or replacement of components.

The fourth extension investigates the portfolio in which the system operates or the system of systems it becomes part of. If the framework recommended here is applied for all participating systems, each of them comes with a high-resolution, realistically operating digital twin. This allows the application of AI methods to optimize the behavior within the portfolio and the guidelines for the overall portfolio behavior. Figure 4 illustrates these extensions.

In summary, the digital twin is realized from the SE tools as a high-resolution, realistic digital representation of the real system and becomes the centerpiece of the ongoing cycle of designing, architecting, and operation. The digital twin is placed together with representations of other systems of the portfolio into a common synthetic situated environment instantiated by real-world data but open for configuration to represent all possible situations of interest. AI and complexity science tools

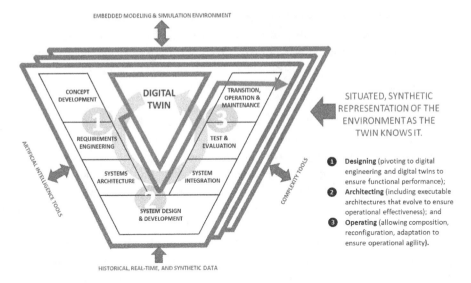

Fig. 4.   Designing, architecting, and operating systems engineering.

are applied for analysis and evaluation and as such are becoming part of the SE tool set needed for CAS engineering.

5.2. *Examples*

Consider the use of digital twin technology and state-of-the-art forecasting models in support of modern data centers. As DeLong and Tolk[27] have observed, U.S. data centers use more than 90 billion kilowatt-hours of electricity a year, and trends showed the need for even more data centers in the future. This insight triggered ongoing research to make data centers more sustainable, and Masanet *et al.*[28] presented a study showing that, indeed, the consequent application of green technology supported this positive development. Some of the green technology discovered in the literature survey looked at hardware solutions; others recommended organizational methods, such as the use of plastic curtains between computers to allow for more efficient air condition. Of particular interest was the development of common metrics and models for energy consumption prediction[29] that were applied to allow for preventative means. The survey also showed the use of digital twins for the planning and operation of new data centers, ensuring that computational loads were distributed in the most efficient way, led to sustainable data center design. Other efforts looked at reconfigurable solutions so that the data center could be modified based on current needs. All these contributions are valuable elements that can be aligned under the proposed framework for CAS engineering, potentially contributing to the increased sustainability needed to offset future data center needs.

The second example is the use of digital twins to improve air traffic control at airports. Academia and industry are actively researching the use of digital twins to analyze and improve safety and performance of traditional aircraft and new entrants such as unmanned aircraft systems (UAS) and urban air mobility (UAM) in preparation for a proliferation of drone taxis and UAS package delivery systems in urban areas.[30] For example, companies such as Deloitte, McLaren, and Airservices are working together to develop digital twins of the environments surrounding airports.[31]

Interestingly, the aircraft "black box" is two orange boxes, one for voice and one for data with over 80 data elements that are continually captured in the data recorder. One envisioned future involves the idea of a fully connected aircraft, where this a type of information that will be provided nearly in real time to terrestrial analysis centers and air traffic control facilities. In addition to using this wealth of aircraft information, a common feature of many proposed digital twins is the addition of an operating environment which includes aircraft, weather, and human–machine systems — as well as their interactions. The value of this expansion of the digital twin is that it allows for the reproduction of a multitude of scenarios related to critical situations in the transport network that require the involvement of a centralized control system trained using machine learning to improve the flow of air traffic.[32] In essence, the inclusion of digital twins as an element of the control system can increase the system stability and resilience in addition to improving performance.[33]

6. Conclusion and Discussion

SE traditionally focuses on designing systems and providing architectures to allow for their composition as well as their integration into a preconceived portfolio. The developments over the recent years require more adaptable and flexible systems that can be combined with a multitude of other systems to provide their functionality in a new, often unforeseen context. This requires supporting the operating phase with much more than just maintenance and updates. Design and architectural elements got interwoven with the operating elements, leading to the proposed SE approach.

This new approach is supported by methods developed in the SE, complexity science, AI, and M&S domains. The resulting tools are based on a common conceptual understanding that allows their technical coordination, enabled by conceptual alignment. We showed the applicability of these ideas by giving examples, where important elements of the new SE approach already are applied. Without digital twins, AI, and simulation, several decisions in design, architecture, and operating would not be feasible. The use of computational means not only provides the means to look at more options but also addresses the need to unambiguously allow for trade-offs or exploration of the solution space when using AI and other computational means that lead to better metrics for capturing measures of merits.

This new approach suggests several research areas for future solutions. The synthetic situated environment offers an opportunity to evaluate the options for automation. Barboza[34] provides an example of a virtual environment which allows for the testing of autonomous behavior of an unmanned surface vehicle until the user trusted the system enough to apply the rules in real-world operations. The ideas were echoed in some contributions by Mittal and Tolk[6] as well. The increased support of engineered systems by AI methods can be seen as one step in the right direction but can also be perceived to be of value by itself. The overlap with engineering efforts that support the development of smart devices — or even smart buildings and smart cities — is another topic of research, as the proposed framework is directly applicable to these efforts as well.

It is worth noting that the concept of digital twins is currently evaluated in the SE as well as in the M&S communities. Examples are given among others by Madni *et al.*,[35] Boschert and Rosen,[23] and Shao and Kibira.[36] Many of these contributions provide valuable insights and innovative concepts, but unfortunately, most of these activities are currently conducted in parallel within the border of the SE and M&S disciplines. As such, this paper is a call for action to conduct synergistic research of experts in SE, AI, M&S, and complexity. The study by Mittal and Tolk[6] is the result of a cross-disciplinary panel on cyber-physical systems.[37] The participating experts from CAS, AI, and M&S were surprised about the significant overlap of their work and the applicability of research results from the other disciplines.

In the various sections of this paper, we showed exemplarily that many of the components needed to support the proposed framework for CAS engineering — which understands designing, architecting, and operating as a perpetual cycle over the full lifetime of a system — are already available in the domains on SE, complexity science, AI, and M&S. What is needed is the conceptual alignment of these methods. The approaches of hybrid modeling, as used in support of cross-disciplinary efforts in operations research, may provide insights on how to overcome the various barriers.[38]

References

1. Gianni D., D'Ambrogio A., Tolk A., *Modeling and Simulation-Based Systems Engineering Handbook*, CRC Press, Baton Rouge, FL, 2015.
2. Sillitto H., Martin J., McKinney D., Griego R., Dori D., Krob D., *Systems Engineering and Systems Definitions*, INCOSE, 2019.
3. Buede D. M., Miller W. D., *The Engineering Design of Systems: Models and Methods*, 3rd edn., Wiley, Hoboken, NJ, 2016.
4. Maier M. W., Architecting principles for system of systems, *J. Int. Council Syst. Eng.* 1(4): 267–284, 1998.
5. Dartmann G., Song H., Schmeink A., *Big Data Analytics for Cyber-Physical Systems: Machine Learning for the Internet of Things*, Elsevier, Amsterdam, Netherlands, 2019.
6. Mittal S., Tolk A., *Complexity Challenges in Cyber Physical Systems: Using Modeling and Simulation to Support Intelligence, Adaptation and Autonomy*, John Wiley & Sons, Inc., Hoboken, NJ, 2019.
7. Barry P., Doskey S., Utilizing artificial intelligence to make systems more human, in Handley H. T. (eds.), *A Framework of Human Systems Engineering*, IEEE Press, 2021.

8. MITRE, *Systems Engineering Guide*, in Rebovich G. (ed.), MITRE Corporation Inc., McLean, VA, 2014.
9. Nuseibeh B. E., Requirements Engineering: A Roadmap. *Inte. Conf. Software Eng.*, ACM, 2000.
10. Jaakkola H. T., Architecture-driven modelling methodologies, in Al A. H. (ed.), *Information Modelling and Knowledge Bases. XXII*, IOS Press, 2011.
11. Mala D., *Integrating the Internet of Things into Software Engineering Practices*, IGI Global, 2019.
12. Mittal S., Extending DoDAF to allow integrated DEVS-based modeling and simulation, *J. Defense Model. Simul.* **3**(2):95–123, 2006.
13. Santa Fe Institute, Overview of the Santa Fe Institute, https://www.santafe.edu/about/overview.
14. New England Complex Systems Institute, Significant points in the study of complex systems,https://necsi.edu/significant-points.
15. Holland J. H., Complex adaptive systems, *Daedalus* **121**(1):17–30, 1992.
16. Holland J. H., Studying complex adaptive systems, *J. Syst. Sci. Complex.* **19**(1):1–8, 2006.
17. Pessa F., What is Emergence? in *Emergence in Complex, Cognitive, Social, and Biological Systems*, Kluwer Academic Publishers, pp. 379–382, 2002.
18. Rouse W. B., Engineering complex systems: Implications for research in systems engineering, *IEEE Trans. Syst. Man Cybernet. C* **33**(2):154–156, 2003.
19. Boden M., Computer models of creativity, *AI Magazine* **30**(3), 2009.
20. Pearl J., Causal and Counterfactual Inference. Technical Report R-485, October 2019, Forthcoming Section in *The Handbook of Rationality*.
21. Pathak M. P., Comparative analysis of search algorithms, *Int. J. Comput. Appl.* **179**:40–43, 2018.
22. Tolk A., Hughes T. K., Systems engineering, architecture, and simulation, in Gianni D., Tolk A. D. (eds.), *Modeling and Simulation-Based Systems Engineering Handbook*, CRC Press, Baton Rouge, FL, pp. 11–41, 2014.
23. Boschert S., Rosen R., Digital twin — The simulation aspect, in Hehenberger P., Bradley, D. (eds.), *Mechatronic Futures*. Springer, Cham, Switzerland, pp. 59–74, 2016.
24. Surowiecki J., *The Wisdom of the Crowds*, Anchor Books, New York, 2005.
25. Taleb N., *The Black Swan: Chapter 1: The Impact of the Highly Improbable*. The New York Times, New York, 2007.
26. Madni A. M., Sievers M., Model-based systems engineering: Motivation, current status, and research opportunities, *INCOSE Syst. Eng. J.* **21**(3):1098–1241, 2018.
27. DeLong S., Tolk A., *Sustainable Computing and Simulation: A Literature Survey*. Winter Simulation Conference. Phoenix, AZ, IEEE Press, 2021.
28. Masanet E., Shehabi, A., Lei, N., Smith, S., Koomey, J., Recalibrating global data center energy-use estimates, *Sci. Mag.* **368**(6481):984–986, 2020.
29. Dayarathna M., Wen Y., Fan R., Data center energy consumption modeling-A survey, *IEEE Commun. Surv. Tutorials* **18**(1):732–794, 2015.
30. NASEM, *Advancing Aerial Mobility: A National Blueprint. National Academies of Sciences, Engineering, and Medicine*, The National Academies Press, Washington, D.C., 2020.
31. Bedo S., Travel, https://www.news.com.au/: https://www.news.com.au/travel/travel-updates/ really-powerful-new-air-traffic-control-system/news-story/c4c490e0ea 505d5785c63952d69c16d5.

32. Saifutdinov F. J., Digital Twin as a Decision Support Tool for Airport Traffic Control. *2020 61st Int. Scientific Conf. Information Technology and Management Science of Riga Technical University (ITMS)*, Riga, IEEE, pp. 1–5, 2020.

33. Yurkevuch E. S., Controlling the security of the airport airspace using the digital twin, *J. Phys. Conf. Ser.* **1864**(1):012128, 2021.

34. Barboza J., Conversion challenges of an autonomous maritime platform: Using military technology to improve civilian security. *MODSIM World Conf. & Expo.* NASA Press, Hampton, VA, 2016.

35. Madni A. M., Madni, C. C., Lucero, S. D., Leveraging digital twin technology in model-based systems engineering, *Systems* **7**(1):7, 2019.

36. Shao G., Kibira D., Digital Manufacturing: Requirements and Challenges for Implementing Digital Surrogates. *Proc. Winter Simulation Conf.*, Piscataway, NJ, IEEE, pp. 1226–1237, 2018.

37. Tolk A., Barros F. J., D'Ambrogio A., Rajhans A., Mosterman P. J., Shetty S. S., Traoré M. K., Vangheluwe H., Yilmaz L., Hybrid simulation for cyber physical systems: A panel on where are we going regarding complexity, intelligence, and adaptability of CPS using simulation. *Proc. Spring Simulation Multi-Conf.*, San Diego, CA, Society for Modeling and Simulation, Inc., pp. 681–698, 2018.

38. Tolk A., Mustafee N., Harper A., Hybrid models as transdisciplinary research enablers, *Eur. J. Oper. Res.* **291**:1075–1090, 2021.

39. Norbert Wiener. 1948. *Cybernetics, or, Control and Communication in the Animal and the Machine.* Cambridge, MA: MIT Press.

40. W. Ross Ashby. 1957. *An Introduction to Cybernetics.* London, UK: Chapman & Hall Ltd.

https://doi.org/10.1142/9789811260186_0003

Chapter 3

DEVS and MBSE: A review

Bernard P. Zeigler

Department of Electrical & Computer Engineering
College of Engineering, The University of Arizona
Tucson, AZ 85721, USA

RTSync Corp., Chandler, AZ 85226, USA
zeigler@rtsync.com

Abstract

Model Based Systems Engineering (MBSE) refers to the trend to use models systematically throughout the design process. MBSE has been struggling to find a way to connect the blue print models that describe the initial architecture with ways to check and evaluate these plans. Simulation has become the preferred means to support this goal. DEVS is a model-based way to perform simulation and a natural enabler of simulation-based MBSE.

In this chapter we first review DEVS in the context of MBSE:

- What it is?
- How/when it started?
- How it compares to other abstractions?
- Where it most makes sense to use?
- Where it will lead?
- The potential benefits of DEVS?
- Some example case studies
- What was (or will be) "made possible" as a direct result of using DEVS?

Then we show how DEVS-based modeling and simulation can connect the stages of MBSE to create a cost-efficient seamless full iterative design cycle.

1. Introduction

Model-based Systems Engineering (MBSE) refers to the trend to use models systematically throughout the design process. MBSE has been struggling to find a way to connect the blueprint models that describe the initial architecture with ways to check and evaluate these high-level plans. Simulation has become the preferred means to support this goal. The Discrete-Event system Specification (DEVS) is a model-based way to perform simulation and a natural enabler of simulation-based MBSE. In this paper, we first review DEVS in the context of MBSE, discussing the DEVS Formalism, associated modeling and simulation (M&S) environments, the hierarchy of system specifications, the DEVS Simulation Protocol, and a timeline history of some key DEVS Developments. As an illustration of application of DEVS methodology to MBSE, we discuss the homomorphic implementation of DEVS-like systems including the hierarchy of system specification morphisms and an application to the design of simulation systems for "as-is" software. The main contribution is discussion of DEVS-based capabilities and tools for MBSE. We outline support for an envisioned MBSE development cycle with DEVS top-to-bottom MBSE capability. As an example, we discuss mapping UML activity diagrams into executable activity-based DEVS models and further elaborated into a family of simulatable architectural variants. We close with conclusions and future research directions.

2. Review of DEVS in the MBSE Context

2.1. *DEVS formalism*

The DEVS Formalism was developed on the firm mathematical systems theory foundation of Wymore[1] and others and constitutes a well-founded computational basis for systems theory-based modeling and simulation needed by today's digital engineering. The mathematical theory helps ensure reliable system implementation and accurate simulation time management. The DEVS hierarchical construction methodology supports the complex system development needed for correct cyber-physical system M&S and downstream implementation. A DEVS model formalization specifies a model's inputs, states, and outputs in a manner similar to a finite state automaton. However, a key difference is that the formal structure includes a time-advance function which allows it to represent discrete-event systems as well as simulated continuous components. Due to its universality of realization,[2] any real-world system, or System of Systems (SoS), can be modeled in DEVS and simulated in a DEVS-compliant computational platform.

We briefly state and stress some key aspects of DEVS. The DEVS Formalism formalizes what a model is, what it must contain, and what it does not contain (for instance, experimentation and simulation control parameters are not contained in the model). Moreover, DEVS is universal and unique for discrete-event system models. Any system that accepts events as inputs over time and generates events as outputs over time is equivalent to a DEVS model. With DEVS, a model of a large system can be decomposed into smaller component models with couplings between them. The DEVS Formalism defines two kinds of models: (i) atomic models that represent the basic models providing specifications for the dynamics of the system components; and (ii) coupled models that describe how to couple several component models (which can be atomic or coupled models) together to form a new model. This hierarchical construction stems from the proof that a coupled model behaves like an atomic model due to DEVS Formalism's closure under coupling which is strongly linked to systems being well defined.[2]

An atomic DEVS model can be considered as an automaton with a set of states and transition functions allowing the state to change when an event occurs or due to the passage of time. When no events occur, the state of the atomic model is updated by the internal transition function upon expiration of its lifetime. When an external event occurs, the atomic model intercepts it and makes a change in state by applying its external transition function. The lifetime of a state is determined by a time-advance function. Each state change can produce output messages via the output function. Examples of such DEVS models, including atomic and coupled models, can be found in Ref. 2.

An abstract simulator algorithm is associated with the DEVS Formalism in order to execute the structure of a model to generate its behavior. This technology-free abstract simulator standard enables DEVS models to be simulated on multiple different execution platforms, including those on desktops (for development) and those on high-performance platforms (such as Clusters or High-Performance Computers).

The DEVS Formalism includes continuous, parallel, coupled, networked, and Markov (stochastic) modeling. The Iterative System Specification and its relation to the DEVS Formalism enable defining various continuous, discrete, and hybrid models for which simulations are possible. The concept of system coupling has been proven within DEVS to allow for coupling of both discrete and continuous systems through closure under coupling. The Iterative Specification of DEVS also allows for use of morphisms to maintain consistency and control deviation throughout the specification of the various system models.[2]

2.2. *M&S environment background*

There are many commercial M&S software environments that cover a large variety of application domains. However, general-purpose environments are relatively rare. Here, we review MS4 Me[3,4] which is an environment to design general systems as well as SoS based on systems theory.[5,6] MS4 Me modeling software uses the DEVS modeling formalism and *System Entity Structure (SES)*[7] ontology to support model composability. MS4 Me supports the collaboration of domain experts and modelers in both top–down and bottom–up system constructions. The state diagram designer supports graphical specification of atomic models and is automatically (and reversibly) converted to constrained natural language text. This text is translated into a Java atomic model class and compiled to execute in the MS4 Me execution environment based on the DEVS abstract simulator. An atomic DEVS model can be constructed within a constrained natural language using constructs such as time advance, input/output ports, state transitions, internal transitions, external transitions, and output specification. However, a model expressed with limited natural language semantics cannot specify a model's detailed behavior. To overcome this problem, the DEVS natural language file introduces tag blocks which enclose actual (Java) computer code to be inserted in specific locations within the Java class file, e.g., within the characteristic functions of the DEVS Java model. Concepts such as these tag blocks facilitate the inclusion of procedural information into atomic model declarative specifications.

2.3. *Hierarchy of system specifications*

Table 1 identifies four basic levels of system specification forming a Systems Specification Hierarchy and informally describes the incremental knowledge of system structure gained at each level. The fourth column shows how the levels are applied to *DEVS-like systems*, a class of systems we will be referring to later.

As in Table 2, orthogonal to the level at which a system is specified is the subclass of systems in which the model resides where the most common subclasses are spanned by the modeling formalisms shown in the table. Note that a model may be designated to lie at a certain level of system specification based on whether it is presented in a variety of ways such as data at the I/O Behavior level, behavior generation instructions in the form of a state diagram, or in the form of interacting components, etc. The system specification formalism of models represents models expressed in types of simulation languages as instances of the basic types of system specification: DESS, DTSS, and DEVS. The table shows that such system specifications can occur at any of the levels of specification. In particular, three types in common use (Discrete-Event Simulation, Agent-based Modeling, and Continuous-time Modeling) are included in the basic DESS, DTSS, and DEVS system specifications of TMS (following, e.g., Ref. 8). Moreover, the wider capability of the Iterative System Specification formalism shows how the class of hybrid simulation models is covered.[2]

2.4. *DEVS simulation protocol*

The DEVS Simulation Protocol is a general distributed simulation protocol that prescribes specific mechanisms for:

- declaring the participants in the simulation (component models = federates);
- declaring how federates exchange data;
- executing an iterative cycle that controls how time advances (time management);
- determines when federates exchange messages (data exchange management);
- determines when federates do internal state updating (state update management).

The protocol guarantees correct simulation in the sense that if the federates are DEVS models then the federation is also a well-defined DEVS coupled model. Distinct from the High-Level Architecture (an IEEE standard for distributed simulation), the DEVS Protocol prescribes specific time, data exchange, and state update management processes. These benefits derive from the fact that based on DEVS only a single set of services is needed for all models obviating the need to align divergent services allowed by the looser HLA standard. Moreover, these benefits do not imply undue performance degradation. The Parallel DEVS Simulation Protocol provides close to the best possible performance except possibly where activity is very low or coupling among components is very small.[9] There are numerous implementations of DEVS simulators (see the list by Wainer,[10] Franceschini *et al.*,[11] and Van Tendeloo and Vangheluwe[12]). In particular, ADEVS[13,14] is distinguished by its support for both discrete-event and continuous dynamic systems, both of which are simulated within the DEVS framework. This gives it the capability to simulate

Table 1. Informal description of the levels of system specification, e.g., DEVS-like systems.

Level	Specification name	What we know at this level	DEVS-like systems
0	I/O Frame	How to stimulate the system with inputs; what variables to measure; and how to observe them over a time base?	The input set, X, and output set, Y, are the names of events that occur at discrete instants of time. DEVS(Z) refers to the set of all discrete-event segments with values in the event Z.
1	I/O Relation	Time-indexed data collected from a source system; consists of input/output pairs.	Pairs of input and output time segments from the cross-product of DEVS(X) and DEVS(Y).
3	I/O System	How states are affected by inputs; given a state and an input what is the state after the input stimulus is over; and what output event is generated by a state?	System that when given an input segment in DEVS(X) and an initial state generates an output segment in DEVS(Y) (more discussion in text).
6	Coupled System (Network of Systems)	Components and how they are coupled together. The components can be specified at lower levels or can even be structure systems themselves — leading to hierarchical structure.	Model specified as a composition of DEVS-like components in the same manner that coupled models of DEVS components are constructed.

Table 2.   System specification levels and types of framework for the simulation model.

System Specification/Level of Specification	Differential Equation System Specification (DESS)	Discrete Time System Specification (DTSS)	Discrete Event System Specification (DEVS)
Observation Frame	✓	✓	✓
I/O Behaviour	✓	✓	✓
I/O Function	✓	✓	✓
State Transition	✓	✓	✓
Coupled Component	✓	✓	✓

hybrid systems involving the interaction of subsystems characterized by discrete-event dynamics (e.g., communication networks and command-and-control systems) and continuous, physical dynamics (e.g., the trajectories of ballistic missiles and their interceptors).

2.5. *Timeline history of some key DEVS developments*

To summarize, DEVS can be considered as a universal computational formalism for systems.[15] Some of the milestones in its thread of development are listed in Table 3.

Table 3.   A historical retrospective on developments including refinements, elaborations, and extensions of the DEVS Formalism with associated references.

Classic DEVS[16]	A formalism for modeling and analysis of discrete-event systems can be seen as an extension of the Moore machine that associates a lifespan with each state and provides a hierarchical concept with an operation, called coupling, based on Wymore's[1] systems theory
Parallel DEVS[17]	Revises the classic DEVS Formalism to distinguish between transition collisions and ordinary external events in the external transition function of DEVS models, extends the modeling capability of the collisions
Hierarchical, Modular DEVS[18]	Implemented DEVS in the object-oriented programming (OOP) and modular programming paradigms[10,12]
System Entity Structure[19]	A structural knowledge representation scheme that contains knowledge of decomposition, taxonomy, and coupling of a system
Dynamic Structure DEVS[20]	Enables representing systems that are able to undergo structural change
DEV & DESS (Discrete-Event and Differential Equation System Specification)[21]	A formalism for combined discrete–continuous modeling which based on system theoretical combines the three system specification formalisms — Differential Equation, Discrete Time, and Discrete Event System Specification formalisms
Quantized State Systems[22]	Dynamical systems are continuous-time systems where the variable trajectories are piecewise constant and can be exactly represented and simulated by DEVS

Table 3. (*Continued*)

GDEVS (Generalized DEVS)[23]	Organizes trajectories through piecewise polynomial segments utilizing arbitrary polynomial functions to achieve higher accuracies in modeling continuous processes as discrete-event abstractions
Modelica & DEVS[24]	Transforms Modelica continuous models into DEVS, thus supporting models with state and time events that comprise differential-algebraic systems with high index
Finite Deterministic DEVS[25]	A powerful subclass of DEVS developed to teach the basics of DEVS that has become the basis implementations of symbolic and graphical platforms for full-capability DEVS
Iterative System Specification[2]	General Mathematical System formalism enables defining various continuous, discrete, and hybrid models extending Wymore's systems theory.[26] Enables DEVS to represent general systems with controlled accuracy

3. Homomorphic Implementation of DEVS-Like Systems

Homomorphisms play a major role in Wymore's systems engineering theory,[26] but so far have not enjoyed corresponding application within the MBSE community. Furthermore, the origin of DEVS as a way to specify a subclass of Wymore's systems definition suggests that employing the homomorphism tools developed in the DEVS context should be applicable to Wymore's systems design theory and MBSE.[26]

Here, we illustrate how DEVS supports using homomorphisms to link system specifications at the various design levels of system specification reviewed in Table 1. We consider design of a simulation environment for SoS models in which one of the components is a software system that is executed "as is" rather than represented as a DEVS component model as are the others. This is interesting because the software component can be tested within the simulated environment established by the others without the development costs incurred in creating a discrete-event model, as well as the risk involved in deriving an inaccurate abstraction. The concept we discuss is to implement a simulation platform to generate the behavior of such model compositions using the DEVS Distributed Simulation Protocol while paying special attention to the "as-is" component. While it is not a conventional discrete-event model, it must still interact with others as if it were DEVS-compliant. In particular, the progress in time of the "as-is" component depends on the execution of its host computer and not on the time scale of the overall simulation. An important instance of such an arrangement occurs when the host is a virtual computer platform and may execute the software at a rate depending on its thread scheduling algorithms. The problem to be illustrated is to establish a homomorphism that provides conditions under which the composite model can be made to be correctly executed on the simulation platform.

3.1. *Hierarchy of system specification morphisms*

To illustrate how homomorphisms apply to the design problem just stated, we first review the hierarchy of system morphisms. The essence of modeling lies in establishing relations between pairs of system descriptions. The Systems Specification Hierarchy of Table 1 is a useful starting point for defining and organizing such model-to-model relationships. The general concepts of homomorphism and isomorphism relate system models at the same level of specification. Corresponding to each of the various levels at which a system may be known, described, or specified, is a relation appropriate to a pair of systems specified at that level. We call such a relation a preservation relation or system morphism because it establishes a correspondence between a pair of systems whereby the features of one system are preserved in the other. Morphisms appropriate to each level of system specification are defined such that higher-level morphisms imply lower-level morphisms. This means that a morphism which preserves the structural features of one system in another system at one level, also preserves its features at all lower levels. Readers can refer to Ref. 2 for a detailed exposition.

3.2. *Application to the design of simulation systems for "as-is" software*

Having reviewed the concept of morphism, we return to the application to the simulation of "as-is" software. As the first step, we model the nonconforming component as a DEVS-like system as mentioned in Table 1. DEVS-like systems are systems whose input and output interfaces are event-like as illustrated in Fig. 1, the systems respond to input segments that are time-indexed discrete events and likewise produce output time segments of the same form. The mathematical representation of DEVS-like systems in Chap. 18 of Ref. 2 allows us to infer that they can respond to external events by immediately changing state and subsequently tracing an input-free state trajectory until a next event occurs. The next event can be another external event occurring later or the generation of an output event. This representation allows us to translate the defining elements of any DEVS-like system into the basic elements of a DEVS.

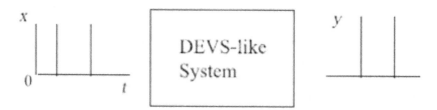

Fig. 1.   Pictorial representation of a DEVS-like system with input events x, output events y, occurring on a continuous-time base.

Thus, by assuming the "as-is" model is a DEVS-like system we can represent it as a DEVS model using the translation from its structural elements to the requisite DEVS elements. We can then specialize a known type of homomorphism for a pair of DEVS models to derive conditions that assure that the "as-is" model can be faithfully represented by the virtualized execution. Application of this homomorphism to the DEVS Simulation Protocol that governs the desired simulation platform involves interpreting the derived requirements for its detailed operation in the context of the virtual host's execution. The details are not given here and considered beyond the scope of this paper.

4. DEVS-Based M&S Capabilities and Tools for MBSE

Alshareef *et al.*[27] proposed an MBSE methodology that can support a full life cycle to design, model, and validate complex SoS. In this section, we review this methodology and relate it to the current litany of commercial MBSE tools as well as the DEVS-based artifacts in the research domain. Figure 2 places the methodology in relation to MBSE life cycle formulated to explicitly include M&S to support iterative stages of development ranging from system requirements to functional and system architectures as well as analysis and design optimization.

Beery[28] emphasized using systems modeling language products to link architecture and analysis. In contrast, the methodology proposed here advocates using the DEVS Formalism as the basic modeling and simulation framework for MBSE methodology to support the critical stages in the design of SoS. Included in Table 4 are columns outlining the development stages with examples from the application to emergency disaster response, commercial-off-the-Shelf (COTS) products that

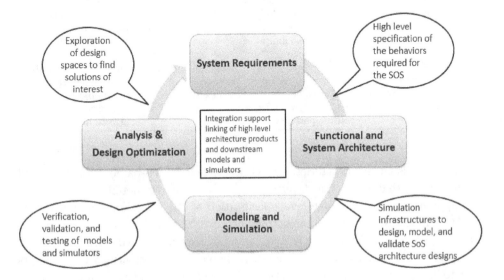

Fig. 2.   MBSE life cycle formulated to explicitly include M&S to support the iterative stages.

Table 4.   M&S support of the envisioned MBSE life cycle.

Development stage support	Example: Design of novel networks with capability to support emergency disaster response	COTS software	DEVS-based environments
High-level specification of the behaviors required for the SoS	High-level specification of packet routing in communication networks	MagicDraw+SysML Cameo Systems Modeler[32] IBM Rational/Raphsody (Mohlin, 2010)	UML/SysML meta-models that map to DEVS simulation models[33,42]
Simulation infrastructures to design, model, and validate SoS architecture designs	Models and simulators focusing on protocol evaluation, environmental representations in the context of hosted applications	STK and Matlab/Simulink (MathWorks, 2018) OMNeT++[36]	CoSMoS (Component-based System Modeling and Simulation) (ACIMS, 2019) MS4 Me (MS4 Systems, 2018)
Integration support linking of high-level architecture products and downstream models and simulators	Virtual communication stack model provides framework for network modeling including one or more OSI layers at different resolution levels	Phoenix Model Center IEEE High-Level Architecture standard	HiLLS (High-Level Language for System Specification)[37] Cadium DEVS[39]
Verification, validation, and testing of models and simulators	Hybrid and co-simulation approaches to packet traffic estimation offer complementary methods that together can overcome the limitations of each one	Cameo Simulation Toolkit (NoMagic, 2020)	Co-simulation of complex networks using DEVS as the formal basis, e.g., MECSYCO[40] Hybrid modeling of packet flow using PowerDEVS[38]
Exploration of design spaces to find the solutions of interest	Incorporation of intelligent search and learning methods to optimize routing parameters	Simulation-enabled multi-objective optimization[41]	DEVS-based parallel framework for multi-objective evolutionary algorithms[42]

support the listed functionalities, as well as current DEVS-based M&S tools and environments that are being developed in these areas. As detailed in the table, the approach starts with high-level specification of the behaviors required by the SoS to support system requirements engineering. This may be done using meta-models (e.g., UML/SysML) that map to simulation models (in formalisms such as DEVS) at an overall schematic level. Alshareef et al.[27] described the concepts and tools to support such specification and illustrated them with application to high-level specification of packet routing mechanisms in communication networks.

The application focused on evaluation of protocols, environmental representations, and included DEVS models of real network applications. DEVS-based simulation infrastructures to design, model, and validate SoS architecture designs were considered next and illustrated with DEVS models and simulators focusing on protocol evaluation, environmental representations in the context of hosted applications. For verification, validation, and testing of earlier developed models and simulators, two DEVS-based alternatives were discussed: (1) co-simulation of complex networks and (2) simulation-based testing using powerful hybrid fluid flow/packet-level mechanisms. The work showed that hybrid and co-simulation approaches based on DEVS offer complementary methods for the verification of SoS designs that together can overcome the limitations of each one. For integration support linking of high-level architecture products and downstream models and simulators, a virtual communication stack model was developed to provide a DEVS-based framework for network modeling that can flexibly include a selection of one or more standard Open Systems Interconnection (OSI) layers for abstraction at different levels of resolution. A DEVS-based framework for multi-objective evolutionary algorithms supports analysis and design optimization by exploration of design spaces to find solutions of interest using intelligent search and learning methods to optimize routing parameters.

4.1. *Mapping activity diagrams into executable activity-based DEVS models*

Alshareef *et al.*[29] discussed the integration of activity-based M&S into the MS4 Me environment demonstrating that support can be developed to link high-level architecture products and downstream models and simulators. Following practices of metamodeling, model transformation, and code generation, they implemented a capability to create UML activity diagrams and to map them into executable activity-based models in the DEVS Markov formalism.[30] This enabled formalization of the flow selection process and state transition in the activity diagram and parameterized specification of stochastic behavior. Such automated code generation supports fast development and simulation of activity-based models for high-level exploration of workflow architectures and illustration of system operation for customers and other stakeholders. Here we provide an example of such development.

Figure 3 illustrates an activity diagram with the graphical elements for input/output (Source/Store), splitting/merging of flow (Random_select/Merge), actions for work on jobs (Compare), and hierarchical construction (BaselineMultiProcessorArch/AlternatMultiProcessorArch) (see Ref. 29 for a more detailed description). At the top level, incoming jobs are randomly directed towards baseline and alternative workflow organizations with subsequent merging of these streams to enable comparison of their throughputs and turnaround times while minimizing the inference with ongoing production. The second-level elaboration of the two

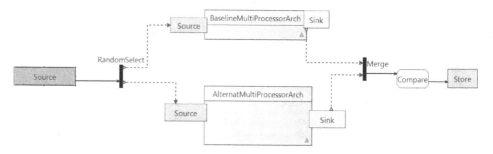

Fig. 3.   Activity diagram determining the processing workflow based on random selection of jobs.

top-level interventions illustrates the capability of hierarchical construction to hide complexity at the top level while exposing it in consistent fashion at the next level down. Notice that although specified at the high level of activity modeling, the subsequent elaboration enables downstream implementation of this workflow.

However, the following limitations were noted:

- Mapped DEVS models in MS4 Me still require a multitude of parameter values to be set to achieve detailed desired behavior, although they are exposed to enable such adjustment.
- Changes in such models may put them outside the scope of activity-based specification, making "round-trip engineering" difficult.
- The current targeted messages and actions have to be enhanced to enable operations that generate the behavior required in other experimental frames. For example, currently the Compare action in Fig. 3 cannot actually perform comparison of intervention outcomes.
- The targeted atomic models cannot easily be used in compositions with other DEVS models.

4.2. *DEVS top-to-bottom MBSE capability*

To illustrate a full top-to-bottom MBSE capability, we proceed to show how the activity model developed in Fig. 3 can be manually integrated into full DEVS reusability. Figure 4(a) illustrates an SES that describes the coupled model structure underlying the activity diagram of Fig. 3. The baseline multi-processor architecture component is further represented in the SES of Fig. 4(b). Note that the same SES is employed for the alternative architecture (therefore not shown here) so that pruning can be done to select desired variants for both architectures from the same template. Roughly, the architecture consists of a coordinator and a group of processors that can implement single processor, multi-server, pipeline, and divide-and-conquer configurations (see Ref. 31 for discussion of such architectures). Figure 5 shows the Simulation Viewer display of an executable DEVS model that is generated by transforming such a pruning. The expanded baseline model shown in the Viewer corresponds to a choice of pipeline workflow model with three processors and its

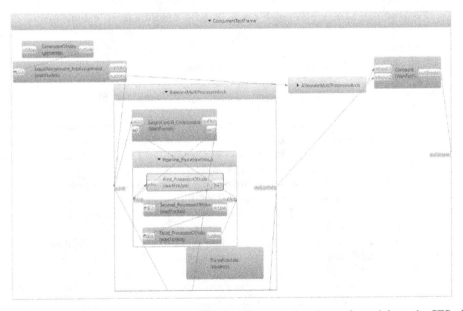

Fig. 4.   SES that describes the coupled model structure underlying the activity diagram of Fig. 3.

Fig. 5.   Simulation Viewer display of a DEVS model pruned and transformed from the SES of Fig. 4.

accompanying coordinator. The alternative, not expanded, is a divide-and-conquer group with accompanying coordinator.

Using capabilities identified in the last column of Table 4 automated pruning and transformation can be instrumented at this point to enable exploration of large design space in which baseline and alternative architectures are sampled for response to various workloads of interest. Thus, to fully support a top-to-bottom design process initiated by the activity diagram would require integration in MS4 Me that also supports semi-automated development of SES and DNL files that then merge with those of other DEVS models. Research is needed to understand whether and how activity diagram specification can be extended to enable such generation of SES and DNL documents to increase model reusability.

5. Summary and Conclusions

Having reviewed DEVS in the context of MBSE, we discussed the application of DEVS methodology to MBSE. We discussed homomorphic implementation of DEVS-like systems including the hierarchy of system specification morphisms and an application to the design of simulation systems for "as-is" software. We then focused on DEVS-based capabilities and tools for MBSE with discussion of support of an envisioned MBSE life cycle with DEVS top-to-bottom MBSE capability. As an example, we discussed a mapping of activity diagrams into executable activity-based DEVS models implemented in the MS4 Me environment. The result was further elaborated into a family of architectural variants using the System Entity Structure. Integrating the activity modeling with the elaborations supported by the latter concepts and tools remains for continued development to achieve.

References

1. Wymore W., *A Mathematical Theory of Systems Engineering: The Elements*, Wiley, New York, 1967.
2. Zeigler B. P., Muzy A., Kofman E., *Theory of Modeling and Simulation,* 3rd edn., Academic Press, New York, NY, 2018.
3. Seo C., Zeigler B. P., Coop R., Kim D., DEVS modeling and simulation methodology with MS4 Me software tool, *DEVS 13: Proc. Symp. Theory of Modeling & Simulation — DEVS Integrative M&S Symp.*, San Diego, CA, The Society for Modeling & Simulation International, San Diego, CA, pp. 33:1–33:8, 2018.
4. MS4 Systems, Inc., MS4 Me, http://ms4systems.com/pages/ms4me.php, 2021.
5. Zeigler B. P., Sarjoughian H. S., *Guide to Modeling and Simulation of Systems of Systems*, 2nd edn., Simulation Foundations, Methods and Applications, Springer International Publishing, London, 2017.
6. Zeigler B. P., Nutaro J., Towards a framework for more robust validation and verification of simulation models for systems of systems, *J. Def. Model. Simul., Appl. Methodol. Technol.* **13**:3–16, 2015, doi:10.1177/1548512914568657.
7. Zeigler B. P., *Multifaceted Modelling and Discrete Event Simulation*, Academic Press Professional, Inc, San Diego, CA, 1984.
8. Paredis, R., Van Mierlo, S., Vangheluwe, H., Translating Process Interaction World View Models to DEVS: GPSS to (Python(P))DEVS, *2020 Winter Simulation Conf. (WSC)*, 2020, pp. 2221–2232, doi: 10.1109/WSC48552.2020.9383952.

9. Zeigler B. P., Nutaro J., Seo C., What's the best possible speedup achievable in distributed simulation: Amdahl's law reconstructed, Proc. 2015 Spring Simulation Multi-Conf., Alexandria, VA, The Society for Modeling & Simulation International, San Diego, CA, pp. 189–196, 2015.

10. Wainer G. A., DEVS tools, http://www.sce.carleton.ca/faculty/wainer/standard/tools.htm, 2012.

11. Franceschini R., Bisgambiglia P.-A., Touraille L., Bisgambiglia P., Hill D., A survey of modelling and simulation software frameworks using discrete event system spec-ification, in Neykova R., Ng N. (Eds.), *2014 Imperial College Computing Student Workshop*, OpenAccess Series in Informatics (OASIcs), Schloss Dagstuhl — Leibniz-Zentrum fuer Informatik, Dagstuhl, Germany, pp. 40–49, 2014.

12. Van Tendeloo Y., Vangheluwe H., An evaluation of DEVS simulation tools, *SIMU-LATION* **93**:103–121, 2017.

13. Nutaro J., On constructing optimistic simulation algorithms for the discrete event system specification, *ACM Trans. Model. Comput. Simul.* **19**:1:1–1:21, 2008.

14. Nutaro J., *Building Software for Simulation: Theory and Algorithms with Applications in C++*, John Wiley & Sons, Hoboken, NJ, 2011.

15. Vangheluwe H., Foundations of modelling and simulation of complex systems, *Elec-tron. Commun. EASST* **10**:1–12. 2008.

16. Zeigler B. P., *Theory of Modeling and Simulation*, Wiley-Interscience, New York, 1976.

17. Chow A., Parallel DEVS: A parallel, hierarchical modular modeling formalism and its distributed simulator, *SIMULATION, Trans. Soc. Comput. Simul. Int.* **13**:55–68, 1996.

18. Zeigler B. P., Hierarchical, modular discrete event models in an object oriented envi-ronment, *SIMULATION* **49**:219–230, 1987.

19. Kim T. G., Lee C., Zeigler B. P., Christensen E. R., System entity structuring and model base management, *IEEE Trans. Syst. Man Cybern.* **20**:1013–1024, 1990.

20. Barros F. J., Dynamic structure discrete event system specification: structural inher-itance in the delta environment, *Winter Simulation Conf. Proc.*, pp. 781–785, 1995.

21. Praehofer H., System theoretic formalisms for combined discrete-continuous system simulation, *Int. J. Gen. Syst.* **19**:226–240, 1991.

22. Kofman E., Junco S., Quantized-state systems: A DEVS approach for continuous system simulation, *SIMULATION, Trans. Soc. Model. Simul. Int.* **18**:2–8, 2001.

23. Giambiasi N., Escude B., Ghosh S., GDEVS: a generalized discrete event specifica-tion for accurate modeling of dynamic systems, *Proc. 5th Int. Symp. Autonomous Decentralized Systems*, Dallas, TX, IEEE, Piscataway, pp. 464–469, 2001.

24. Nutaro J., An extension of the OpenModelica compiler for using Modelica models in a discrete event simulation, *SIMULATION* **90**:1328–1345, 2014.

25. Hwang M. H., Taxonomy of DEVS subclasses for standardization, *Proc. 2011 Symp. Theory of Modeling & Simulation: DEVS Integrative M&S Symp.*, Boston, MA, The Society for Modeling & Simulation International, San Diego, CA, pp. 152–159, 2011.

26. Wach P., Zeigler B. P., Salado A., Conjoining Wymore's systems theoretic framework and the DEVS modeling formalism: Toward scientific foundations for MBSE, *Appl. Sci.* **11**:4936, 2021.

27. Alshareef A., Blas M. J., Bonaventura M., Paris T., Yacoub A., Zeigler B. P., Using DEVS for full life cycle model-based system engineering in complex net-work design, in Nicopolitidis P., Misra S., Yang L. T., Zeigler B., Ning Z. (eds.), *Advances in Computing, Informatics, Networking and Cybersecurity.* Lecture Notes in Networks and Systems, Vol. 289, Springer, Cham, 2022, https://doi.org/10.1007/978-3-030-87049-2_8.

28. Beery P., A model based systems engineering methodology for employing architecture in system analysis: Developing simulation models using systems modeling language products to link architecture and analysis, Master's Thesis, Naval Postgraduate School, Monterey, CA, 2018.
29. Alshareef A., Kim D., Seo C., Zeigler B. P., DEVS Markov modeling and simulation of activity-based models for MBSE application, *Proc. Winter Simulation Conf. 2021*, Phoenix, AZ, 2021.
30. Seo C., Zeigler B. P., Kim D., DEVS Markov modeling and simulation: Formal definition and implementation, *Proc. Theory of Modeling and Simulation Symp.*, Baltimore, MA, The Society for Modeling & Simulation International, San Diego, CA, pp. 1–12, 2018.
31. Alshareef A., Sarjoughian H. S., Hierarchical activity-based models for control flows in parallel discrete event system specification simulation models, *IEEE Access* **9**:80970–80985, 2021, doi:10.1109/ACCESS.2021.3084940.
32. NoMagic (2020). Cameo Systems Modeler. Available at https://www.nomagic.com/products/cameo-systems-modeler (Accessed July 1, 2020).
33. Alshareef, A., Kim, D., Seo, C., Zeigler, B. P., Activity diagrams between DEVS-based modeling and simulation and fUML-based model execution, in *Proc. 2020 Summer Simulation Conf.*, Society for Computer Simulation International, 2020.
34. Blas, M. J., Gonnet, S., Leone, H., Routing structure over discrete event system specification: A DEVS adaptation to develop smart routing in simulation models, Winter Simulation Conf. (WSC), IEEE, pp. 774–785, 2017.
35. Mohlin, M. (2010). Model simulation in rational software architect: Simulating UML models. Cupertino, CA: IBM.
36. Varga, A., Hornig, R., An overview of the OMNeT++ simulation environment, *Proc. 1st International Conf. Simulation Tools and Techniques for Communications*, Networks and Systems & Workshops, Simutools'08, ICST, Brussels, Belgium, pp. 60:1–60:10, 2008, http://dl.acm.org/citation.cfm?id=1416222.1416290, http://dl.acm.org/citation.cfm?id=.
37. Kehinde, G., and Mamadou, K. T., A DEVS-based pivotal modeling formalism and its verification and validation framework, *Simulation J.* **96**(12) (2020) 969–992.
38. Bonaventura, M., Castro, R., Fluid-flow and packet-level models of data networks unified under a modular/hierarchical framework: Speedups and simplicity, combined, *Proc. of 2018 Winter Simulation Conf.* (WSC), 2018.
39. Wainer, G. A., 2020, http://www.sce.carleton.ca/faculty/wainer/standard/tools.htm.
40. Camus, B., Paris, T., Vaubourg, J., Presse, Y., Bourjot, C., Ciarletta, L., Chevrier, V., Cosimulation of cyber-physical systems using a DEVS wrapping strategy in the MECSYCO middleware. *SIMULATION*, 2018, doi:10.1177/0037549717749014.
41. Wade, B. M., A multi-objective optimization of ballistic and cruise missile fire plans based on damage calculations from missile impacts on an airfield defended by an air defense artillery network, *J. Defense Model. Simul.*, 1–15, 2018, doi: 10.1177/1548512918788503.
42. Astorga, A. M. *et al.*, DEVS-based parallel framework for multi-objective evolutionary algorithms, in *The Fourth Int. Workshop on Parallel Architectures and Bioinspired Algorithms — The Twentieth Int. Conf. Parallel Architectures and Compilation Techniques*, 2011.

Chapter 4

XDEVS: A hybrid system modeling framework

Kunyu Xie[*], Lin Zhang[†], Yuanjun Laili[‡] and Xiaohan Wang[§]

School of Automation Science and Electrical Engineering
Engineering Research Center of Complex Product Advanced
Manufacturing Systems Ministry of Education
Beihang University, No. 37, Xueyuan Road, Beijing, China
[*]zy1903114@buaa.edu.cn
[†]zhanglin@buaa.edu.cn
[‡]lailiyuanjun@buaa.edu.cn
[§]by1903042@buaa.edu.cn

Abstract

When Discrete Event System Specification (DEVS) is used as a modeling tool, there is a semantic gap between a DEVS model and the mathematical representation, which may result in understanding difficulties. To provide a more intuitive form of modeling, XDEVS expands the concept of states in DEVS. The continuous state is introduced in XDEVS, which enhances the ability to model hybrid systems. Based on the DEVS simulation framework, a simulation engine is developed to drive the XDEVS model safely and efficiently and avoid the wrong location of state events during the simulation of the continuous model. A hybrid model is constructed and simulated using XDEVS. A comparison between the XDEVS model and models described by DEV&DESS and GDEVS shows that XDEVS can clearly express the structure of the model and reduce the burden on modelers.

1. Introduction

With the development of computer science and technology, modeling and simulation have been used in many complex systems such as manufacturing, healthcare, transportation, and military exercise. The Discrete Event System Specification (DEVS)[1] is one of the most widely used discrete system simulation frameworks. Other formalisms (such as differential equation system specification (DESS)) can be unified into DEVS under its formalism framework.

DEVS can model a continuous system by unifying it into discrete event simulation frameworks, such as DEV&DESS.[2] In this way, however, the generated model is more difficult to understand than a mathematical model. Hybrid system modeling and simulation theories have been developed based on DEVS. Giambiasi puts

---

[†]Corresponding author.

forward the general discrete event system specification (GDEVS) in Ref. 3. GDEVS uses polynomials to model continuous models, which is more convenient than DEVS, but at the expense of precision. In Refs. 4 and 5, PowerDEVS was built, which used the quantized state systems (QSS)-based method to model and solve the continuous part of the hybrid model. In Ref. 6, a way to divide the hybrid model into continuous and discrete parts is proposed. The numerical integration algorithm is used to simulate the continuous part of the model. However, this method has specific technical difficulties and is not easy to popularize in engineering. Later, in Ref. 7, Nutaro proposed a tool to directly transform the continuous part of the model constructed by Modelica into DEVS based on the above tearing method. This tool maps the DAE model to the ADEVS using OpenModelica. Users can integrate and use the transformed continuous model in ADEVS. However, this tool has a limitation to the modeling of the Modelica model. Moreover, it uses two independent platforms, which require modelers to have considerable knowledge to complete the modeling task.

Aiming at the above problems, a state-based XDEVS modeling specification is proposed in this paper. XDEVS extends the concept of the continuous state in DEVS and puts forward the definition, which can realize more intuitive modeling of hybrid models. XDEVS is the discrete-event modeling specification of complex system modeling language, X language.[8] In the literature,[9-11] the supporting technologies of the X language have been developed. Details about X language will be introduced in Chapter 5.

The rest of the paper is composed as follows: Section 2 introduces the XDEVS specification and its background. Section 3 introduces the simulation of XDEVS models. Section 4 presents a modeling case. Section 5 ends with the summary and future work.

2. XDEVS Specification

2.1. *DEVS*

XDEVS is built based on the DEVS specification, which includes two classes of models: Atomic models and Couple models. A couple model defines the connection and hierarchy of the system, and an atomic model defines the function of the model.[1]

An atomic model can be defined as follows:

$$\mathrm{AM} = \langle X, Y, S, \delta_{\mathrm{ext}}, \delta_{\mathrm{int}}, \lambda, ta \rangle, \tag{2.1}$$

where

X : set of input values,

Y : set of output values,

S : set of states,

$\delta_{\text{ext}} : Q \times X \to S$ is the external transition function,

$Q = \{(s, e) \mid s \epsilon S, 0 \le e \le ta(s)\}$,

$\delta_{\text{int}} : S \to S$ is the internal transition function,

$\lambda : S \to Y$ is the output function,

$ta : S \to \mathbb{R}_{0,\infty}^{+}$ is the time advance function.

In atomic models, internal interfaces, external interfaces, and states formed the static structure of the model. The external state functions, internal transition functions, output functions, and forward time functions define the dynamic behavior of the model. The duration of each state is defined in the function. Suppose the external transition function is not triggered within the period. In that case, the corresponding behavior of the state in the internal transition function is triggered, and the next state of the model is calculated. Meanwhile, the λ function is activated to produce the output. External state functions define the system's behavior when it receives the corresponding external inputs.

The duration of the model state is defined in the function. The external function defines the model's behavior when it receives external inputs. The internal function defines the behavior of the model when the state duration ends, while the function defines the output of the model when the internal event occurs.

A couple model can be defined as follows:

$$\text{CM} = \langle X, Y, D, M_d \mid d\epsilon D, \text{EIC}, \text{EOC}, \text{IC}, \text{Select} \rangle, \tag{2.2}$$

where

$X = \{(p, v)|_p \in IPorts, v \in X_p\}$: set of input ports and values,

$Y = \{(p, v)|_p \in OPorts, v \in Y_p\}$: set of output ports and values,

D : set of the component names.

Component requirements for each $d\epsilon D$

M_d is a discrete atomic model or a continuous model.

With $X_d = (p, v)|_p \in IPorts_d, v \in X_p$,

$Y_d = (p, v)|_p \in OPorts_d, v \in Y_p$.

Coupling requirements

External input coupling connects external inputs to component inputs:

$\text{EIC} \subseteq \{((N, i_p N), (d, ip_d)) \mid ipN \in IPorts, d \in D, ip_d \in IPorts_d\}$.

External output coupling connects component outputs to external outputs:

$\text{EOC} \subseteq \{((d, op_d), (N, opN)) \mid opN \in OPorts, d \in D, op_d \in OPorts_d\}$.

An internal coupling connects component outputs to component inputs:

$$IC \subseteq \{((a, op_a), (b, ip_b)) \mid a, b \in D, op_a \in OPorts_a, ip_b \in IPorts_b\}.$$

The input interfaces, output interfaces, the set of models, and the connections in a couple model define the static structure of the model. Of the three classes of coupling connects, the IC defines the interoperation between internal components; the EIC establishes the interaction of external interfaces with its internal components; and the EOC defines the outward output of internal components.

2.2. *XDEVS*

DEVS specification clearly defined the system's architecture, but as a modeling specification, the differences between a DEVS model and a mathematical model bring a semantic gap, which leads to difficulties in understanding. In DEVS, the state is a part of the atomic model's definition. However, its various attributes are divided into multiple functions and put in different places, as shown in Fig. 1. In this way, DEVS realizes the consistency of the simulation framework and system structure but loses the intuitiveness of the model description, which will make the model difficult to understand.

To enhance the intuitiveness of modeling, in XDEVS, the state exists as an independent element. The state's behavior (internal event behavior and external event behavior) and duration will be directly defined in it.

In XDEVS, a state can be defined using the following formula:

$$\text{State} = \langle \Delta_{\text{ext}}, \Delta_{\text{int},\lambda}, ta, f \rangle, \quad \text{where}$$

$$\Delta_{\text{ext}} : \text{Set of external function};$$

$$\Delta_{\text{int},\lambda} : \text{Set of internal function and corresponding output};$$

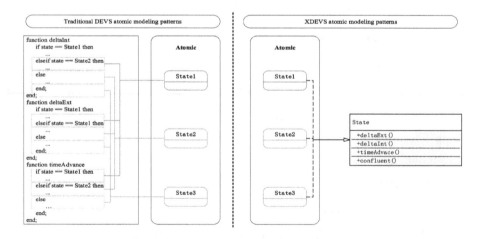

Fig. 1.   Comparison of the two design patterns.

ta : The duration of state;

f : The behavior during the duration of a state   (2.3)

Δ_{ext} represents a set of external events. That is, the response of the system to various external events, which may be received when the system is in this state, means a collection of internal affairs and their corresponding outputs; ta defines the duration of the state; and f defines the behavior of the system during the time of the state.

In addition, XDEVS expands the definition of the state. The state definition in DEVS is the stage where the state variable remains unchanged. This definition has encountered difficulties in describing a continuous system. Because in a continuous approach, the state variable remains constant for only a one-time step. Or similar to QSS, the state variable remains constant until it changes by more than one quantum. This modeling method is more difficult to understand than the commonly used differential equations for continuous models. The problem is that the requirements of modeling and simulation are inconsistent. That is, DEVS' way of modeling is more based on simulation requirements, with the hope that the model will be similar to its mathematical model. To overcome this inconsistency, in XDEVS, the state is redefined as follows:

Definition 1. The state is a stage in which the state variable remains unchanged or subject to consistent constraints.

The state's definition is similar to Newton's static law: An object perseveres in its state of rest or uniform motion in a right line. Therefore, the description of the continuous state is introduced in XDEVS, as shown in Definition 2:

Definition 2. The system's continuous state is the state that the state variables of the system change with the given constraints. The continuous state ends when an event (internal or external) is triggered.

The constraints in Definition 2 are mathematical models of the system's behavior, usually algebraic differential equations in continuous systems. In addition, the internal events that lead to the end of the continuous state are more extensive than those defined in DEVS. The internal events in DEVS occur when the duration of the system state ends, that is, time events. However, the state variable can change over time when in a continuous state. So not only does the state ends when the time condition is met, but when the state variable meets a specific condition, it can also trigger an internal event. This kind of event is called a state event. Because the state event is also triggered internally by the model, in XDEVS, it is classified as internal events.

By introducing the definition of a continuous state, a description of a hybrid model is presented in XDEVS.

Definition 3. A hybrid model is a model that includes both the continuous state and discrete state.

3. Simulation of XDEVS Models

3.1. *Simulation of DEVS models*

XDEVS's simulator is based on the DEVS simulator. The DEVS simulator can efficiently simulate a complex multilevel model.[1]

In the DEVS simulator, a coupled model can be simulated by the following steps:

(1) The top layer of the coupled model triggers the event. There are two kinds of events. One is the internal events triggered by its internal atomic model. The other is the external event triggered by the model, which receives the external input. Let us call the model that triggers the event D. Let T denote the time at which the event will occur.
(2) Then, the DEVS simulator advances the simulation time to T and executes the atomic model triggered by events (external events and internal events).
(3) If an internal event occurs in D, the DEVS simulator will calculate the output generated by the event and send the output result to the target models. And if an external event occurs in D, the DEVS simulator will execute the model's external event function.
(4) Check whether the simulation is finished. If not, return to the first step.

Zeigler *et al.* have implemented the hierarchical control algorithm with DEVS in the literature.[1] The hierarchy corresponding to the algorithm is shown in Fig. 2. It can be seen that the DEVS simulator and DEVS models are all hierarchical. The couple model corresponds to a *Coordinator* in the DEVS model, and the atomic model corresponds to a *Simulator*. The *Simulator* schedules internal and external events of its corresponding atomic model, and the *Coordinator* manages events of all its submodels. At the top level of the DEVS simulator, a root coordinator is defined to organize the event progression of the entire simulation system.

3.2. *Simulation engine for XDEVS*

To simulate the XDEVS model, based on the DEVS simulator,[1] we built the XDEVS simulator. In the XDEVS simulator, a coupled model can be simulated by the following steps:

(1) The top layer of the coupled model triggers the event. There are two kinds of events. One is the internal events triggered by its internal atomic model. The other is the external event triggered by the model, which receives the external input. Let us call the model that triggers the event D. Let T denote the time at which the event will occur.
(2) Then, the DEVS simulator advances the simulation time to T and executes the atomic model triggered by events (external events and internal events).
(3) Remember the atomic model set that triggered internal events as D'. For each atomic model in D', the XDEVS simulator will find out the current state and then execute the events to get the output and the next state of the model. If

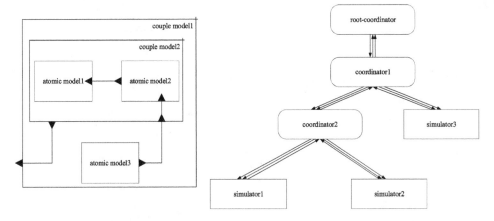

Fig. 2.   DEVS hierarchical model and simulation scheme time.

the next state of the atomic model is continuous (denoted as S_{continue}), the duration of the state defined in S_{continue} or the constraint equation of state variables will be solved and sent to the XDEVS simulator.

(4) If an internal event occurs in D, the XDEVS simulator will calculate the output generated by the event and send the output result to the target models. And if an external event occurs in D, the DEVS simulator will execute the model's external event function.

(5) Check whether the simulation is finished. If not, return to the first step.

The XDEVS simulator adds a step compared to DEVS. In step 3, the state is used to perform the behavior that is performed in the atomic model in DEVS. The hierarchy corresponding to the algorithm is shown in Fig. 3. It can be seen that in addition to the couple model corresponding to the coordinator and the atomic model corresponding to the simulator in DEVS, the corresponding state and *Solver* are added in the XDEVS simulator. For the ordinary state, the *Solver* provides the state duration, internal event function, and external event function to the *Simulator*. For the continuous state, the *Solver* also provides the solution function and root location function of the state constraint equation except those provided in the ordinary state.

Based on the simulation engine for XDEVS simulator, a simulation engine (a software tool) for XDEVS was developed with C++, and its class diagram is shown in Fig. 4. As shown in Fig. 4, in the XDEVS simulation engine, the continuous state exists as a particular state, and the solution of the constraint equation defined in the continuous state is completed in the simulation process. In this way, we can integrate most of the equation solving software tools into the XDEVS engine. In the engine, the solution of the constraint equation in the continuous state is provided by GNU Scientific Library (GSL). The state event location algorithm used in the engine is the binary location algorithm.

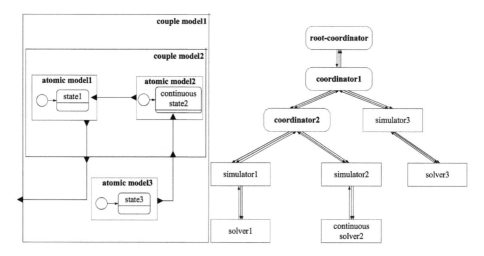

Fig. 3.   XDEVS hierarchical model and simulation scheme.

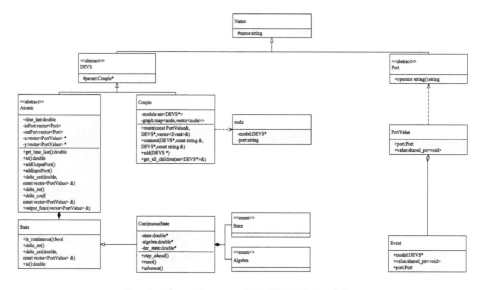

Fig. 4.   Class diagram of the XDEVS simulator.

In the XDEVS simulation engine, the *Solver* uses the equation solving tool and state event location algorithm to simulate the continuous state. This method is easy to use, but as Ref. 7 says, any root-finding algorithm will cause the wrong location of the state event due to the error tolerance P. The error location of the state event in XDEVS is shown in Fig. 5. At t_0, *atomic*1 is in *continuous state*2. Due to the error tolerance, the root function incorrectly locates the time of the state event as t_1, but the actual state event occurs at t_0. At the same time, *atomic*2 sends an external event to *atomic*1 at t_0. *atomic*1 should trigger both the state event and the external event at t_0. However, due to the incorrect positioning of the state

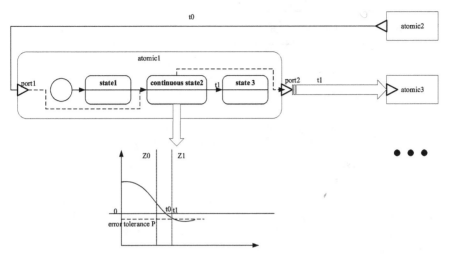

Fig. 5.   State event incorrect location.

event, *atomic*1 could not trigger its internal event at t_0, which causes its output to *atomic*3 to be canceled and finally leads to a wrong event trigger chain. By this example, it can be seen that a false state event location will cause the model to shift to the incorrect event trigger chain. Under extreme conditions, a wrong state event location will let all models in the simulation system miss an event.

This result is caused by the existence of error tolerance P. Suppose the time of the calculated state event is $t_{\delta 1}$, and the actual time of the system event is t_δ. This means that at $t_{\delta 1}$ and t_δ, the zero-crossing function has $Z(t_\delta, x, w) = 0$ and $|Z(t_{\delta 1}, x, w)| < P$. Assuming that, it means a difference $t_{\delta 1} - t_\delta$ between the exact time of the state event and the calculation result. If the atomic model receives an external input, the model should trigger parallel events. But due to the calculation errors, it can only trigger external events and ignore the internal events, leading to errors in model state transitions.

To avoid these errors, we need to test whether the value of the zero-crossing function is consistent at two-time points (e is the state duration when the state event is triggered). The test is that the zero-crossing function has been evaluated after the state event calculation. It only needs to detect zero-cross and determine whether there is a state event. That is, when $Z(t_0, x, w)! = Z(t_{0+e}, x, w)$, a state event will occur during this period.

After solving the detection problem, the overall execution flow of the engine still needs to be changed. Because in the execution flow, the output of all the models that execute the internal transfer in the system will be sent to the target through the coupling relationship. This means that once a state event has been located incorrectly, the events triggered at the current moment in the engine are all possibly be wrong. So, the engine needs to re-detect all models and find the correct event. The model's relocation algorithm is shown in Algorithm 1. The idea

---

Algorithm 1. Re-location of state event

Input: activeModels
Output: reActivedModels
  1: *if_loop ← false{repeat flag}*
  2: *reActiveModels ← [ ]*
  3: **for** model in activeModels **do**
  4:    *missEvent ← model.testMissEvent(){Check if state*
          event was missed}
  5:   **if** missEvent **then**
  6:     *if_loop ← true*
  7:     *reActiveModels.append(model){Recollect the actived model}*
  8:   **end if**
  9: **end for**
10:
11: *activeModels ← reActiveModels*
12: *reActiveModels ← [ ]*
13:
14: **while** if_loop **do**
15:   *if_loop ← false*
16:   **for** model in activeModels **do**
17:     *Regenerate output for model and sent it*
18:   **end for**
19:
20:   **for** model in activeModels **do**
21:     *missEvent ← model.testMissEvent(){Check if state*
          event was missed}
22:     **if** missEvent **then**
23:       *if_loop ← true*
24:       *reActiveModels.append(model){Recollect the actived model}*
25:     **end if**
26:   **end for**
27: **end for**
28:

---

is to perform loop detection on all models in the simulator until there are no more incorrect state event locations.

4. Case Study

In this section, we will verify the modeling capabilities of XDEVS for hybrid models through the vehicle cruise model that is derived from an example in Ref. 12.

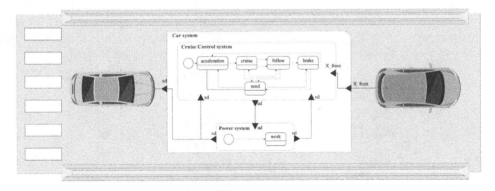

Fig. 6.   Car cruising model.

4.1. *Model description*

In this model, the car is controlled by an automatic cruise model. As shown in Fig. 6, the automatic cruise model includes five states. They are *acceleration, cruise, follow, brake,* and *send.* The *send* state is responsible for shipping the system control signal to the power system; The *acceleration* state accelerates the vehicle after the vehicle has started. After the car speed reaches the rated value, it turns the *cruise* state and travels at the cruising speed. And finally, if the distance between the car and the car in front is less than the set safety value, it will turn to the *follow* state and control the vehicle to keep the same speed with the vehicle in front. In case of emergency, the distance from the front car is less than the minimum safe distance. The car will enter the *brake* state for emergency braking until the distance from the front vehicle is restored to normal. The car's engine is controlled by the cruise system and consists of two states: *idle* and *work,* in which the engine provides power to the vehicle.

To highlight the advantages of XDEVS for hybrid system modeling, we will introduce XDEVS mainly through the power system. XDEVS can describe the power system as follows:

$$\text{XDEVS}_{\text{power}} = \langle X, Y, S, Q \rangle, \quad \text{where}$$

$$X = \{U_d\}, \quad \text{where } U_d \in \mathbb{R}$$

$$Y = \{V_d, X_d\}, \quad \text{where } V_d, \ X_d \in \mathbb{R} \tag{4.1}$$

$$S = \{\text{idle, work}\} \times V_d \times X_d, \quad \text{where } V_d, \ X_d \in \mathbb{R}$$

$$Q = v \times x, \quad \text{where } v, \ x \in \mathbb{R}.$$

The state idle and work can be, respectively, described as follows:

$$\text{State}_{\text{idle}} = \langle \Delta_{\text{ext}}, \Delta_{\text{int}}, \lambda, ta, f \rangle, \quad \text{where}$$

$$\Delta_{\text{ext}}(U_d) = (\text{work}, V_d, X_d)$$

$$\Delta_{\text{int},\lambda} = \{\}$$

$$ta = \text{infinite}$$

$$f = \{\} \tag{4.2}$$

$$\text{State}_{\text{work}} = \langle \Delta_{\text{ext}}, \Delta_{\text{int},\lambda}, ta, f \rangle, \quad \text{where}$$

$$\Delta_{\text{ext}}(U_d) = \begin{cases} (\text{idle}, V_d, X_d) & \text{when } U_d < 0 \\ (\text{work}, V_d, X_d) & \text{when } U_d \geq 0 \end{cases}$$

$$\Delta_{\text{int},\lambda} = (\text{work}, v, x)$$

$$ta = 0.01 \ s$$

$$f = \begin{cases} \dfrac{dx}{dt} = v \\ 1000 \cdot \dfrac{dv}{dt} + 5v \cdot abs(v) = -5000 \cdot tau. \end{cases}$$

$$\tag{4.3}$$

However, when DEV&DESS represent the same model, the entire model requires two submodels. The first is the DEVS model that is responsible for controlling the state.

$$\text{DEVS}_{\text{power}} = \langle X, Y, S, \delta_{\text{ext}}, \delta_{\text{int}}, \lambda, ta \rangle, \quad \text{where}$$

$$X = \{U_d\}, \quad \text{where } U_d \in \mathbb{R}$$

$$Y = \{V_d, X_d\}, \quad \text{where } V_d, X_d \in \mathbb{R}$$

$$\Delta_{\text{ext}}(\text{idle}, U_d, e) = (\text{work}, (V_d, X_d), e)$$

$$\Delta_{\text{ext}}(\text{idle}, U_d, e) = \begin{cases} (\text{idle}, (V_d, X_d), e) & \text{when } U_d < 0 \\ (\text{work}, (V_d, X_d), e) & \text{when } U_d \geq 0 \end{cases} \tag{4.4}$$

$$\Delta_{\text{int}}(\text{work}) = \text{work}$$

$$\lambda(\text{work}) = (v, x)$$

$$ta(\text{idle}) = \text{infinite}$$

$$ta(\text{work}) = 0.01 \ s.$$

Then, the differential equation of the power system needs to be solved using the DESS model.

$$\text{DESS} = (X, Y, Q, f, \lambda), \quad \text{where}$$

$$X = \{U_d\}, \quad \text{where } U_d \in \mathbb{R}$$

$$Y = \{V_d, X_d\}, \quad \text{where } V_d, X_d \in \mathbb{R}$$

$$Q = \{v, x\}, \quad \text{where v, } x \in \mathbb{R}$$

$$f = \begin{cases} \dfrac{dx}{dt} = v, x_{\text{new}} = x + \dfrac{dx}{dt} \cdot \Delta_t \\[2mm] \dfrac{dv}{dt} = 5U_d - 0.005v \cdot abs(v), v_{\text{new}} = v + \dfrac{dv}{dt} \cdot \Delta_t \end{cases}$$

$$\lambda = \{V_d = v, X_d = x\}. \tag{4.5}$$

Finally, the two are coupled together to form a car engine model through a coupling model.

In addition to DEV&DESS, we also used GDEVS[13] to describe the model. GDEVS uses a segmented approach to construct the hybrid model, a commonly used DEVS hybrid modeling method.

When constructing the model with GDEVS, it is necessary to divide it into segments. In the automobile model, segments are divided once for every $0.1\,\text{m/s}$ change of the automobile speed, and the differential equation of the POWER model can be modeled as follows:

$$\text{GDEVS}_{\text{integration}} = (X, Y, S, \delta_{\text{int}}, \delta_{\text{ext}}, \lambda, D, \text{Coeff}), \quad \text{where}$$

$$X = \{in\}, \quad \text{where } in \in \{\text{true, false}\}$$

$$Y = \{\text{sigm}, u, v\}, \quad \text{where sigm} \in \mathbb{R}$$

$$S = \{\text{work, send}\}$$

$$D = 1$$

$$\text{Coef} = \{(a_v, b_v), (a_x, b_x)\}$$

$$\Delta_{\text{int}}(\text{send}, \{(a_v, b_v), (a_x, b_x)\}, x, v)$$

$$= \begin{cases} \text{sigm} = 0.1/a_v \\ (\text{work}, \{(a_v, b_v), (a_x, b_x)\}, x, v) \end{cases}$$

$$\Delta_{\text{ext}}(\text{work}, \{(a_v, b_v), (a_x, b_x)\}, x, v, in, e)$$

$$= \begin{cases} \text{if}(in = \text{true}) \begin{cases} b_x = x, a_x = v, x = b_x + a_x \cdot e \\ b_v = v, a_v = 5U_d - 0.005v \cdot abs(v), v = b_v + a_v \cdot e \\ (\text{send}, \{(a_v, b_v), (a_x, b_x)\}, x, v) \end{cases} \\ \text{if}(in = \text{false})(\text{work}, \{(a_v, b_v), (a_x, b_x)\}, x, v) \end{cases}$$

$$\lambda(\text{work}) = (\text{sigm}, u, v)$$

$$ta(\text{work}) = \text{infinite}$$

$$ta(\text{send}) = 0 \tag{4.6}$$

Then, just like DEV&DESS, the differential equation solving model constructed by GDEVS also needs an additional atomic model to control its state so that it can genuinely meet the interface of the power model. The control model is modeled as follows:

$$\text{GDEVS}_{\text{power}} = \langle X, Y, S, \delta_{\text{ext}}, \delta_{\text{int}}, \lambda, ta \rangle, \quad \text{where}$$

$$X = \{U_d, \text{sigm}\}, \quad \text{where } U_d \in \mathbb{R}$$

$$Y = \{V_d, X_d, \text{Out}\}, \quad \text{where } V_d, X_d \in \mathbb{R}$$

$$S = \{\text{idle}, \text{work}\}$$

$$\Delta_{\text{ext}}(\text{send}, U_d, e) = (\text{work}, (V_d, X_d, \text{Out}), e)$$

$$\Delta_{\text{ext}}(\text{idle}, U_d, e) = \begin{cases} (\text{idle}, (V_d, X_d, \text{Out}), e) & \text{when } U_d < 0 \\ (\text{work}, (V_d, X_d, \text{Out}), e) & \text{when } U_d \geq 0 \end{cases} \quad (4.7)$$

$$\Delta_{\text{int}}(\text{work}) = \text{work}$$

$$\lambda(\text{work}) = (v, x, \text{Out})$$

$$ta(\text{idle}) = \text{infinite}$$

$$ta(\text{work}) = \text{sigm}.$$

The two models are connected through port pair (power. in, integration. out) and (integration. sigm, power. sigm). The integration model is controlled by the POWER model for the integral calculation to obtain the speed and position of the car at this time.

4.2. XDEVS simulation result

We have constructed a car cruise model using the above car model consisting of five cars. The initial positions of the five vehicles in the model are 0, 300, 600, 900, and 1200. The expected speeds of 100, 65, 60, 50, and 25 km/h are assigned. All other cars start the simulation at the expected speed except for the first car. With the XDEVS simulation engine, the results can be obtained (shown in Figs. 7 and 8).

It can be seen from the simulation results that all vehicles finally maintained a speed of 25 km/h and cruised at an interval of 100 m after the adjustment of the control system.

4.3. Specification comparison

In this example, XDEVS only used an atomic model to complete the model's construction without changing the system's original structure. But when using DEV&DESS and GDEVS, it can be found that the structure of the constructed model has changed. In DEV&DESS, the power model is only responsible for control, and the actual system behavior needs to be executed in the DESS models. In this way, there is a difference between the simulation structure of the model and its mathematical model, and the intuitiveness of model representation is lost. Similarly, GDEVS has a similar problem in building a hybrid model that requires using

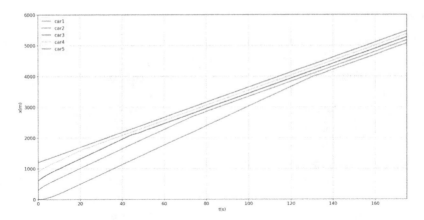

Fig. 7.   Positions of cars in a platoon.

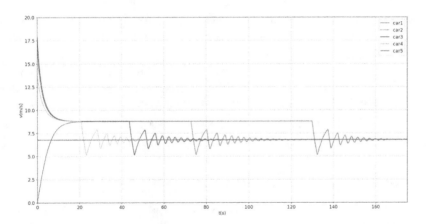

Fig. 8.   Velocity of cars in a platoon.

two atomic models simultaneously, one as an integrator and the other to control the integration behavior.

It can be seen from the simulation result that the built XDEVS model can be simulated in the XDEVS simulation engine by C++ programs. By introducing high-precision equation-solving software tools, the engine can solve the hybrid model with high precision. But this approach will also trigger more additional events in simulation, thus reducing the simulation efficiency.

In the XDEVS work pattern, the modeler can focus on modeling during the modeling phase, and then, the programmer can write the program simulated in the XDEVS simulator. Compared to GDEVS and DEV&DESS, which combine modeling and simulation, this decoupled pattern can effectively improve the efficiency of modeling tools when building large and complex models.

5. Conclusions

For the problem of hybrid system modeling, this paper proposes an XDEVS hybrid modeling framework based on DEVS. New elements are added to enhance the capability of state description in DEVS. The concept of the continuous state is introduced to simplify the hybrid model structure.

By comparing the construction of a vehicle cruise model with DEV&DESS and GDEVS, it can be found that a model can be constructed with XDEVS in a form closer to the mathematical formalism. XDEVS emphasizes more on model expression and has the ability of simulating a hybrid model.

As a modeling specification, the XDEVS model currently requires programmers to program the XDEVS model into the XDEVS simulation engine with C++. This design process introduces efficient modeling and a simulation work pattern, making XDEVS suitable for complex models. But this work pattern also leads to the need for an XDEVS model building platform and programmers to write the built models into simulation codes. In addition, the high-precision equation solving software tool introduced in the XDEVS simulation engine can provide high-precision solutions for the model, but it will also trigger too many additional events in the simulation, reducing the simulation efficiency.

In the future, a more powerful software platform to support XDEVS modeling and simulation is needed. Together with the platform, model libraries of different industrials and supporting tools, such as VV&A tools, analysis tools, and visualization tools, should be developed. A ecosystem based on X language is important to embody the values of MSBSE.

Acknowledgment

This work is supported by National Key R&D Program of China, No. 2018YFB1701600.

References

1. Zeigler B. P., Praehofer H., Kim T. G., *Theory of Modeling and Simulation: Integrating Discrete Event and Continuous Complex Dynamic Systems*, Academic Press, San Diego, 2000.
2. Zeigler B., Embedding DEV&DESS in DEVS: Characteristic behavior of hybrid models, *Simul. Series* **38**, 2006.
3. Giambiasi N., Carmona J. C., Generalized discrete event abstraction of continuous systems: GDEVS formalism, *Simul. Model. Practice Theory* **14**(1):47–70, 2006, https://doi.org/10.1016/j.simpat.2005.02.009.
4. Kofman E., Lapadula M., Pagliero E., PowerDEVS: A DEVS-based environment for hybrid system modeling and simulation, School of Electronic Engineering, Universidad Nacional de Rosario, Tech. Rep. LSD0306, 1–25, 2003.
5. Bergero F., Kofman E., PowerDEVS: A tool for hybrid system modeling and real-time simulation, *Simulation* **87**(1–2):113–132, 2011, https://doi.org/10.1177/0037549710368029.

6. Nutaro J., Kuruganti P. T., Protopopescu V., Shankar M., The split system approach to managing time in simulations of hybrid systems having continuous and discrete event components, *Simul.-Trans. Soc. Model. Simul. Int.* **88**(3):281–298, 2012, https://doi.org/10.1177/0037549711401000.

7. Nutaro J., An extension of the OpenModelica compiler for using Modelica models in a discrete event simulation. *Simulation* **90**(12):1328–1345, 2014.

8. Zhang L. *et al.*, X language: An integrated intelligent modeling and simulation language for complex products, *2021 Annual Modeling and Simulation Conf. (ANNSIM)*, IEEE, pp. 1–11, 2021.

9. Zhang L., Laili Y., Ye F., Research on new generation of multi-domain unified modeling language for complex products. *Methods and Applications for Modeling and Simulation of Complex Systems, Asian Simulation Conf.*, Singapore, 30 October–1 November, 2019, pp. 237–242.

10. Zhang L. *et al.*, An integrated intelligent modeling and simulation language for model-based systems engineering, *J. of Industrial Information Integration*, **28**:100347, 2022, https://doi.org/10.1016/j.jii.2022.100347.

11. Chen Z., Zhang L., Wang X., Gu P., Ye F., A conversion framework of the continuous modeling languages based on ANTLR4, *33rd European Modeling & Simulation Symp., 18th Int. Multidisciplinary Modeling and Simulation Multiconf.*, 15–17 September, 2021, Krakow, Poland.

12. Elmqvist H. *et al.*, State machines in Modelica, *Proceedings of the 9th Int. MODELICA Conf.*, September 3–5, 2012, Munich, Germany, Linköping University Electronic Press, pp. 37–46, 2012.

13. Giambiasi N., Escude, B., Ghosh S., GDEVS: A generalized discrete event specification for accurate modeling of dynamic systems, *Proc. 5th Int. Symp. Autonomous Decentralized Systems*, IEEE, pp. 464–469, 2001.

Chapter 5

An integrated intelligent modeling and simulation language for model-based systems engineering

Lin Zhang*, Fei Ye*,**,‖, Kunyu Xie*,**, Pengfei Gu*,**, Xiaohan Wang*,**, Yuanjun Laili*, Chun Zhao†, Xuesong Zhang‡, Minjie Chen§, Tingyu Lin¶ and Zhen Chen*

*Beihang University; Xueyuan Road No. 37, Beijing, China
†Beijing Information Science and Technology University; North Ring No. 35, Chaoyang District, Beijing, China
‡Jilin University; Qianjin Street No. 2699, Chaoyang District Changchun, Jilin Province, China
§Beijing Huaru Technology Co., Ltd; Dongbeiwangxi Road No. 10 Haidian District, Beijing, China
¶Beijing Institute of Electronic System Engineering; Yongding Road No. 52, Haidian District Beijing, China

Abstract

Modeling and simulation are now leading the way in supporting analysis and development of system of systems. At present, to support the unified modeling formalism and dynamic simulation for different domain specific models across MBSE process, system modeling languages (such as SysML) are often required to cooperate with multi-physics modeling languages and simulation platforms (such as Modelica, Simulink), which makes it challenging to ensure the true unity of the whole system models, the consistency between the various system layers and the traceability of the modeling and simulation processes. In response to the above problems, this paper develops a new integrated intelligent modeling and simulation language, which can uniformly describe the system-level architecture and physical behavior models as a whole. On this basis, models can be simulated directly to support system verification for MBSE. Compiler and simulation engine are developed to enable X language to support the simulation of continuous, discrete event and agent models. Finally, an intelligent car system is taken as a case to verify the modeling and simulation capabilities of X language.

1. Introduction

In recent years, Model-based Systems Engineering (MBSE) has become an essential means to support the development of complex systems, especially system of systems (SoS).[1-3] Taking complex products as an example, MBSE transforms the traditional research and development (R&D) method based on documents and physical models into a model-driven R&D method. This formal description method renders MBSE reusable, unambiguous, intelligible, and easy to spread. MBSE employs Systems

---

‖Corresponding authors. zhanglin@buaa.edu.cn, yefei@buaa.edu.cn, zy1903114@buaa.edu.cn, by2003151@buaa.edu.cn, by1903042@buaa.edu.cn, lailiyuanjun@buaa.edu.cn, zhao_chun@189.cn, xs_zhang@126.com, jimi_chen@163.com, lintingyu2003@foxmail.com, czhen@buaa.edu.cn
**These authors contribute equally to this work.

Modeling Language (SysML) to realize the model-based integrated management and optimization of the whole product development process.[4] Since a SysML model cannot be directly simulated, it is necessary to use other simulation methods to verify the correctness and completeness.

One of the mainstream approaches is to uniformly describe system components of different domains based on a unified modeling language to achieve seamless integration and data exchange of multi-domain models.[5] For complex products that incorporate mechanical, electrical, hydraulic, and control engineering, the requirement description and architecture design are first conducted based on system modeling languages (such as SysML, IDEF, etc.). Then the physical models are developed and integrated in accordance with the physical modeling languages (such as Modelica, etc.) and the integration standards (FMI, HLA, etc.). Finally, different stages of product development are uniformly managed through mappings and transformations between the system models and the physical models for full system modeling and simulation.

However, due to the disconnection between the system modeling languages and the physical domain simulation languages, the connection needs to be realized through a transformation. Therefore, this approach falls behind in ensuring the consistency and traceability of the whole system modeling and simulation process. Worse still, this method lacks the ability of intelligent modeling and simulation, which is of vital importance for intelligent actions in development processes and/or intelligent functions of complex products.

Thus, this paper develops a new integrated intelligent modeling and simulation language, which can uniformly describe the system-level architecture and physical behavior models as a whole. On this basis, models can be simulated directly to support system verification for MBSE. At the system modeling level, six parts of the definition, requirement, connection, equation, action, and state machine are designed based on the object-oriented approach to represent the architecture and behavior.[6] At the level of simulation and verification, the continuous, discrete event, and agent models are incorporated into the couple models of DEVS (Discrete Event System Specification).[7] A specific tool XLab is developed to realize the modeling and simulation of the whole system.

The remainder of this paper is organized as follows. Section 2 presents related work from the perspective of system modeling, physical modeling, agent modeling, as well as the integration of system design and verification. In Section 3, we elaborate on the overall structure of X language, including the hierarchical structure of X language, the correspondence between graphics and text, and the design of X language classes. Section 4 gives an introduction to the essential elements and grammatical structure of X language, mainly in the form of classes. In Section 5, we introduce the compiler of X language. In Section 6, we demonstrate the modeling and simulation capabilities of X language using an intelligent car system. Finally, we summarize this paper and briefly outline the further research work.

2. Related Work

When it comes to system modeling, typical practices include, to cite but a few, the modeling methods based on the DEVS, system modeling methods based on the SysML language, multidisciplinary unified modeling methods based on the Modelica language, Bond diagram-based system dynamic structure modeling method, European simulation language (ESL)-based software and hardware coordination modeling method, Dymola language-based system dynamics modeling method, and high-level architecture (HLA)-based distributed simulation system modeling method. These languages and methods have been studied and applied to varying degrees in industry and academia.

2.1. *System modeling language*

Before the advent of SysML, many modeling languages and tools were used in systems engineering, such as IDEF, N2 diagrams, behavior diagrams, etc. These modeling languages employed different symbols and semantics, which cannot be interoperated and reused, thus restricting the effective communication between systems engineers and those of other disciplines on system requirements and design, and affecting the quality and efficiency of systems engineering. To meet the actual needs of systems engineering, the INCOSE International Council of Systems Engineering) and the OMG (Object Management Organization) decided to propose a new system modeling language — SysML on the basis of reusing and extending a subset of UML 2.0 as a standard modeling language for systems engineering.[5] SysML supports the specification, analysis, design, verification, and validation of a broad range of complex systems. These systems may include hardware, software, information, processes, personnel, and facilities.[8] It supports multiple structured and object-oriented methods and multiple procedures. However, native SysML models are static and cannot be directly used to verify the correctness and completeness. Thus, the SysML models should be transformed into domain-specific models, such as Modelica models.[9] There has been a lot of work in this direction.[10-15]

Generally, for systems with different characteristics, the types of SysML diagrams adopted are also different. Literature[16] proposes a method of using SysML parameter diagrams to describe the behavior of continuous systems. Literature[12] and[17] elaborate on the description of discrete event systems based on SysML action, sequence, or state machine diagrams. Although SysML models can be extracted and used by the transformation methods, system engineers have to add a large number of simulation codes, especially those related to system behavior, to obtain executable simulation models, which is a tedious process and not very versatile.[18]

2.2. *Physical property modeling language*

A complex system generally contains different domains, such as mechanics, electronics, control, hydraulics, and pneumatics. As a result, the cost is surging to verify and optimize characteristics of a complex system through physical experiments, and modeling and simulation of multiple domain physical properties prove to be a more efficient way.

For modeling and simulation of physical systems in a single domain, traditional software generally establishes system state equations for a single energy domain based on fundamental physical laws (such as Newton's laws of mechanics, Kirchhoff's laws, etc.), solves the equations through computer programming and finally obtains the system response characteristics. According to the known mathematical models, the typical software, such as Matlab and Simulink of MathWorks, is formed on the block diagram modeling methods. Other software such as Power DEVS and Modelica also employs similar modeling methods.

Although most simple systems can be simulated by the above methods of a single domain, the actual engineering systems often incorporate the couple of multiple energy forms, such as mechanical, electromagnetic, hydraulic, and chemical energy. In this case, only interface-based co-simulation is feasible. It is difficult to obtain a mathematical model of a multi-domain system using a single-domain method or to realize the automatic generation and simulation analysis of the model in a unified form on the computer. To address this problem, in 1961, Professor Herry Paynter of the Massachusetts Institute of Technology, from the viewpoint of energy system dynamics, proposed a theoretical framework for a unified modeling method of system dynamics suitable for the coexistence of multiple energy domains.[19] It lays the foundation for dynamic analysis, modeling, and simulation of multi-energy domain couple systems. Since then, various bond graph technologies have been proposed for modeling and simulation applications of different systems.[20]

The modeling method based on bond graphs can solve the modeling problems of multi-domain physical systems; however, the construction of model details based on graphs is not convenient enough. In 1997, the theoretical framework of energy conservation based on the bond graph and the equation-based Modelica language was proposed to support object-oriented modeling, declarative modeling, non-causal modeling, and multi-domain unified modeling as well as modeling of hybrid, i.e., both continuous and discrete, systems.[21] The Modelica language has then risen to be the mainstream language for multi-domain physical system modeling due to its high model reusability, ease of use, no symbol processing, and many other advantages. At the same time, the system standard library of Modelica language also provides essential components and typical system models in many fields, including electricity, fluids, thermodynamics, machinery, etc.,[22] which offers great convenience in model development and simulation of physical systems.

Despite the fact that Modelica is able to model and simulate hybrid models, the equation-based language characteristics make it inept to support discrete event simulation well, resulting in to inconvenient description and low simulation efficiency.[23–25] Therefore, the application of Modelica lies more suitable in multi-domain physical system modeling rather than in modeling large-scale discrete systems.

2.3. *Intelligent extension of modeling languages*

To meet the requirements of modeling intelligent activities and behaviors of complex systems, modeling languages need to be extended with intelligent factors to better describe the complex agent and neural network models and to strengthen the capability in interaction, sensing, and learning. As an essential method to achieve complex system modeling and simulation, agent-based models and multi-agent systems have seen ever-widening applications in the fields of simulation, artificial intelligence, and control. In order to efficiently construct various agent models, some modeling languages supporting agent models were proposed in different aspects.

As one of the most commonly used languages in modeling and simulation, Modelica has also been applied in the research of agent models. However, due to the insufficient support for discrete system modeling, it is not suitable for agent modeling. Therefore, the research on agent modeling based on Modelica mainly focuses on the support of third-party libraries. Bünning[26] pointed out that native Modelica is unsuitable for modeling agents and built a third-party library for multi-agent systems based on Modelica. Sanz[27] designed the ABMlib library rfor the type, behavior, communication, and environment of agents to improve the performance of Modelica based on agent models. In addition, some studies focus on applying Modelica to describe the continuous behavior or action of an agent rather than modeling the agent or the overall system agent.[28,29]

SysML plays a vital role in the system-level model design. Some works revolve around SysML to provide support for the construction of agent models. Sha[30] introduced the concept representation of agents with SysML, supported and verified the early conceptual model of agents, and provided a case to demonstrate the method proposed in the article. Literature[31] proposed a set of dynamic modeling methods based on SysML to establish agent models and emphasized the important influence of the environment, including the fact that the environment determines the action and updates the parameters of agents. As a system-level language, SysML can describe the event relationship among agents and can easily establish an agent conceptual model. However, as the native SysML model is static, the simulation of agent models needs to rely on third-party simulation tools. Besides, SysML is also insufficient in describing the detailed behaviors and actions of agents, as well as some specific multi-agent algorithms.

As a kind of discrete models, agents can be modeled and simulated by DEVS. In the literature,[32] a complex agent perception architecture is constructed based on multiple types of atomic models with the BDI (Belief-Desire-Intention) model as its component. However, the entire model is too bulky and redundant as many parts are uncommon to most agent models. In addition, the BDI part in the paper is only represented in the form of symbols rather than in the atomic model. Akplogan[33] used the DEVS couple model to build a BDI agent model to solve the problem of agent decision-making in agricultural applications and provided a specific application to prove its feasibility of the overall architecture. From the perspective of multi-agents, Müller[34] built a set of system models using DEVS and modified the expression of the original DEVS atomic model to adapt to the multi-agent characteristics. However, this method is not applicable when facing a single complex agent, as the specification of DEVS is rudimentary compared with the agent models.

In summary, although several representative modeling languages may support the construction of agent models and multi-agent systems, they only apply agent models at the level of basic methods or integration with third-party libraries, lacking the ability of autonomy. In other words, these languages themselves are not designed for modeling multi-agent models, which can make intelligent and dynamic decisions by reasoning and learning, so it is difficult to avoid problems such as poor interpretability, poor algorithm representation, low autonomy, and low modeling efficiency.

2.4. *Integration of system modeling and simulation*

SysML has the ability to describe the system model but cannot be directly used to verify its correctness and completeness. Therefore, it needs to be transformed into an executable one to make up for the deficiency, which is the common practice used by current engineers and researchers.

Schamai et al.[35,36] proposed a mapping method ModelicaML based on the UML extension method for Modelica transformation. It uses state machine diagrams as the carrier for hybrid modeling of discrete and continuous behavior and adds annotations to state transformation to describe continuous behavior, thereby providing a more complete solution for integrating design and simulation behavior. However, this method lacks formal model expression. The description based on plain text can not effectively express and manage models, and the parameter correspondence between the state machine diagrams and structure models is not attained, which makes ModelicaML unable to fully support all grammar standards of Modelica. Gauthier et al.[37] used the ATL (Atlas Transformation Language) to map a SysML model to a Modelica model based on the SysML4Modelica extension package[38] proposed by the OMG to verify the accuracy and completeness of a design model. Compared with the QVT (Query/View/Transformation) mapping method applied by OMG, Gauthier et al. have some innovations in the mapping method. However, due to the incomplete definition of the SysML4Modelica extension package, the description of the Modelica syntax is not perfect. Cao et al.[39] proposed a unified behavior model extension method based on SysML. This method is combined with Matlab/Simulink to realize the automatic transformation between the design and simulation models by establishing a supplementary simulation model. On the flip side, this method is more focused on the simulation of the control system field and is weak in supporting the multi-domain modeling and simulation of the physical system, so it is not applicable to the simulation of complex systems engineering. Li et al.[40] developed a modeling language that supports modeling and simulation of the continuous and discrete systems, providing parallel solutions for the simulation optimization problem, but not good at system-level modeling. Li *et al.*[41] proposed a SysML-based visualization model transformation method from the perspective of a meta-model. They determined the transformation relationships between the SysML source and Modelica target models by hierarchical instantiation modeling of the transformation rule and transformation activity meta-model, thereby implementing the dynamic transformation activities. Despite that, this method does not extend SysML but establishes a mapping relationship with Modelica based on the existing model elements of SysML. Therefore, the specific description of complex products is insufficient, making the transformation between the two languages incomplete. Zhou *et al.*[42] constructed the SysML extension package M-Design for Modelica based on the Modelica meta-models, and then defined the mapping rules between the two according to the extended SysML and Modelica meta-models, thus implementing the automatic transformation from the SysML design models to Modelica simulation models. Even so, the extension package only defines the basic meta-model of Modelica, and some advanced features escape the description. Besides, the ATL-based mapping method only implements the one-way model transformation from SysML to Modelica and fails to implement the bidirectional model transformation.

In addition, complex systems involve models in multiple domains. These models use different formalisms, modeling languages, and tools to solve specific problems, bringing significant challenges to consistency management. Different techniques were proposed to alleviate the consistency problem in systems engineering studies. MBSE tools like SCADE Architect can be directly integrated into SCADE Suite, providing system and software teams with the same environment to synchronize requirements, avoiding duplication and inconsistency.[43] Herzig *et al.*[44] presented a conceptual basis for inconsistency management in MBSE that a model can be represented by a graph and that inconsistencies manifest as subgraphs. To identify inconsistencies, graphs can be queried using partially defined graph patterns. However, the authors did not provide proof of the technical viability and practicability. Feldmann *et al.*[45] introduced a conceptual approach based on semantic web standards allowing for identifying inconsistencies in heterogeneous models and demonstrating its technical viability. A possible disadvantage is that the evaluation of the conceptual frame-work's viability is preliminary since only a small system was used as a demonstration case. Jongeling *et al.*[46] proposed the idea of extending the OpenMBEE platform to include code as a view. They believe that this extension will allow simple structural consistency checks between the SysML system model and C/C++ code and provide engineers and managers with insight into model-code consistency. Berriche *et al.*[47] proposed a model synchronization approach to actively check for model consistency in a continuous way during the multidisciplinary design process. However, this method has some limitations: the model synchronization method is only applicable to structural and hierarchical models. In addition, the classification and resolution of differences is a manual process that relies on the activities of the project manager.

In summary, the existing modeling languages are mainly aimed at a specific part of modeling and simulation. They lack the ability of full-process (the entire lifecycle) collaborative design and verification. Although the integration of system design and verification can realize the unified management of different stages during product development, it is still achieved through the mapping and transformation between languages. It may be effortless to deal with a single domain model but challenging to support the modeling and simulation of complex systems that contain the continuous, discrete event and intelligent properties.

3. Overall Structure of X Language

As can be seen from above, the existing modeling languages cannot achieve full system modeling and simulation. Aiming at this problem, this paper proposes a new integrated intelligent modeling and simulation language-X language. As shown in Figure 1, at the level of system modeling, six parts of the definition, requirement, connection, equation, action, and state machine are designed to represent structure and behavior. At the model construction and simulation level, the continuous, discrete event, and agent models are regarded as part of the couple model of DEVS, which supports the simulation verification of physical behavior. Based on the design, X language is endowed with the capabilities to: 1) support two modeling forms of graphics and text, and based on XLab, the two forms of models can be converted to each other. 2) support system-level architecture and physical behavior modeling and simulation verification. 3) support modeling for various complex agent models,

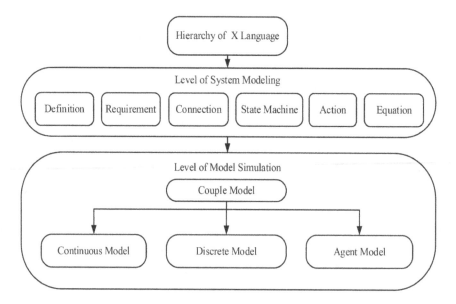

Fig. 1.   Hierarchy of X language

including agent learning, communication, and multi-agent parallel simulation. 4) support continuous, discrete event, and hybrid simulation.

X language is a modeling language that supports model-based systems engineering. As shown in Figure 2, from the perspective of modeling process, it includes two modeling forms of graphics and text, as well as an engine for simulation. As for language elements, there are structural elements, behavioral elements, and other essential elements. Figure 3 shows the one-to-one correspondence between the graphic and textual forms of X language and its six types of diagrams: definition diagram, requirement diagram, connection diagram, state machine diagram, equation diagram, and action diagram. Each diagram corresponds to the language text and exists as a part of the class. Therefore, a single part can only describe an aspect of the class rather than the complete one. That is, a class is a collection of contents described by multiple parts.

The six parts of X language have their respective focuses. The definition part and the connection part define the system model from the system structure level, explaining which components the system contains and the connection relationships among them. The requirement class is defined for requirement description, analysis, and tracking. Modelers generally use a variety of relationships to establish the trace-ability between requirements, and the traceability from requirements to the structure and behavior of the system models.

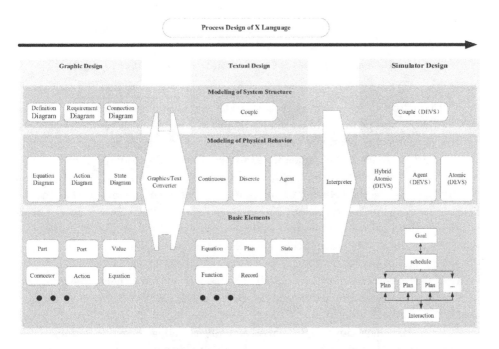

Fig. 2.   Design process and elements of X language

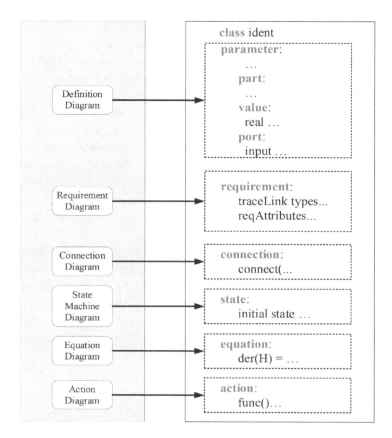

Fig. 3.　Correspondence between graphical and textual syntax of X language

The equation part, action part, and state machine part describe the system behavior from the perspective of the mathematical equation, assignment process, and state machine, respectively. Different modeling elements are selected depending on the characteristics of the model; for example, continuous models can be modeled by equations, while discrete models by state machines. Therefore, different forms are required to describe the behavior of different types of system models or components. On this basis, the restricted classes of X language are classified: the continuous class is used to describe continuous multi-domain physical systems, the discrete class describes discrete systems, and the agent class describes agent systems.

X language supports model-based systems engineering and has the ability to verify the entire process of system design. The models built in either graphics or text can be directly translated into executable DEVS codes via the compiler. X language simulation engine is a multi-domain engine designed based on XDEVS (introduced in Chapter 4), which can support cross-domain modeling in multiple domains of continuous, discrete events, and agents. The results obtained by the simulation can be directly fed back to the engineer to realize the functional verification of the system design.

4. Essential Elements and Grammatical Structure of X Language

Class is the basic unit of a model in X language, which can be further divided into basic classes and restricted classes. The basic classes are modified by the keyword *class* and applied to describe the structural and behavioral characteristics of any entities. The restricted classes are mainly used to describe models of different characteristics more accurately and improve the readability. They are modified by specific keywords, including *continuous, discrete, couple, agent, requirement, record, function*, and *connector*. The types and functions of the classes are shown in Table 1.

X language provides two modeling forms: graphics and text. The concept of class is for the entire language; that is, it is applicable to both text and graphic model forms. Diagrams refer to the elements of the graphical models, including definition diagram, requirement diagram, connection diagram, state machine diagram, equation diagram, and action diagram. Correspondingly, the text models also contain 6 parts, namely the definition part, requirement part, connection part, state part, equation part, and action part. A class is often a combination of multiple components, as shown in Table 2, which lists the components contained in each class.

The following content will specify the essential elements and grammatical structure of each class, and the extended BNF[6] of each component is demonstrated in Appendix A.

4.1. *Continuous class*

According to the behavior characteristics of models, they can be divided into continuous models, discrete models, and hybrid models. The continuous class is defined for models with continuous behavior that constantly changes over time and can be abstracted by mathematical equations. The structural properties of entities with continuous behavior contain the definitions of parameters and their types, state

Table 1. Functions of X language classes

Types	Functions
Class	Supporting the description of any types of model entities
Continuous	Supporting the description of model entities with continuous behavior
Discrete	Supporting the description of model entities triggered by events
Agent	Supporting the description of model entities with intelligent behavior
Couple	Supporting the description of system-level model entities with multiple components
Requirement	Supporting the description, analysis and tracking of requirements
Record	Supporting the description of complex data structures in various model entities
Function	Supporting the description of algorithms required for various model entities to solve procedural modeling
Connector	Supporting the description of connectors that follow Kirchhoff's law in various model entities

Table 2.   Composition of the two forms of X language classes

Class	Composition of diagrams	Composition of text
Class	Definition diagram, Requirement diagram, connection diagram, equation diagram, state machine diagram, action diagram	Definition part, Requirement part, connection part, equation part, state machine part, action part
Continuous	Definition diagram, equation diagram	Definition part, equation part
Discrete	Definition diagram, state machine diagram	Definition part, state machine part
Agent	Definition diagram, action diagram	Definition part, action part
Requirement	Requirement diagram	Requirement part
Couple	Definition diagram, connection diagram	Definition part, connection part
Record	Definition diagram	Definition part
Function	Definition diagram, action diagram	Definition part, action part
Connector	Definition diagram	Definition part

Table 3.   Definition of continuous class

Continuous class	Related properties of continuous class	Descriptive objects of different properties
Definition diagram/ Definition part	Parameter	Definition of instantiation parameters and their types
	Value	Definition of state variables
	Port	Definition of ports
Equation diagram/ Equation part	Equation	Definition of behavior described based on mathematical equations

variables, and ports. At the same time, the behavior properties can be defined by mathematical equations. Based on this, in graphics and text modeling, the continuous class in X language describes the structural attributes by the definition diagram and the definition part, and the behavior characteristics by the equation diagram and the equation part, respectively. The details are shown in Table 3.

4.2. *Discrete class*

The discrete class is defined for discrete models. The behavior of discrete models are triggered by events and can be regarded as an abstraction of a series of states. The structural properties of discrete models generally include the definitions of the parameters and their types, state variables, and ports. The behavior parameters are defined based on the state machine theory. Accordingly, in graphics and text modeling, the discrete class in X language describes the structural characteristics by the definition diagram and the definition part, and the behavior characteristics by the state machine diagram and the state machine part, respectively. The details are presented in Table 4.

Table 4. Definition of discrete class

Discrete class	Related properties of discrete class	Descriptive objects of different properties
Definition diagram/ Definition part	Parameter	Definition of instantiation parameters and their types
	Value	Definition of state variables
	Port	Definition of ports
State machine diagram/ State machine part	State	Definition of behavior based on state machine description

Table 5. Definition of couple class

Couple class	Related properties of couple class	Descriptive objects of different properties
Definition diagram/ Definition part	Port	Definition of ports
	Part	Definition of components
Connection diagram/ Connection part	Connection	Definition of the connection relationship between components

4.3. *Couple class*

The couple class is defined to endow X language with the ability to describe couple models. Its principal function is to describe the components included in the couple model and the connections among them. Based on this, the couple class in X language adopts the definition diagram and the definition part to describe the system composition, and the connection diagram and the connection part to describe the component connection relationship, respectively. The details are shown in Table 5.

4.4. *Agent class*

The agent class is defined for multi-agent models that emphasize more on the autonomy of agents, which can make intelligent and dynamic decisions by reasoning and learning. The design of the agent class in X language follows the BDI architecture and has been simplified. Among them, the most critical content is retained; that is, goals guide the execution of plans. A series of content such as environmental perception is left to users to define, thereby improving the extensibility of the language. For modeling with the agent class, the entire structure can be divided into two parts, the definition part and the action part. The former is used to initialize the values of parameters and variables, as well as the declaration of functions and plans. The latter is to control the execution of the plan and set the start and end conditions of the agent simulation.

The architectural correspondence between the agent class and the BDI is illustrated in Figure 4. The left side is the architecture of the agent class, and the BDI

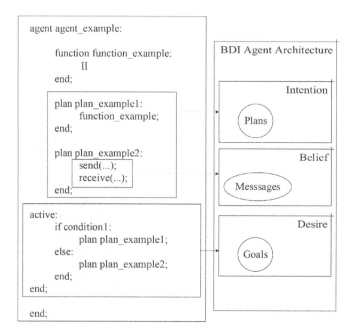

Fig. 4.   The architectural correspondence between the agent class and the BDI

Table 6.   Definition of agent class

Agent class	Related properties of agent class	Descriptive objects of different properties
Definition diagram/ Definition part	Parameter	Definition of instantiation parameters and their types
	Value	Definition of state variables
	Plan	Definition of Agent behavior sequence
Action diagram/ Action part	Active	Definition of plan execution logic

architecture is on the right. The plan corresponds to the intention part of the BDI architecture. The content defined in the execution part is associated with the goal part and the belief part is integrated into the entire process of interaction process between the agent and the environment. On the basis of retaining the characteristics of the original BDI architecture, the agent class is integrated with the syntax and semantics of X language, giving X language intelligent characteristics.

The agent models generally contain the behavior of communication and interaction with other entities, the agent class in X language describes the structure characteristics by the definition diagram and the definition part, and the behavior characteristics by the action diagram and the action part, respectively. The details are shown in Table 6.

4.5. *Requirement class*

The requirement class is defined for requirement description, analysis, and tracking. It contains two parts, namely *Requirement Attributes* and *TraceLink Types*. The former describes the relevant attributes of requirements to illustrate the inherent characteristics of a specific requirement, such as ID, Name, Level, Type, etc. The latter is used to manage links between requirements and requirements and other modeling elements (including stakeholders, sources, and system development elements), forming links for demand tracking, such as Compose, Satisfy, Verify, etc. The details are shown in Table 7.

4.6. *Record class*

The record class is defined for models with different data types. Accordingly, the record class in X language uses definition diagrams and definition parts to describe the types of data contained in graphics and text modeling, as shown in Table 8.

Table 7.   Definition of requirement class

Requirement class	Related properties of requirement class		Descriptive objects of different properties
Requirement diagram/ Requirement part	Requirement Attributes[48]	Identifier	Unique identifier of the requirement
		Name	Name of the requirement
		Level	Level of the requirement (Stakeholder/ System/Component)
		Type	Type of the requirement (General/Functional/ Non Functional/Physical/Design)
		Risk	Security level of the requirement (High/ Medium/Low)
		Source	Where the requirement originated from
		Stakehodler	Stakeholder who is in charge
		Text	Description text defined by the modeler
	TraceLink Types[48]	Compose	Relates requirement to its parent requirement
		Copy	The same requirement that appears in a different level
		Derive	Relates requirement to its derived requirement
		Refine	Relates requirement to its refined requirement
		Satisfy	Relates requirement to the block that fulfills it
		Verify	Relates requirement to test cases
		Mapped To	Relates requirement to a particular attribute, operation, state or value of the artifact
		Originated From	Relates requirement to its source
		Responsible Of	Relates requirement to its stakeholder

Table 8.   Definition of record class

Record class	Related properties of record class	Descriptive objects of different properties
Definition diagram/Definition part	Value	Definition of different data types

Table 9.   Definition of agent class

Function class	Related attributes of record class	Descriptive objects of different properties
Definition diagram/ definition part	Value	Definition of input/output parameters
Action diagram/ action part	Active	Definition of function realization process

Table 10.   Definition of connector class

Connector class	Related attributes of record class	Descriptive objects of different properties
Definition diagram/ definition part	Value	Definition of input/output data types

4.7. *Function class*

The function class is defined for models with complex functional behavior. Generally, the function class is composed of the definition part and the action part. The former is used to define input and output parameters, while the latter is to specify specific functions of the function class. The details are shown in Table 9.

4.8. *Connector class*

The connector class is defined for models with connectors that follow Kirchhoff's law. The connectors define the types of data transferred between the entity and other entities. On this basis, the connector class is defined to describe non-causal connector ports as well as the types of data transferred between models or components. Generally, the connector class in X language describes the types of data transmitted through the definition diagram and the definition part when graphics and text are modeled, as shown in Table 10.

A class is a collection of contents described by multiple parts, and X language modeling framework consists of 6 parts. Therefore, a single part can only describe an aspect of the class rather than the complete one.

5. Compiler and Simulation Engine

X language is an object-oriented multi-domain system modeling and simulation language. It includes not only the characteristics of object-oriented programming languages but also those of equation-based modeling languages. These two kinds of languages usually employ different interpretation routes, leading to different technical routes in X language interpretation.

The framework of X language compiler is shown in Figure 5. The interpretation process is divided into three stages, namely the pre-processing stage, the intermediate processing stage, and the post-processing stage.

The pre-processing stage is responsible for lexical analysis and grammatical analysis of the source code to obtain the abstract syntax tree and collect the information of the elements in the model to make a symbol table.

In the intermediate processing stage, the compiler processes the abstract syntax tree that has been obtained by the pre-processing stage. Different technical methods are applied according to the types of models included in the interpreted document. For continuous models based on equations, the first step is to flatten the model to obtain a flattened equation set. Then in the stage of casualization, the equations are transformed into a form suitable for being solved by the differential equation solver. For assignment-based models, i.e., the agent models and the DEVS-models, the static type checking is first performed for each sentence contained in the model with the help of the symbol table constructed in the previous stage. Then different technical methods are selected according to different model types. The reason to adopt different compilation routes here is that the interpretation and code generation of the DEVS model can correspond to the simulation code one by one, while the representation of the upper model of an agent model differs drastically from the lower one, thus requiring the parameter correspondence and the integration of

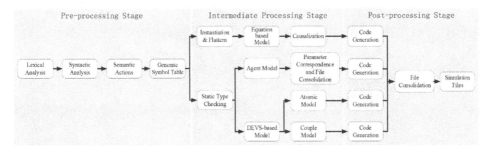

Fig. 5.   Framework of X language compiler

generated files to ensure that the necessary information is not lost. Therefore, the complexity of the two compilation routes is also quite different.

In the last stage, the processed data structures obtained in the different technical routes are traversed and the simulation files of the respective models are obtained. If the model has a hierarchical structure, the file level integration is required to obtain simulation files of the entire model.

A X language simulation engine based on XDEVS has been introduced in Chapter 4. Together with the compiler, integrated modeling and simulations with X language can be conducted.

6. Case Study

An intelligent car driving system is illustrated here to prove the simulation capability of X-language for hybrid systems, which means the hybrid of a continuous system and discreet event system. The system is simplified into three modules: continuous module, discrete event module, and agent module. Figure 6 shows the structure of the system, where *Car1* is a manned vehicle, regarded as an intelligent car, and *Car2* is an unmanned vehicle, as a non-intelligent car. *Car1* contains three modules: *driver* as an agent model, *car* as a discrete event model, and *power* as a continuous model. *Car2* only has a discrete event model named *autocar*.

In order to show more clearly the entire modeling and simulation process based on X language, the connection relationship and action sequence among various models of the system are explicitly defined in Figure 6. The agent model (*driver*) first uses the trained policy to make decisions and passes the action results to the

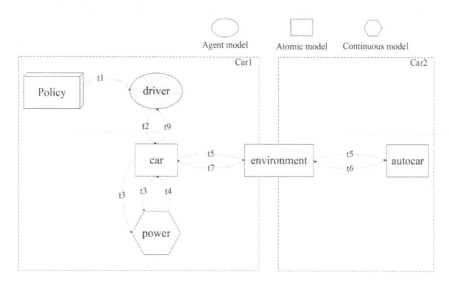

Fig. 6.   An intelligent car driving system

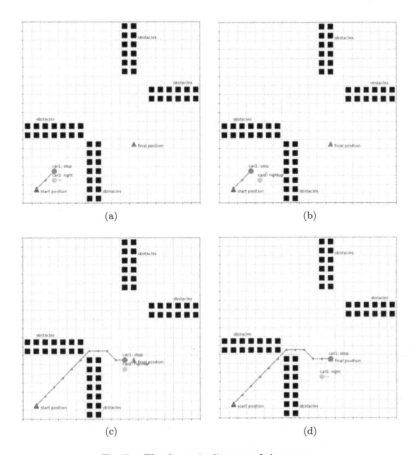

Fig. 7.   The dynamic diagram of the system

discrete event model (car). The *car* transmits the driver's actions to the *power* module to generate dynamic feedback based on the actions. Finally, the *car* changes its actual position according to the *power* feedback. During this process, the *environment* also keeps track of the positions of *Car2* and feeds them back to *Car1* so that *Car1* will make way for *Car2* to prevent accidents.

The dynamic diagram of the system is shown in Figure 7, where (a), (b), and (c) show the three interaction stages that *Car1* and *Car2* experience on the way to the destination. At each encounter, *Car1* will stop its current action and give way to Car2 until *Car2* leaves. The entire trajectory of *car1* from the initial position to the final position is illustrated in (d). In this process, *Car1* traverses the t1-t8 stages shown in Figure 6.

For this case, the top-level model of the entire system is firstly established, which is composed of the *car, autocar, environmental, driver*, and *power* module. The definition diagram and connection diagram of the system are shown in Figures 8 and 9, respectively defining the components and the connection relationship among

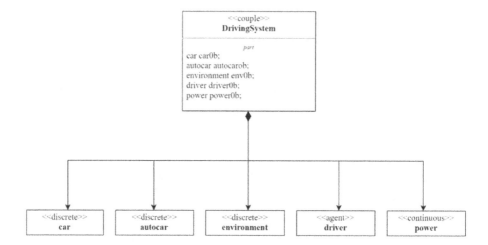

Fig. 8.   Definition diagram of the top-level model

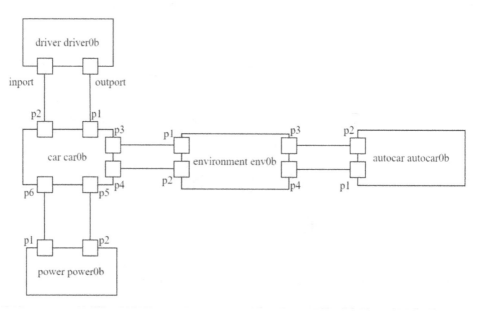

Fig. 9.   Connection diagram of the top-level model

the above 5 modules. Figure 10 indicates the modeling text of the top-level model. Obviously, Figure 8 and Figure 9 are the graphic forms of the couple class, and Figure 10 is the text forms; they all represent the same models. Similarly, Figures 11 and 12 are, respectively, the definition diagram and state machine diagram of the *car*. Figure 13 shows the modeling text of the *car*. In view of the fact that the modeling process is the same, the other system models will not be described in

```
couple simulation                              connection:
    import car;                                     connect(driverOb.outport, carOb.p1);
    import autocar;                                 connect(carOb.p2, driverOb.inport);
    import environment;
    import driver;                                  connect(carOb.p3, envOb.p1);
    import power;                                   connect(envOb.p2, carOb.p4);

part:                                              connect(carOb.p6, powerOb.p1);
    car carOb;                                      connect(powerOb.p2, carOb.p5);
    autocar autocarOb;
    environment envOb;                              connect(envOb.p4, autocarOb.p1);
    driver driverOb;                                connect(autocarOb.p2, envOb.p3);
    power powerOb;
                                               end;
```

Fig. 10.   Modeling text of the top-level model

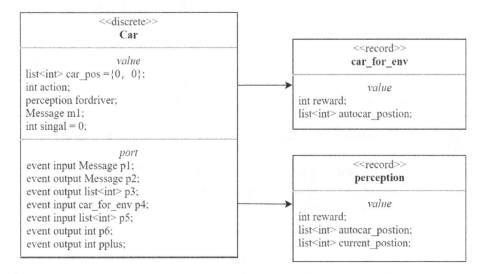

Fig. 11.   Definition diagram of the car

detail. It should be noted that the modeler can use X language-specific tool XLab to realize the automatic transformation of the graphic model to the text model or can directly perform the text modeling and skip the graphic modeling according to the actual needs.

Since X language simulation engine is built based on XDEVS, there is a time advancement process of discrete events during the simulation of the system, as shown in Figure 14, where a point represents an event occurrence of each DEVS-based

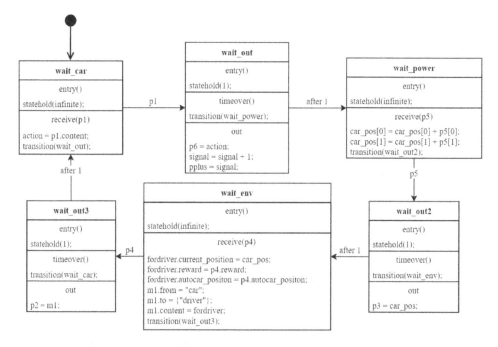

Fig. 12.   State Machine diagram of the car

atomic model. The abscissa represents the simulation advancing time, and the ordinate represents each atomic model. When time = 0, the *driver goal* first output a signal to the *driver watchfor* plan. Then the *driver makedecision ext* model is activated to generate an agent action-decision for the car, thus activating the *car* model. Afterward, the *car* model outputs a signal to the *power* model, whose actions are continuous as shown in a line in Figure 14. The *power* model returns a signal to the *car*, and the *car* outputs a signal to the *environment* at the same time. The processes described above are the signal transition processes between different models in the car system.

It can be found from Figure 14 that the running sequence of the entire model is consistent with the modeling sequence of Figure 6, presenting the simulation process of the couple model composed of continuous, discrete, and agent models. In this case, the *power output* is continuous throughout the simulations and interacts with the *car* when the interaction conditions are met. Due to the discrete nature, the agent model has a consistent simulation process with the operation of the discrete model.

This case shows the modeling processes of X language in multi-domain models and demonstrates the support of X language for the continuous, discrete event, and agent models from the perspective of modeling and simulation.

```
discrete car
import car_for_env;
import perception;
value:
    list<int> car_pos = {0, 0};
    int action;
    perception fordriver;
    Message m1;
    int signal = 0;

port:
    event input Message p1;
    event output Message p2;

    event output list<int> p3;
    event input car_for_env p4;

    event input list<int> p5;
    event output int p6;
    event output int pplus;

state:
    initial state wait_car
        when entry() then
            statehold(infinite);
        end;
        when receive(p1) then
            action = p1.content;
            transition(wait_out);
        end;
    end;

    state wait_out
        when entry() then
            statehold(1);
        end;
        when timeover() then
            transition(wait_power);
        out
            p6 = action;
            signal = signal + 1;
            pplus = signal;
        end;
    end;

    state wait_power
        when entry() then
```

```
            statehold(infinite);
        end;
        when receive(p5) then
            car_pos[0] = car_pos[0] + p5[0];
            car_pos[1] = car_pos[1] + p5[1];
            transition(wait_out2);
        end;
    end;

    state wait_out2
        when entry() then
            statehold(1);
        end;
        when timeover() then
            transition(wait_env);
        out
            p3 = car_pos;
        end;
    end;

    state wait_env
        when entry() then
            statehold(infinite);
        end;
        when receive(p4) then
            fordriver.current_position = car_pos;
            fordriver.reward = p4.reward;
            fordriver.autocar_positon=p4.autocar_positon;
            m1.from = "car";
            m1.to = {"driver"};
            m1.content = fordriver;
            transition(wait_out3);
        end;
    end;

    state wait_out3
        when entry() then
            statehold(1);
        end;
        when timeover() then
            transition(wait_car);
        out
            p2 = m1;
        end;
    end;
end;
```

Fig. 13.   Modeling text of the car model

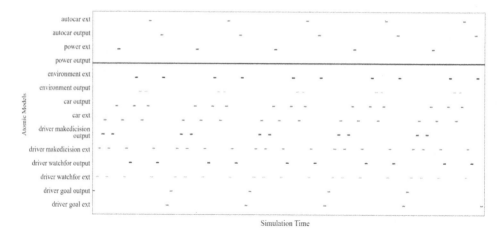

Fig. 14.   Simulation time series of each atomic model of the system

7. Conclusion

MBSE transforms the traditional R&D method based on documents and physical models into a model-driven R&D method, which renders MBSE reusable, unambiguous, intelligible, and easy to spread, enabling it to be an important tool in supporting system modeling and development. As the name suggests, models are the foundation of MBSE, and how to ensure the accuracy of the model has become an important research content. However, the modeling language SysML employed by MBSE needs to corporate with physical modeling languages rather than directly verifying the correctness and completeness of the model, which makes it challenging to ensure the consistency and traceability of the whole system modeling and simulation process. This method also lacks the support for intelligent products in modeling and simulation.

In response to this problem, this paper introduces a new integrated modeling and simulation language and the corresponding compiler and simulation engine developed by the authors' team that supports MBSE. X language has two modeling forms, namely graphics and text, and can be converted to each other through XLab. It is able to support both system modeling and physical simulation, ensuring that a unified language can run through the entire process of architecture design, multi-domain modeling, and simulation verification, thus realizing multi-disciplinary and cross-staged collaborative modeling and simulation of complex products. In addition, the agent class adding to the language enables X language not only to realize the modeling of continuous, discrete, and hybrid models, but also to support the modeling of various complex agent models, thereby giving the language the capability of intelligence modeling. Table 11 shows the comprehensive capabilities of X language through comparison with other mainstream modeling languages.

In Table 11, the mainstream modeling languages are compared from the perspectives of design, simulation, and verification, from which it can be seen that the

Table 11.   Capability comparison of X language and other modeling languages

Capability	Languages X Laguage	SysML[49]	AADL[50]	Modelica[51,52]	KARMA[53,54,56]	SIMAN[57]
Multi-view Modeling	★★①	★★	★	—	★★	—
Qualitative Modeling	★★	★★	★	★	★★	—
Simulation Execution	★★	—	★	★★	★	★
Integrated Modeling and Verification②	★★	—	★	★	—	—
Continuous System Modeling	★★	★	★	★★	★★	★
Discrete Event Modeling	★★	★	★★	★	★★	★★
Hybrid System Modeling	★★	★	★	★	★★	★
Multi-agent modeling	★★	★	★	★	★	—

Notes: ① "—" means do not have this capability, "★" means have this capability but not enough, "★★" means good at this capability
② Models can be simulated directly to verify whether the performance meets stakeholder needs and objectives, without resorting to model transformation.

existing languages have their own advantages in some aspects, but fails to independently complete the whole process of MBSE. For example, SysML[49] is good at top-level architecture modeling, Modelica[50] is dedicated to multi-domain physical system simulation, and AADL[50] focuses on safety analysis for embedded systems, each of which has its capability shortcomings. It is worth noting that a new modeling language recently proposed, KARMA,[53,54] can support the unified formalisms across MBSE models and simulations for different domain-specific models and performs well in each function listed in Table 11. However, as an architecture-driven technology-based language, the KARMA language still realizes verification through model transformation. In the follow-up study,[55] the syntax of hybrid automata is integrated into KARMA to describe the behavior models more precisely and facilitate verification, which is an improvement. In contrast, models built in X language can be directly simulated to verify whether the performance associated with the system meets stakeholder needs and objectives without resorting to model transformation, which genuinely achieves the integration of modeling and verification by using a unified language.

So far, a large number of models and systems built in X language have been simulated and verified, just as the intelligent car system in this paper, fully validating the effectiveness of the proposed approach. To better support MBSE, for one thing, many development efforts still have to be done for XLab, including 1) developing model libraries for different industrial applications, 2) integrating with more software used in the lifecycle of product development, e.g. Computer-Aided Design (CAD), Computer-Aided Engineering (CAE), Software Engineering tools, 3) improving the compatibility with current modeling and/or simulation languages, 4) enriching software interfaces to improve compatibility with other software, such as support for FMI (Functional Mock-up Interface), 5) cloudification and servitization of XLab, etc. For another thing, A lot of research related to X language will be conducted, for example, X language-based comprehensive optimization for complex product design, digital twin construction with X language, X language-based multi-scale and multi-view modeling, model composition, and reuse with X language so on.

Acknowledgments

This work was supported by the National Key R&D Program of China, No. 2018YFB1701600.

Appendix

Appendix A
BNFs for components of classes are shown in Figures 15–20.

Appendix B

The processes of modeling and simulation using XLab are shown in Figures 21, 22.

---

definition_section ::={(import_clause | extends_clause
   | class_definition
   | parameter_component_clause)';'}
   { port_section
   | part_section
   | value_section
   | plan_definition}
import_clause ::= 'import' (IDENT '=' name | name ('.' ('*' | '{' import_list '}'))?)
extends_clause ::= 'extends' type_specifier [class_modification]
class_definition   ::= ('encapsuate')?   class_prefixes class_specifier
parameter_component_clause ::= 'parameter' type_specifier component_list
port section ::= 'port:'{port component clause}
part_section ::= 'part:'{component_clause';'}
value_section ::= 'value:'{component_clause';'}
import_list ::= IDENT {',' IDENT}
component_clause ::=['replaceable'] type_prefix type_specifier component_list

---

Fig. 15.   BNF of Definition Part

requirement_section ::= ('requirement'| 'traceble requirement') {statement';'}
statement ::= {traceLink types} {requirement name} {requirement contents}
traceLink types ::= compose|copy|derivedFrom|refinedBy|satisfiedBy|verifiedBy
    |mappedTo
    |originatedFrom
    |responsibleOf
requirement attributes::= identifier : id
    |name
    |level: Level
    |type: Type
    |risk: Risk
    |source
    |stakehodler
    |text: description
Level ::= Stakeholder|System|Component
Type ::= General|Functional|NonFonctional|Physical|Design
Risk ::= High|Medium|Low

Fig. 16. BNF of Requirement Part

connection_section ::= 'connection:'{connect_clause';'}
connect_clause ::= 'connect' '(' component_reference ',' component_reference ')'

Fig. 17. BNF of Connection Part

state_section ::= 'state:' {state_definition}
state_definition ::= 'initial' 'state' IDENT (state_statement)* 'end";'
    | 'state' IDENT (state_statement)* 'end";'
    | 'state' IDENT catch_clause ((when_receive_clause';')|(when_statement';'))*
'end";'
    state_statement ::= (when_entry_clause
    | when_receive_clause
    | when_goto_out_clause)';'

Fig. 18. BNF of State Machine Part

equation_section ::= 'equation:' {equation ';'}
equation ::= simple_equation
    | if_equation
    | for_equation
    | when_receive_equation
    | when_equation

Fig. 19. BNF of Equation Part

```
action_section ::= 'action:' {statement';'}
statement ::= send_clause
            | simple_statement
            | function_call
            | break  statement
            | continue_statement
            | return_statement
            | if_statement
            | for_statement
            | while_statement
            | when_statement
            | statehold_clause
            | run_statement
            | agentover_statement
            | transition_clause
```

Fig. 20.   BNF of Action Part

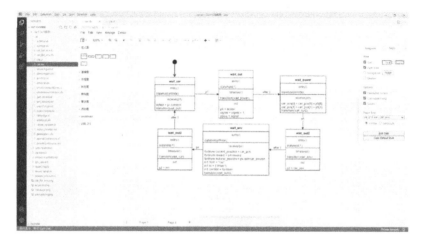

Fig. 21.   State Machine diagram of the car in XLab

Fig. 22.   State Machine text of the car in XLab

References

1. Zeigler, B. P., Zhang, L., Service-oriented model engineering and simulation for system of systems engineering, Concepts and Methodologies for Modeling and Simulation, Springer, Cham, pp. 19–44, 2015.
2. Ramos, A. L., Ferreira, J. V., Barceló, J. Model-based systems engineering: An emerging approach for modern systems, *IEEE Transactions on Systems, Man, and Cybernetics, Part C (Applications and Reviews)* **42**(1) 101–111, 2011.
3. Zhang, L., Liu, Y., Laili, Y. *et al.*, Model maturity towards modeling and simulation: Concepts, index system framework and evaluation method, *International Journal of Modeling, Simulation, and Scientific Computing* **11**(03), 2040001, 2020.
4. Hause, M., OMG systems modeling language (OMG SysML^{TM}) tutorial, *INCOSE international symposium* **19**(1) 1840–1972, 2009.
5. Shao, G., Latif, H., Martin-Villalba, C. *et al.*, Standards-based integration of advanced process control and optimization, *Journal of Industrial Information Integration* **13** 1–12, 2019.
6. Zhang, L., Ye, F., Laili, Y. *et al.*, X language: an integrated intelligent modeling and simulation language for complex products. *2021 Annual Modeling and Simulation Conference (ANNSIM)*, IEEE, pp. 1–11, 2021.
7. Zeigler, B. P., Muzy, A., Kofman, E., *Theory of modeling and simulation: discrete event & iterative system computational foundations*, Academic Press, pp. 19–23, 2018.
8. Walden, D. D., Roedler, G. J., Forsberg, K. INCOSE systems engineering handbook version 4: Updating the reference for practitioners, *INCOSE International Symposium* **25**(1) 678–686, 2015.
9. Kerzhner, A. A., Jobe, J. M., Paredis, C. J. J., A formal framework for capturing knowledge to transform structural models into analysis models, *Journal of Simulation* **5**(3) 202–216, 2011.
10. Huang, E., Ramamurthy, R., McGinnis, L. F., System and simulation modeling using SysML. *2007 Winter Simulation Conference*, IEEE, pp. 796–803, 2007.
11. Schönherr, O., Rose, O., First steps towards a general SysML model for discrete processes in production systems. *Proceedings of the 2009 Winter Simulation Conference (WSC)*, IEEE, pp. 1711–1718, 2009.
12. Batarseh, O., McGinnis, L. F., System modeling in SysML and system analysis in Arena. *Proceedings of the 2012 Winter Simulation Conference (WSC)*, IEEE, pp. 1–12, 2012.
13. Paredis, C. J. J., Bernard, Y., Burkhart, R. M. *et al.*, 5.5. 1 An overview of the SysML-Modelica transformation specification, *INCOSE International Symposium* **20**(1) 709–722, 2010.
14. Nikolaidou, M., Kapos, G. D., Tsadimas, A. *et al.*, Simulating SysML models: Overview and challenges. *2015 10th System of Systems Engineering Conference (SoSE)*, IEEE, pp. 328–333, 2015.
15. Bajaj, M., Zwemer, D., Peak, R. *et al.*, Slim: collaborative model-based systems engineering workspace for next-generation complex systems. *2011 Aerospace Conference*, IEEE, pp. 1–15, 2011.
16. Peak, R. S., Burkhart, R. M., Friedenthal, S. A. *et al.*, 9.3.2 Simulation-based design using SysML Part 1: A parametrics primer, *INCOSE international symposium* **17**(1) 1516–1535, 2007.
17. Wang, R., Dagli, C. H. An executable system architecture approach to discrete events system modeling using SysML in conjunction with colored Petri Net. *2008 2nd annual IEEE systems conference*, IEEE, pp. 1–8, 2008.

18. Kapos, G. D., Dalakas, V., Tsadimas, A. *et al.*, Model-based system engineering using SysML: Deriving executable simulation models with QVT. *2014 IEEE International Systems Conference Proceedings*, IEEE, pp. 531–538, 2014.
19. Paynter, H. M. *Analysis and design of engineering systems*, Cambridge MIT Press, 1961.
20. Jenny, M. D., Marisol, D., Claude, B., A survey of bond graphs: theory, applications and programs, *Journal of the Franklin Institute* **328**(4) 565–606 1991.
21. Fritzson, P., Bunus, P., Modelica-a general object-oriented language for continuous and discrete-event system modeling and simulation. *Proceedings 35th Annual Simulation Symposium.* SS 2002, IEEE, pp. 365–380, 2002.
22. Fritzson, P., *Introduction to modeling and simulation of technical and physical systems with Modelica*, John Wiley & Sons, 2011.
23. Nutaro, J., Kuruganti, P. T., Protopopescu, V. *et al.*, The split system approach to managing time in simulations of hybrid systems having continuous and discrete event components, *Simulation* **88**(3) 281–298, 2012.
24. Elmqvist, H., Gaucher, F., Matsson, S. E. *et al.*, State machines in Modelica, in: *Proceedings of the 9th International Modelica Conference*; September 3–5, 2012, Linköping University Electronic Press, Munich; Germany, pp. 37–46, 2012.
25. Beltrame, T., Cellier, F. E., Quantised state system simulation in Dymola/Modelica using the DEVS formalism, *Proceedings 5th International Modelica Conference.* The Modelica Association, 73–82, 2006.
26. Bünning, F., Sangi, R., Müller, D., A Modelica library for the agent-based control of building energy systems, *Applied energy* **193** 52–59, 2017.
27. Sanz, V., Bergero, F., Urquia, A. An approach to agent-based modeling with Modelica, *Simulation Modelling Practice and Theory* **83** 65–74, 2018.
28. Aertgeerts, A., Claessens, B., De Coninck, R., *et al.*, Agent-based control of a neighborhood: a generic approach by coupling Modelica with Python, *Proceedings of Building Simulation 2015.* 2015.
29. Schaub, A., Hellerer, M., Bodenmüller, T., Simulation of artificial intelligence agents using Modelica and the DLR visualization library. *9th International Modelica Conference*, Linköping University Electronic Press, Munich, Germany, pp. 339–346, 2012.
30. Sha, Z., Le, Q., Panchal, J. H. Using SysML for conceptual representation of agent-based models, *International Design Engineering Technical Conferences and Computers and Information in Engineering Conference* **54792** 39–50, 2011.
31. Maheshwari, A., Kenley, C. R., DeLaurentis, D. A. Creating executable agent-based models using SysML, *INCOSE international symposium* **25**(1) 1263–1277, 2015.
32. Zhang, M. Constructing a cognitive agent model using DEVS framework for multi-agent simulation. *Proc. 15th Eur. Agent Syst. Summer School (EASSS)*, 1–5, 2013.
33. Akplogan, M., Quesnel, G., Garcia, F. *et al.*, Towards a deliberative agent system based on DEVS formalism for application in agriculture. *Proceedings of the 2010 Summer Computer Simulation Conference* 250–257, 2010.
34. Müller, J. P., Towards a formal semantics of event-based multi-agent simulations. *International Workshop on Multi-Agent Systems and Agent-Based Simulation*, Springer, Berlin, Heidelberg, pp. 110–126, 2008.
35. W. Schamai, *Modelica modeling language (ModelicaML): A UML profile for Modelica*, Linköping University Electronic Press, 2009.
36. Schamai, W., Pohlmann, U., Fritzson, P., *et al.*, Execution of umlstate machines using Modelica. *3rd International Workshop on Equation-Based Object-Oriented Modeling Languages and Tools*; Oslo; Norway; October 3. Linköping University Electronic Press, 2010 (047): 1–10.

37. Gauthier, J. M., Bouquet, F., Hammad, A. *et al.*, Tooled process for early validation of SysML models using Modelica simulation. *International Conference on Fundamentals of Software Engineering*, Springer, Cham, pp. 230–237, 2015.

38. Paredis, C. J. J., Bernard, Y., Burkhart, R. M., *et al.*, 5.5. 1 An overview of the SysML-Modelica transformation specification. *INCOSE International Symposium* **20**(1) 709–722, 2010.

39. Cao, Y., Liu, Y., Fan, H. *et al.*, SysML-based uniform behavior modeling and automated mapping of design and simulation model for complex mechatronics, *ComputerAided Design* **45**(3) 764–776, 2013.

40. Li, B. H., Song, X., Zhang, L. *et al.*, CoSMSOL: Complex system modeling, simulation and optimization language, *International Journal of Modeling, Simulation, and Scientific Computing* **8**(02) 1741002, 2017.

41. Li, X. G., Liu, J. H. A method of SysML-based visual transformation of system design-simulation models, *Journal of Computer-Aided Design & Computer Graphics* **11** 2016.

42. Zhou, S. H., Cao, Y., Zhang, Z. *et al.*, System design and simulation integration for complex mechatronic products based on SysML and Modelica, *Journal of Computer-Aided Design & Computer Graphics. Beijing* **30** 728–738, 2014.

43. Berry, G. SCADE: Synchronous design and validation of embedded control software. *Next Generation Design and Verification Methodologies for Distributed Embedded Control Systems*, Springer, Dordrecht, pp. 19–33, 2007.

44. Herzig, S. J. I., Paredis, C. J. J. A conceptual basis for inconsistency management in model-based systems engineering, *Procedia Cirp* **21** 52–57, 2014.

45. Feldmann, S., Herzig, S. J. I., Kernschmidt, K. *et al.*, Towards effective management of inconsistencies in model-based engineering of automated production systems, *IFAC-PapersOnLine* **48**(3) 916–923, 2015.

46. Jongeling, R., Cicchetti, A., Ciccozzi, F., *et al.*, Towards boosting the OpenMBEE platform with model-code consistency. *Proceedings of the 23rd ACM/IEEE International Conference on Model Driven Engineering Languages and Systems: Companion Proceedings.* 1–5, 2020.

47. Berriche, A., Mhenni, F., Mlika, A., *et al.*, Towards model synchronization for consistency management of mechatronic systems. *Applied Sciences* **10**(10) 3577, 2020.

48. Haidrar, S., Bencharqui, H., Anwar, A. *et al.*, REQDL: a requirements description language to support requirements traces generation. *2017 IEEE 25th International Requirements Engineering Conference Workshops (REW)*, IEEE, pp. 26–35, 2017.

49. Hause, M. The SysML modelling language, *Fifteenth European Systems Engineering Conference* **9** 1–12, 2006.

50. Feiler, P. H., Gluch, D. P., Hudak, J. J. The architecture analysis & design language (AADL): An introduction, Carnegie-Mellon Univ Pittsburgh PA Software Engineering Inst, 2006.

51. Fritzson, P., Engelson, V. Modelica — A unified object-oriented language for system modeling and simulation. *European Conference on Object-Oriented Programming*, Springer, Berlin, Heidelberg, pp. 67–90, 1998.

52. Cellier, F. E., Sanz, V., Mixed quantitative and qualitative simulation in Modelica. *Proceedings of the 7th International Modelica Conference*, Linköping University Electronic Press, Como; Italy, pp. 86–95, 2009.

53. Lu, J., Wang, G., Ma, J. *et al.*, General modeling language to support model-based systems engineering formalisms (part 1), *INCOSE International Symposium* **30**(1) 323–338, 2020.

54. Guo, J., Wang, G., Lu, J. *et al.*, General modeling language supporting model transformations of mbse (part 2), *INCOSE International Symposium* **30**(1) 1460–1473, 2020.

55. Ding, J., Reniers, M., Lu, J., *et al.*, Integration of modeling and verification for system model based on KARMA language. *Proceedings of the 18th ACM SIGPLAN International Workshop on Domain-Specific Modeling.* 41–50, 2021.

56. Chen, J., Wang, G., Lu, J., *et al.*, Model-based system engineering supporting production scheduling based on satisfiability modulo theory. *Journal of Industrial Information Integration*, 100329, 2022.

57. Pegden, C. D. Introduction to SIMAN. *Proceedings of the 17th conference on Winter simulation*, 66–72, 1985.

Chapter 6

Modeling for heterogeneous objects based on X language: A modeling method of algorithm-hardware

Yue Liu[*] and Chun Zhao[†]

School of Computer
Beijing Information Science and Technology University
Beijing, 100101, P. R. China
*liuyue@bistu.edu.cn
†zhaochun@bistu.edu.cn

Abstract

With the development of systems engineering and related technology, modeling and simulation of complex systems need to include many disciplines, modeling languages, simulation environments, etc. By using unified modeling language to build models, barriers between different fields can be broken, the efficiency of model integration can be improved. In this paper, a unified modeling language is introduced, which is called X language, and a modeling method of algorithm-hardware based on the X language is proposed. In this method, according to the characteristics of the hardware algorithm, X language is used to build the algorithm-hardware model. Then the X language models are converted to Very-High-Speed Integrated Circuit Hardware Description Language (VHDL). At last, a model of Kalman filter is built by the method proposed in this paper. Results show that the feasibility of modeling method of algorithm-hardware based on X language is verified.

1. Introduction

Multi-disciplinary modeling is integrating models from different fields such as machinery, control, electronics, and software into whole-life of a system.[1] Model integration[2] is an important issue of multi-disciplinary modeling. At present, the most commonly used methods of model integration include interface-based methods[3] and Unified Modeling Language (UML)-based methods.[4,5] The interface-based method uses the modeling software for different domains to modeling, so as to implement the model integration using interfaces of the modeling software.[6,7] The modeling and simulation software must provide interfaces to each other, which is the limitation of the interface-based method. If a software cannot provide interfaces between others, multi-domain modeling cannot be implemented. The UML-based method uses unified modeling language to build heterogeneous models.[8] Because

---

[†]Corresponding author.

the models are described by the same structure, syntax, and rules, the UML-based method can enable models' integration in different domains.[9]

Integrated circuit is a typical heterogeneous object in multi-disciplinary modeling. Field Programmable Gate Array (FPGA) is an integrated circuit which can be used to verify complex integrated circuits. The FPGA has the characteristics of parallel and reconfigurable.[10] FPGAs are used in many complex systems in recent years, such as Internet of Things (IoT),[11,12] edge computing,[13] Cyber-Physical Systems (CPS),[14] and acceleration of algorithm.[15,16] The hardware-implemented algorithm is configured on FPGA, which can effectively improve the calculation speed of the algorithm.[17] The traditional method to describe hardware-implemented algorithm is using hardware description language. Very-High-Speed Integrated Circuit Hardware Description Language (VHDL),[18] for instance, a language for circuit design, can describe the structure, behaviors, functions, and interfaces of hardware-implemented algorithms.

In the process of the whole complex system modeling, not only the structure of the system is needed to model, but also the internal structure and behavior of the heterogeneous integrated circuit. The main differences between system model and integrated circuit model are the resolution of modeling and the description method of mathematical algorithm. System model built as high- or low-resolution depends on the requirements of simulation. Nevertheless, to meet the availability of model in simulation or practice, the integrated circuit model needs to be described in as much detail as possible. In complex systems, mathematical or physical models can be represented in various ways, such as differential equations, difference equations, and algebraic equations. However, in an integrated circuit model, equations cannot be used directly to represent hardware-implemented algorithm models. To solve the problem mentioned above, there are many related researches about modeling and simulation of multi-domain that include integrated circuit. The VHDL-AMS is an extension language of VHDL; VHDL-AMS differs from VHDL in that VHDL is only used to describe digital circuits, while VHDL-AMS can describe digital–analog hybrid circuits or even physical models.[19,20] Using VDHL-AMS can simplify the process of system modeling,[21] but the field of modeling is limited in electronic and physical systems. At present, there are many modeling languages that can model the complex systems, including SysML,[22] Modelica,[23] etc., but all of them cannot cover the whole process of system. For example, SysML cannot simulate directly,[24] and Modelica is suitable for physical model modeling[25] rather than describing system structure.

In order to integrate the integrated circuit model with models in other domain, a modeling method of integrated circuit based on X language is proposed in this paper. X language is a new integrated intelligent modeling and simulation language, which supports the modeling and simulation of system structure and physical behavior and supports the simulation of event of continuous, discrete, and hybrid.[26] The X language supports modeling from top-level to bottom-level and can describe models at different resolutions from low to high. In this paper, the method of modeling hardware-implemented algorithm by X language is introduced; these models include graphic description and text description. To verify the usability of X language, the conversion rules of X language to VHDL are designed. Based on the method proposed, the model of Kalman filter is used as a case study to verify the feasibility of the method. Then the model built by X language is converted to VHDL code according to the conversion rules for verification on FPGA. The main contribution of the paper is using X Language to describe the hardware-implemented algorithm, so as to model the complex system including integrated circuit. The ability of X language to modeling hardware-implemented algorithm of integrated circuit is proved.

The remainder of this paper is organized as follows. First, X language and VHDL are introduced in Sec. 2. Second, the method of modeling by using X language and the method of converting X language to VHDL are presented in Sec. 3. In Sec. 4, a case study of the method proposed is provided in detail and the analysis of the simulation is presented. Finally, Sec. 5 concludes the paper.

2. Background

In this section, the basic elements and grammatical structure of the X language and VHDL are introduced.

2.1. *X language*

X language is a new modeling and simulation language, which is used for modeling, simulation, and verification of multi-domain model. X language supports the full-process, multi-disciplinary, cross-stage collaborative modeling, and simulation.

In the layer of system modeling, the framework of X language is divided into five parts, including *definition, connection, statemachine, equation*, and *action*, which are used for describing structure and behavior.

In the layer of physical modeling and simulation, X language supports the simulation of continuous model, discrete model, and agent model. Using X language the models of the whole system can be built directly; there is needless to design the special interfaces for the model of hardware-implemented algorithm, so the difficulty and complexity of model integration can be reduced.

2.1.1. *Class of model*

The class is basic unit of X language. Different classes describe the models with different characteristics. The types of classes are as follows:

- class: Supporting to describe all models.
- couple: Describing coupled model with sub-modules.

- continuous: Describing model with continuous behavior.
- discrete: Describing model based on event-triggered behavior.
- agent: Describing model with intelligent behavior.
- record: Describing complex data structures in model.
- function: Describing the algorithms of the model.
- connector: Describing the connection among models.

2.1.2. *Graphical model of X language*

- definition
  Describing the top-level architecture model of the entire system or subsystem.
- connector
  Used to connect two modules to represent the two modules can access each other and pass data or events.
- equation
  Describing the equations contained in the model, including simple-equation, when-equation, for-equation, if-equation, etc.
- state machine
  Describing the states of the model, including definitions of states, the transitions between states and the durations of states.

2.1.3. *Text model of X language*

The graphical model built by X language has corresponding text description. As shown in Fig. 1, the text description of the model can include these parts. The *class*, *part*, *port*, *value*, and *parameter* correspond to a definition diagram. The connection corresponds to connection diagram. The equation corresponds to equation diagram. The state corresponds to state machine diagram.

2.2. *VHDL*

VHDL is a kind of hardware description language,[27] which can be used to describe entities, architecture, behavior, states, etc. of hardware-implemented algorithm. The process of describing hardware-implemented algorithm using VHDL can also be referred to the modeling of integrated circuit. Generally, the top-down modeling approach is used,[28] first, modeling the top-level modules, then modeling the sub-modules, and next, defining the connections among the modules and the behavior within the modules. The following statements are used to describe the integrated circuit in VHDL.

- entity
  Including some libraries, packages, configurations, the description of the external interface of an entity and the connection to other modules.

```
class class_name
part :
  //declaration of component
port :
  //declaration of I/O port
parameter :
  //declaration of parameter
value :
  //declaration of variable
connection :
  //describing connections between submodules
state :
  //definition of state and state transition
equation :
  //description of model behavior
  //and definition of internal event
end ;
```

Fig. 1.   Text description of X language.

- port
  Defining the ports of the entity, including port name, port mode and data type.
- component
  Used to instantiate sub-modules of entities. The entity name and port description of the referenced module need to be specified.
- signal
  Describing the connections of the circuit modules. Signal can be used to transmit information between different entities or statements.
- port map
  Describing the connection between a component and the signal of the upper-module.
- process
  Describing the behavior of circuits. The process can describe sequential circuits, combinatorial logic circuits, etc. Within process, VHDL defines three sequential description statements, including if, case, and loop.
- state machine
  Describing states of the model and the condition which trigger a state. There are two types of state machines including Mealy and Moore. The output of a Mealy is only related to the current state; the Moore is related to both the state and the input signal.

3. Methodology

In this section, the method of modeling the algorithm-hardware by X language is introduced. In this method, first of all, the hardware-implemented algorithm is described with the graphical modeling of X language, and then, the model of hardware-implemented algorithm is described with the text of X language according to the graphical model. Next, according to the syntax of X language and VHDL, the conversion rules of X language to VHDL are given. According to the rules, X language can be converted to VHDL.

3.1. *Modeling hardware-implemented algorithm by X language*

3.1.1. *Definition diagram*

Definition diagram is used to define basic properties of each module in the model of hardware-implemented algorithm, including the I/O ports, signal, component, variable, etc. The definition diagram is shown in Fig. 2.

Entity of VHDL is equivalent to the *continuous/discrete/couple* model of X language; the class of model is based on the functionality that the module implementation.

IP core is a special type of entity. Generally, the cores are frequently used modules designed and packaged by FPGA manufacturers. In the use of these IP cores, designers only need to pay attention to the functions, ports, and parameters of IP cores and do not need to understand the internal circuit.[29] Because IP core is a black-box model, the class of IP core is *record*, and only ports need to be defined; the internal structure and behavior are not described. *port* of X language is used to define the external ports of entities and IP cores. *part* of X language is used to describe the sub-modules of a module. *parameter* of X language is used to define signals of circuit model.

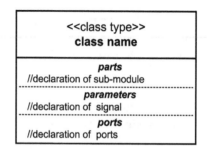

Fig. 2.   Definition diagram of X language.

3.1.2. *Connection diagram*

The connection diagram is used to describe the connections among modules. The information of connected port is defined in the definition diagram. In the process of building the connection diagram, paying attention to the direction of the two ports connected together is necessary to ensure the data can be transmitted from the output port to the input port. Figure 3 shows the connection diagram of module A and module B.

3.1.3. *Equation diagram*

Equation diagram can be used to describe the behavior of model. As shown in Figs. 4 and 5, the *for-equation* and *if-equation* of X language are mainly used to describe the behavior of hardware-implemented algorithm model such as sequential logic and combinational logic.

3.1.4. *State machine diagram*

The state diagram is used to describe the state and transition in the hardware-based algorithm. As shown in Fig. 6, *statement*1 and *statement*2 are states, and the

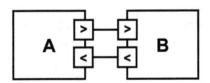

Fig. 3.   Connection diagram of X language.

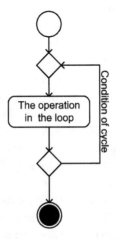

Fig. 4.   The for-equation of X language.

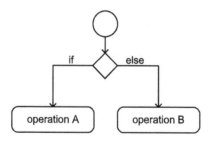

Fig. 5.   The if-equation of X language.

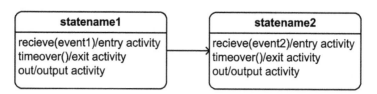

Fig. 6.   The state machine in X language.

arrows represent transitions of states. The $receive(event1)/entryactivity$ represents the event $event1$ received in the state $statement1$. The $entryactivity$ is description of the behavior in current state. The $Timeover()/exitactivity$ represents internal event which in current state is over, and then entering the next state $statename2$. $out/outputactivity$ represents the output of the state.

3.2. *Model conversion*

X language and VHDL language have some similarities in description of model; both have strict hierarchical and structured description. For example, the couple model of X language includes a header part, an attribute part, and a connection part. The header part imports the external model, the attribute part describes the basic attributes of the model, and the connection part describes the connection relationship among different sub-models. The VHDL describes the model as *package*, *entity*, and *portmap*. The *package* is used to import external models, methods, data types, etc., the *entity* is used to describe basic properties of circuit modules, and *portmap* is used to connect modules. The attribute part of X language includes *parameter*, *port*, and *part*, which are used to describe the inherent attribute of class, definition of port, and instantiation of sub-module. In VHDL, the corresponding definition to the attribute part of X language is the *signal*, *port*, and *component*, respectively, describes the internal signal, port of module, and instantiation of sub-module. The rigorous and structured modeling method makes X language has ability to describe hardware-implemented algorithm models accurately. Using the proposed conversion rules, valid VHDL code can be generated from the hardware-implemented algorithm model built by X language.

In this section, the method of converting X language to VHDL is introduced. A series of VHDL model templates are built, and the conversion rules of X language to VHDL are designed. Based on templates and conversion rules, models built in the X language can be automatically converted to VHDL models.

3.2.1. *Model templates of VHDL*

According to the syntax of VHDL, this paper builds a series of model templates of VHDL and removes the key information which describes the model and keeps the common parts of each model. Templates constructed in this paper are shown in Figs. 7–13.

3.2.2. *Conversion rule*

A series of conversion rules from X language to VHDL are designed in this section. The conversion rules specify the corresponding relation of X language and VHDL.

```
library IEEE;
use IEEE.STD_LOGIC_1164.ALL;
use IEEE.STD_LOGIC_UNSIGNED.ALL;
use IEEE.STD_LOGIC_ARITH.ALL;
use IEEE.NUMERIC_STD;
entity  _Temp<entityname>_  is
   port( _Temp<entityport>_);
end _Temp<entityname>_ ;
architecture Behavioral of _Temp<entityname>_ is
begin
end Behavioral;
```

Fig. 7.   Model template of entity.

```
component   _Temp<component name>
   port(_Temp<port>_);
end component;
```

Fig. 8.   Model template of component.

```
<port name>:<in/out> <data type> <(data width)>;
```

Fig. 9.   Model template of port.

```
signal <signal name>:<data type> <(data width)>;
```

Fig. 10.   Model template of signal.

```
<component name> port map (_Temp<map_detail >);
```

Fig. 11.   Model template of port map.

```
<port name>  ⇒  <signal name>,
```

Fig. 12.   Model template of the detail of port map.

```
process
begin
//description of behavior
end process;
```

Fig. 13.   Model template of process.

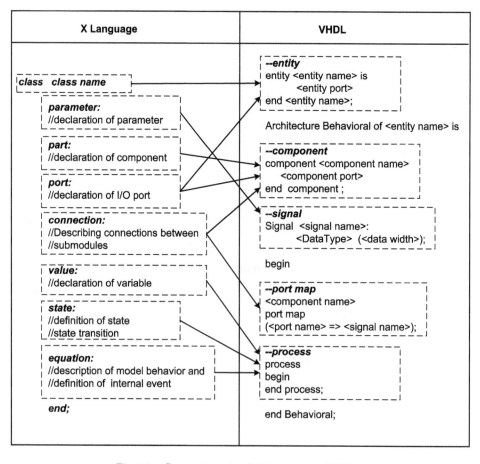

Fig. 14.   Conversion rule of X language to VHDL.

The mapping of the various parts of the X language to the various parts of the VHDL is shown in Fig. 14.

As shown in Fig. 15, a model in the X language corresponds to an entity in VHDL, and the *classname* corresponds to the *entityname*.

The mapping of VHDL's IP core is shown in Fig. 16. The class type of X language is *record*. The class name corresponds to the name of IP core.

Both the X language model and the VHDL model use *port* to represent the external ports of the module. The mapping rules are shown in Fig. 17.

In X language, *parts* are used to represent the submodules of a module, and VHDL is using *component*. The mapping rules are shown in Fig. 18.

In X language, *connection* is used to describe the connection between modules, and that is represented as *portmap* in VHDL. Figure 19 shows the mapping rules of connection between X language and VHDL.

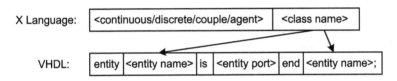

Fig. 15.   Conversion rule of X-class to VHDL-entity.

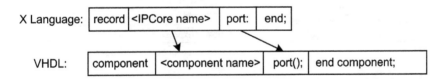

Fig. 16.   Conversion rule of X-class to VHDL-IP core.

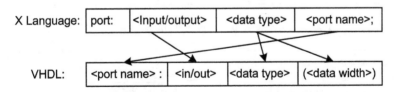

Fig. 17.   Conversion rule of X-port to VHDL-port.

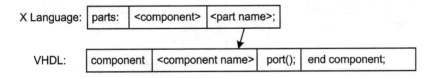

Fig. 18.   Conversion rule of X-part to VHDL-component.

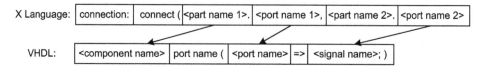

Fig. 19.   Conversion rule of X-connection to VHDL-port map.

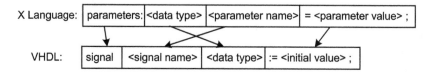

Fig. 20.   Conversion rule of X-parameter to VHDL-signal.

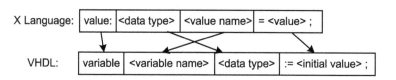

Fig. 21.   Conversion rule of X-value to VHDL-variable.

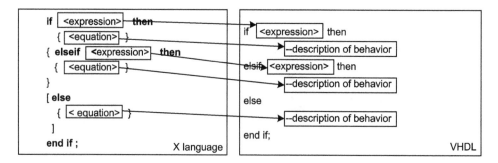

Fig. 22.   Conversion rule of X-if equation to VHDL-if.

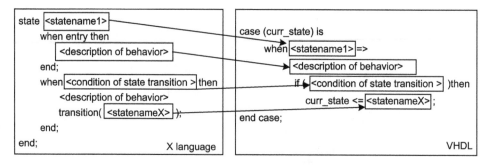

Fig. 23.   Conversion rule of X-state to VHDL-state machine.

As shown in Figs. 20 and 21, *parameter* of X language corresponds to the *signal* of VHDL; the *value* of X language corresponds to the *variable* of VHDL.

As shown in Figs. 22 and 23, the *if-equation* in X language corresponds to the *if* statement in VHDL. The state machine in X language is described by *state*. In VHDL, the *case*, *when* and *if* statements are used together to describe the state machine.

4. Case Study

In this section, the Kalman filter is used as an example to verify the feasibility of the method proposed in this paper. The model of the Kalman filter is built using X language, and according to the conversion rules, the VHDL code of the Kalman filter is generated.

4.1. *Brief of Kalman filter*

Filtering is to eliminate the noise in the signal. The process of signal processing of Kalman filter is a multi-iteration process.

First of all, the signal at a moment is predicted to get the predicted value. Then, the error of the predicted value is obtained according to the actual measurement. Next, the optimal estimation of the signal is carried out.[30]

The Kalman filter consists of the following five equations. Equations (1) and (2) are time update equations. Equations (3)–(5) are state update equations.

$$\hat{x}_{k+1}^- = A_k \hat{x}_k + B u_k, \tag{1}$$

$$P_{k+1}^- = A_k P_k A_k^T + Q_k, \tag{2}$$

$$K_k = P_k^- H_k^T (H_k P_k^- H_k^T + R_k)^{-1}, \tag{3}$$

$$\hat{x}_k = \hat{x}_k^- + K(z_k - H_k \hat{x}_k^-), \tag{4}$$

$$P_k = (I - K_k H_k) P_k^-. \tag{5}$$

4.2. *Modeling by X language*

First, the top-level model of the whole algorithm-hardware is built, including graphical model and text model. As shown in Fig. 25, the top-level model of Kalman filter is defined as the couple model, and in the definition diagram, six submodules, two parameters, and two ports are defined. As shown in Fig. 26, the connection diagram defines the connection of sub-modules which is defined in the definition diagram. Figure 24 shows the text description of the top-level model.

Next, the model of each submodule is built in detail. Figure 27 is the definition diagram of module *Kalman_Forecast_01*, which implements Eq. (1). Figure 28 shows the definition diagram of module *Kalman_Forecast_02*, which implements Eqs. (2) and (3). Figure 29 shows the definition diagram of module *Kalman_update*,

```
1  couple  KalmanFilter
2          import  IPCore;
3          import  component;
4      part:
5          IPCore RAM01  ;
6          component  Kalman_forecast_01;
7          component  Kalman_forecast_02;
8          component  Kalman_update;
9          component  control01;
10         component  control02;
11     port:
12         VHDLInput  array [31:0]  inputSignal;
13         VHDLOutput  array [31:0]  kalman_res;
14     parameter:
15         array [0:0]  wea_01;
16         array [9:0]  addra_01;
17         ...
18     connection:
19         connect (RAM01. clka , clk );
20         connect (RAM01. ena , wea_01 );
21         ...
22     equation:
23         if  rising (clk )  then
24         {...}
25         end if;
26 end;
```

Fig. 24.   Text description of top-level model.

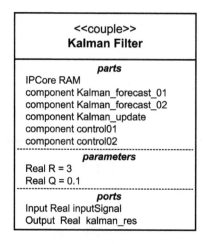

Fig. 25.   Definition diagram of top-level model.

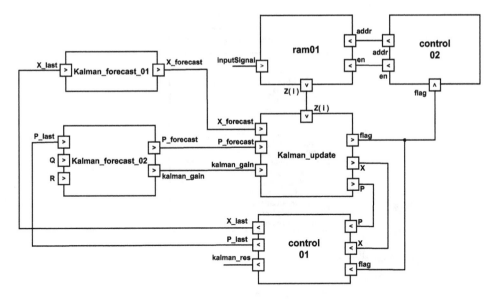

Fig. 26.   Connection diagram of top-level model.

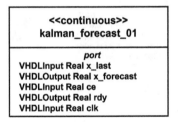

Fig. 27.   Definition diagram of kalman_forecast_01.

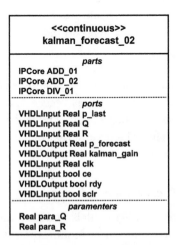

Fig. 28.   Definition diagram of kalman_forecast_02.

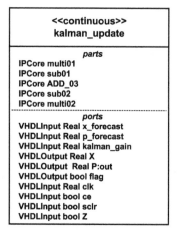

Fig. 29.   Definition diagram of kalman_update.

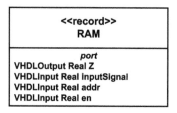

Fig. 30.   Definition diagram of RAM.

which implements Eqs. (4) and (5). As shown in Fig. 30, the module $RAM01$ is used to store the signal before filtering, which is formed by the superposition of sine wave and random noise. The module $Control01$ in top-level model is used to control the iteration of the whole model, and module $Control02$ is used to control the accessing of RAM.

The connection diagrams of $Kalman\_forecast\_02$ and $Kalman\_update$ are shown in Figs. 31 and 32. Specially, the type of module $ram01$, ADD_01, ADD_02, DIV_01, $multi01$, $multi02$, $sub01$, $sub02$ is $record$ class, which represents the IP core in the hardware-implemented algorithm. The IP core belongs to the black box model, that only needs to define the external ports, needless to define the behavior inside the module.

4.3. *Generating VHDL code of Kalman filter*

In the previous section, the graphic models and text models of Kalman filter are built. In this section, the information of modules is extracted by C++ language, which includes the name of the module, the information of the port, etc. The conversion rules designed in this paper are used to map the information in X language

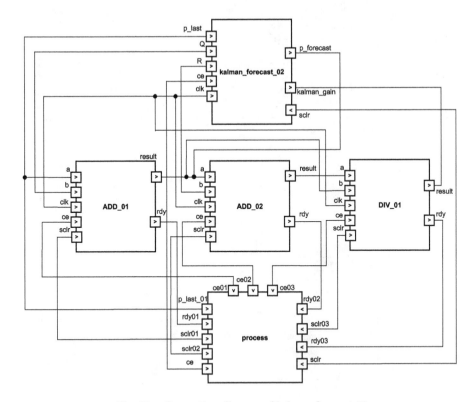

Fig. 31.   Connection diagram of kalman_forecast_02.

model and the information in the VHDL code. The model templates are used to automatically generate a series of *.vhd* files. The schematic of generating the VHDL code is shown in Fig. 33. The generated codes of top-level model are shown in Fig. 34.

4.4. *Verification of algorithm*

In this section, the generated VHDL codes are verified. The codes are imported into ISE 14.7 to check the syntax and generate RTL diagrams. Figure 35 shows the schematic of the model and Fig. 36 shows the simulation results in ISim. From the schematic generated, X language can correctly describe the structure characteristics of integrated circuit. From the waveform of simulation, the model built by X language can describe the behavior of the algorithm. The input signal is original data, and output is filtered data. Driven by the clock, the model performs a filtering calculation each 1 μs.

In order to observe the simulation results of the model more intuitively, the simulation results are exported, and the results before and after filtering are compared. Figure 37 shows the original data. Figure 38 shows the data filtered. The original data are the superposition of sinusoidal wave and random noise, and the waveform

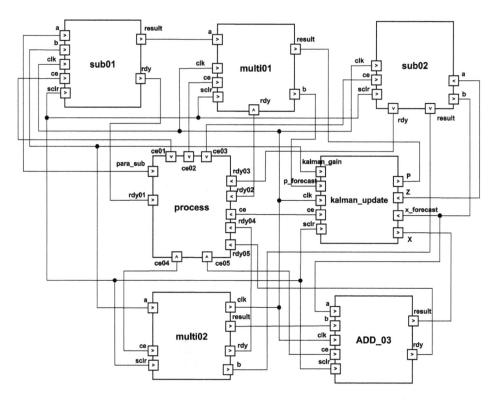

Fig. 32.   Connection diagram of kalman_update.

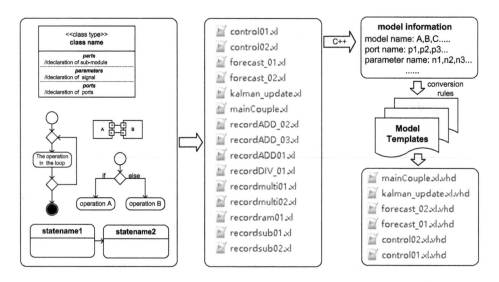

Fig. 33.   The schematic of generating the VHDL code

```
1    library IEEE;
2    use IEEE.STD_LOGIC_1164.ALL;
3    ...
4    entity  KalmanFilter
5    port(
6    inputSignal:in std_logic_vector(31 downto 0);
7    kalman_res:out std_logic_vector(31 downto 0)
8    );
9    end KalmanFilter;
10   architecture Behavioral of     KalmanFilter
11   component RAM01
12   port(
13   ena:in std_logic;
14   ... );
15   end component;
16   signal   wea_01 : STD_LOGIC_VECTOR(0  downto  0);
17   signal   addra_01 : STD_LOGIC_VECTOR(9  downto  0);
18   ...
19   begin
20   RAM01 port map(clka=>clk,ena=>wea_01,...);
21   ...
22   process(clk)
23   begin
24   if(clk='1' and clk'event) then
25   ...
26   end process;
27   end Behavioral;
```

Fig. 34.   Generated code of top-level model.

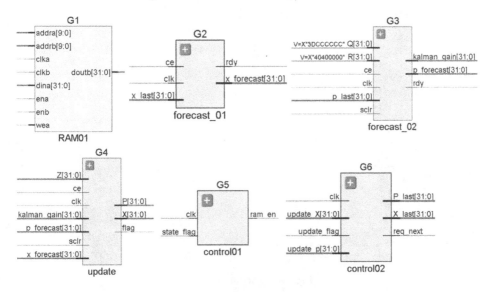

Fig. 35.   RTL of Kalman filter.

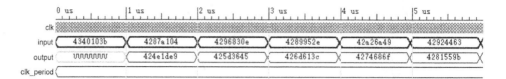

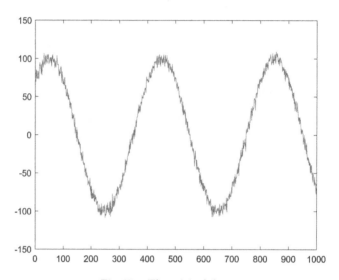

Fig. 36.   Wave of Kalman filter.

Fig. 37.   The original data.

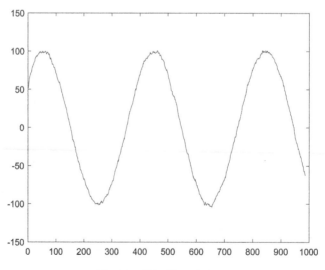

Fig. 38.   The filtered data.

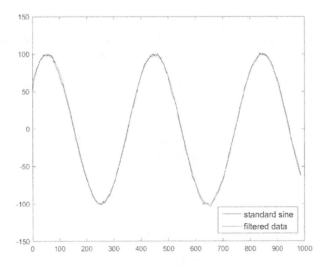

Fig. 39.   Comparison of filtered data with standard sine.

contains much irregular sawteeth. After filtering, the waveform becomes smooth. As shown in Fig. 39, the filtered data are compared with the standard sine that shows the effect of filtering meets the requirements.

5. Conclusion

Complex system often includes multiple domain models, and integrated circuit is a heterogeneous object in complex system. This paper proposes a method for modeling the algorithm-hardware of integrated circuit using X language, and the conversion rules from X language to VHDL language are designed, which can automatically generate VHDL code from the X language model. Using the method proposed in this paper, the algorithm of Kalman filter is built. As the results, the feasibility of the proposed method is verified, and the modeling ability of X language for hardware algorithm is proved.

In the future, the method can be applied to modeling other hardware-implemented algorithms expediently. In the current method, we need to build some circuit modules for basic operations, such as addition, subtraction, multiplication, and division, which leads to a cumbersome modeling process. We can further optimize the basic operation and establish a direct mapping from the operator to the operation module. In addition, some common hardware-implemented algorithms can be packaged as functions, which can be called directly in X language using $function()$, further simplifying the modeling process.

Acknowledgments

This work is supported by the National Key R&D Program of China (Grant No. 2018YFB1701600).

References

1. Ivanov D., Tang C. S., Dolgui A., Battini D., Das A., Researchers' perspectives on Industry 4.0: Multi-disciplinary analysis and opportunities for operations management, *Int. J. Product. Res.* **59**(7):2055–2078, 2021.

2. Dolk D. R., Kottemann J. E., Model integration and a theory of models, *Decis. Support Syst.* **9**(1):51–63, 1993.

3. Belete G. F., Voinov A., Laniak G. F., An overview of the model integration process: From pre-integration assessment to testing, *Environ. Model. Softw.* **87**:49–63, 2017.

4. Li B. H., Song X., Zhang L., Liu J., Chi P., Lin T., Li T., CoSMSOL: Complex system modeling, simulation and optimization language, *Int. J. Model. Simul. Sci. Comput.* **8**(2):1741002.

5. Elmqvist H., Mattsson S. E., Otter M., Modelica-a language for physical system modeling, visualization and interaction, *Proc. 1999 IEEE Int. Symp. Computer Aided Control System Design (Cat. No. 99TH8404)*, pp. 630–639, 1999.

6. Neema H., Sztipanovits J., Steinbrink C., Raub T., Cornelsen B., Lehnhoff S., Simulation integration platforms for cyber-physical systems, *Proc. Workshop on Design Automation for CPS and IoT*, NY, United States, pp. 10–19, 2019.

7. Conquet J. C. R., Third party model integration in a modeling and simulation platform, 2020.

8. Wortmann A., Barais O., Combemale B., Wimmer M., Modeling languages in Industry 4.0: An extended systematic mapping study, *Softw. Syst. Model.* **19**(1): 67–94, 2020.

9. Missaoui S., Mhenni F., Choley J., Nguyen N., Verification and validation of the consistency between multi-domain system models, *2018 Annual IEEE Int. Systems Conf. (SysCon)*, Vancouver, BC, Canada, pp. 1–7, 2018.

10. Ganorkar S., Sharma S., Jain A., Soft computing algorithms and implementation on FPGA-A review. Available at SSRN 3851220, Tamil Nadu, India, 2021.

11. Chamola V. *et al.*, FPGA for 5g: Re-configurable hardware for next generation communication, *IEEE Wirel. Commun.* **27**(3):140–147, 2020.

12. Samir N. *et al.*, ASIC and FPGA comparative study for IoT lightweight hardware security algorithms, *J. Circuits Syst. Comput.* **28**(12):1930009, 2019.

13. Rodrguez A. *et al.*, FPGA-based high-performance embedded systems for adaptive edge computing in cyber-physical systems: The artico3 framework, *Sensors* **18**(6):1877, 2018.

14. Grimm T. *et al.*, The value of FPGAs as reconfigurable hardware enabling cyber-physical systems, *2015 IEEE 20th Conference on Emerging Technologies & Factory Automation (ETFA)*, IEEE, pp. 1–8, 2015.

15. Crosbie R., Using field-programmable gate arrays for high-speed real-time simulation, *Int. J. Model. Simulat. Sci. Comput.* **1**(01):99–115, 2010.

16. Dang L. K. *et al.*, Simulink model and FPGA-based OFDM communication system: A simulation and hardware integrated platform, *Int. J. Model. Simulat. Sci. Comput.* **1**(3):369–404, 2010.

17. Boutros A., Betz V., FPGA architecture: Principles and progression, *IEEE Circuits Syst. Mag.* **21**(2):4–29, 2021.

18. Gschwind M., Salapura V., A VHDL design methodology for FPGAs, *Int. Workshop on Field Programmable Logic and Applications*, Springer, Berlin, Heidelberg, pp. 208–217, 1995.

19. Otter M., Multi-domain modeling and simulation, in *Encyclopedia of Systems and Control*, 2019.

20. Pcheux F., Lallement C., Vachoux A., VHDL-AMS and Verilog-AMS as alternative hardware description languages for efficient modeling of multidiscipline systems, *IEEE Trans. Comput. Aid. Des. Integr. Circuits Syst.* **24**(2):204–225, 2005.
21. Benhamadouche A. D. *et al.*, FPGA-based hardware-in-the-loop for multi-domain simulation, *Int. J. Model. Simulat. Sci. Comput.* **10**(4):1950020, 2019.
22. Nigischer C. *et al.*, Multi-domain simulation utilizing SysML: State of the art and future perspectives, *Proc. CIRP* **100**:319–324, 2021.
23. Elmqvist H. and Otter M., Innovations for future Modelica, *Proc. 12th Int. Modelica Conf.*, Linköping University Electronic Press, Prag, Tschechische Republik, pp. 693–702, 2017.
24. Kapos G.-D. *et al.*, A declarative approach for transforming SysML models to executable simulation models, *IEEE Trans. Syst. Man Cybernet. Syst.* 2019.
25. Wu J., The key technology research for integrated simulation of multi-disciplinary complex product system, *Int. J. Model. Simulat. Sci. Comput.* **8**(02):1741001, 2017.
26. Zhang L., Ye F., Laili Y. *et al.*, X language: An integrated intelligent modeling and simulation language for complex products, *Annual Modeling and Simulation Conf.*, Fairfax, VA, USA, pp. 1–11, 2021.
27. Ashenden P. J., VHDL standards, *IEEE Des. Test Comput.* **18**(5):122–123, 2001.
28. Salcic Z., Introduction to VHDL, in *VHDL and FPLDs in Digital Systems Design, Prototyping and Customization*, Springer, Boston, MA, pp. 3–21, 2001.
29. Ferrandi F. *et al.*, VHDL to FPGA automatic IP-Core generation: A case study on Xilinx design flow, *Proc. 20th IEEE Int. Parallel and Distributed Processing Symp.*, IEEE, pp. 219–219, 2006.
30. Welch G., Bishop G., An introduction to the Kalman filter, 127–132, 1995.

Chapter 7

Data-driven modeling method with reverse process

Guodong Yi[*,‡,**], Lifan Yi[*,§], Zaizhao Zhang[*,¶] and Chuihui Li[†,‖]

*State Key Laboratory of Fluid, Power & Mechatronic
Systems, Zhejiang University
Hangzhou 310027, P. R. China*

†*Xiangyang Boya Precision Industrial
Equipment Co., Ltd., China*
‡*ygd@zju.edu.cn*
§*22025117@zju.edu.cn*
¶*zhangzaizhao_zju@163.com*
‖*lchuihui2021@163.com*

Abstract

The factors that affect the performance of the equipment are numerous and complicated, which makes it difficult to establish a performance calculation model. This paper puts forward a data-driven modeling method with reverse process for this problem. Based on the Partial Least Squares (PLS) algorithm and the Gray Relational Analysis (GRA) method, the analysis method of the performance related factors, the extraction method of characteristic variables, and the performance modeling method are studied. The related factors of the energy consumption of an industrial steam turbine are analyzed, and an energy consumption calculation model is established, and the effectiveness of the above-mentioned modeling methods is verified with sample data, which provides a basis for the energy-saving optimization of the steam turbine.

1. Introduction

The performance calculation model is the basis for the analysis and optimization of equipment performance. There are many factors that affect the performance of the equipment. If too many factors that have a small impact on the performance are included in the modeling, it will not only increase the amount of calculation, but also reduce the stability of the model. On the contrary, if some key energy consumption-related factors are omitted, the modeling results will be inaccurate. Therefore, it is very important to select the characteristic variables that are most conducive to modeling from a large number of performance-related factors.

**Corresponding author.

Aiming at the problems of which factors that affect the performance of the equipment are numerous and complicated, this paper proposes a data-driven modeling method with reverse process. The operating data of the equipment is used to study the factors that affect performance, that is, the "cause" is inferred from the "result". The relationship between independent variables and dependent variables is clarified, which helps to improve the accuracy of equipment performance analysis and optimize performance design for specific factors.

The rest of this paper is organized as follows. Section 2 reviews the related works. Section 3 analyzes modeling based on partial least squares (PLS). Section 4 introduces the details of gray relational analysis (GRA) method. Section 4 introduces the details of GRA method. Case analysis and experimental results are presented in Sec. 5. Finally, the conclusion and perspectives are stated in Sec. 6.

2. Related Work

At present, the mechanism analysis method, that is, the forward modeling method, is widely used.[1] The method studies the relationship between independent variables and dependent variables through quantitative mathematical models based on the operating mechanism of the target object. The mathematical model used for quantitative calculation of performance mainly establishes a differential equation or transfer function based on the parameter transfer relationship between the various devices of the system, but the process is typically abstract and complicated. Therefore, a lot of research work has been done on mathematical modeling, analysis and simulation based on the mechanism analysis method.

Colonna and Van Putten used SimECS to conduct dynamic modeling and simulation of a 600 MW coal-fired thermal power plant, and established a steam cycle dynamic model of the power plant. The experimental verification results show that this model shows good performance.[2,3]

Kulkowski *et al.* proposed three nonlinear models of NPP steam turbine.[4] The experimental verification results show that due to its complexity and the resulting long calculation time, dynamic models are not suitable for advanced control methods. However, the introduced simplifications significantly reduce the computational load, enabling the use of simplified models for online control.

Yu *et al.* proposed a hybrid modeling method based on operation data and first-principle mechanism for performance monitoring of control stage systems.[5] This model was validated via two case studies of a 330 MW subcritical steam turbine and a 1000 MW ultra-supercritical steam turbine. The results show that the average relative error between the simulated and measured values of the outlet pressure and outlet temperature of the control stage is within 1%.

Chaibakhs and Ghaffari established a nonlinear mathematical model of the unit to study the transient dynamics of the steam turbine.[6] Based on the unit's real-time operating data, the genetic algorithm was used to calculate the relevant parameters in the model. The model has high accuracy and a wide range of practicability.

Morini and Piva established a modular simulation library for various equipment of industrial steam turbines based on the mass and energy balance equation, used the library to model and simulate each module, and then packaged the simulation modules to form a thermal power plant simulation model.[7,8]

Liu *et al.* combined the improved neural network model with the thermodynamic model to develop an online calculation model for industrial steam turbines, which is used to analyze the system's heat consumption and parameter deviations.[9] Compared with the traditional methods, this model has higher accuracy and stability.

Yu *et al.* proposed a method for estimating the pressure and temperature after the regulating valve, which laid a foundation for using the actual operating data of the steam turbine to establish a mathematical model of the variable-condition characteristics of the regulating stage.[10] The experimental results for 330 MW steam turbine show that the model can accurately calculate the pressure and temperature after the control stage.

Yan *et al.* proposed a general physical model and mathematical model for thermal economic analysis of thermal power units based on the laws of thermodynamics, and calculated the model through specific examples to verify its correctness.[11]

Valero *et al.* used BP neural network to establish an online calculation model for turbine heat consumption analysis and parameter deviation analysis. Compared with the conventional method, this model has higher accuracy and stability.[12,13]

Penning and De Lange used MMS to establish a nuclear power plant's full-condition simulation model and a control system simulation model, and conducted simulation calculations.[14] The developed models and calculation methods will easily be extended to other systems.

Mavromatis and Kokossis established a steam turbine model for the design and selection of steam turbines, which was capable of accurately predicting the efficiency of a turbine simple on the basis of its maximum capacity. This model was general and applies to single as well as complex turbines.[15]

Hubka established a model of reheaters and turbine based on actual process measurement and ARX model, and verified the accuracy of the model.[16] This model allowed researchers to test and develop a new control algorithm for the power plant.

In these studies, the models based on the mechanism analysis method are typically very complicated, and too many simplified assumptions will bring relatively large errors. Therefore, it is necessary to propose a new modeling method to solve this problem.

Therefore, on the basis of the above-mentioned research, this paper puts forward a data-driven modeling method with reverse process, and a novel energy consumption calculation model is established, which provides a basis for the energy-saving optimization of the steam turbine. It will provide reference for related research.

3. Modeling Based on Partial Least Squares (PLS)

The parameters of equipment are usually multi-correlated, which means that changes in parameters will not only affect the performance of the equipment, but may also lead to changes in other parameters. In data analysis and modeling, multiple correlations will cause large errors in parameter estimates and undermine the stability of the model. The PLS algorithm extracts the most explanatory independent variables as characteristic variables by filtering, decomposing and combining the data in the sample, so as to reduce the influence of multiple correlations of variables on modeling.[17]

The key to the modeling of PLS algorithm is the selection of the appropriate number of principal components, which is important to improve modeling efficiency and reduce modeling difficulty.

First, n variables are preselected as principal components based on mechanism analysis and empirical knowledge to establish a preliminary PLS model as follows:

$$y = b_0 + b_1 x_1 + b_2 x_2 + b_3 x_3 + \cdots + b_n x_n, \tag{1}$$

where b_0 represents the intercept, $b_1, b_2 \ldots b_n$ represent the regression coefficients of the corresponding independent variables, respectively.

Second, the leave-one-out cross-validation method is used to calculate the prediction residual error sum of squares ss_h as follows to optimize the number of principal components.

$$ss_h = \sqrt{\sum_{i=1}^{n} (y_i - y_{h(-i)})^2}, \tag{2}$$

where n is the number of samples, and y_i is the value obtained by substituting the ith sample into Eq. (1), and $y(h(-i))$ is the predicted value obtained by substituting the ith sample into the regression equation modeled by the PLS method for $n-1$ samples except the ith sample and fitted by selecting h components.

ss_h can be used as a standard to measure the predictive ability of the model. When ss_h is the smallest, the predictive ability of the model is the best. Therefore, the h when ss_h is the smallest is selected as the principal component number for modeling.

Equations (1) and (2) are used to verify the accuracy of the test samples. If the error is within a reasonable range, the model is considered correct; otherwise, the modeling principal component calculation is performed again until the accuracy meets the requirements.

4. Gray Relational Analysis of Characteristic Variables

On the basis of the least square method, the GRA method is used to evaluate the correlation between factors according to the similarity between data curves, which is suitable for the extraction of characteristic variables of performance correlation factors.[18]

The operating parameters of the equipment are mostly sequences with time as the independent variable, thus the correlation coefficient is calculated according to the value of the correlation between the comparison sequence and the reference sequence of performance factors at each time. Too much or too scattered correlation coefficients are not conducive to comparison, thus the correlation coefficients at each time are averaged as the correlation degree between the two sequences. The gray slope correlation coefficient and gray slope correlation degree are calculated based on the GRA method as follows.

The reference sequence X_0 and the comparison sequence X_i are expressed as follows:

$$X_0 = x_0(j); \quad X_i = x_j(j) \quad j = 1, 2, \ldots, m, \tag{3}$$

where n is the time sequence and m is the number of samples.

The jth correlation coefficient $\vartheta(j)$ between X_0 and X_i is

$$\vartheta(j) = \frac{1}{1 + |k_i - k_0|}, \tag{4}$$

where k_0 and k_i are the slopes of X_0 and X_i at j, respectively.

The correlation degree γ between X_0 and X_i is

$$\gamma = \frac{1}{n-1} \sum_{k=1}^{n-1} \vartheta(j). \tag{5}$$

The value of γ indicates the strength of the correlation between the parameters represented by the reference sequence and the comparison sequence.

5. Case Analysis

This paper takes an industrial steam turbine as the object of analysis and verification. Steam turbines are complex high-energy-consuming equipment, so how to reduce energy consumption while maintaining high-efficiency operation is challenging. An important part of energy-saving optimization is to extract the related factors of energy consumption to calculate the energy consumption of the steam turbine. The parameters of steam turbines are diversified, coupled, time-varying,

Table 1. Calculation results of ss_h and h.

h	1	2	3	4	5	6	7
ss_h	146.42	141.30	138.94	74.84	14.81	39.28	13.37

Table 2.   The data and the errors according to Eq. (6) and 66 modeling samples.

Number	1	2	3	...	13	14	15	...	63	64	65
Actual	287.91	286.78	287.69	...	288.54	288.48	288.61	...	289.36	288.68	287.84
Calculate	288.02	286.28	286.65	...	286.91	286.36	287.97	...	288.44	287.65	288.89
Error	0.11	0.50	1.04	...	1.63	2.12	0.64	...	0.92	1.03	1.05
Relative error	0.04%	0.17%	0.36%	...	0.56%	0.73%	0.22%	...	0.32%	0.36%	0.36%

nonlinear, and boundary uncertain, which leads to large errors in the calculation of energy consumption, thus it is very difficult to study the influence of each parameter on energy consumption.[19] The improvement method is proposed to reduce energy consumption only when the details of energy consumption related factors affecting steam turbines are clarified.

The statistical analysis software SPSS is used to classify and compress the operating data of the steam turbine, and 266 samples are randomly selected, 66 of which are selected for modeling, and the rest are used for testing.

Eight parameters that affect the energy consumption of the steam turbine are selected as independent variables: the pressure of reheated steam x_1, the volume of desuperheated water x_2, output coefficient x_3, the pressure of exhaust steam x_4, the temperature of main steam x_5, the temperature of feed water x_6, the temperature difference of heater x_7, the clearance of blade tip x_8. The energy consumption y is selected as the dependent variable.

The PLS model is established based on the above variables, and the calculation results are shown in Table 1. The value of ss_h is the smallest when $h = 7$.

Since the correlation between x_3 and y is the smallest according to the calculation of the correlation coefficient, the rest seven principal components except x_3 are selected to establish the PLS model as follows:

$$y = 9.24 - 0.17x_1 - 1.62x_2 + 0.15x_4 + 160.46x_5 + 21.83x_6 + 0.21x + 7 + 2.05x_8.$$

$$(6)$$

The data and the errors between the actual energy consumption of the steam turbine and the calculated energy consumption according to Eq. (6) and 66 modeling samples are shown in Table 2. The comparison curves are shown in Fig. 1.

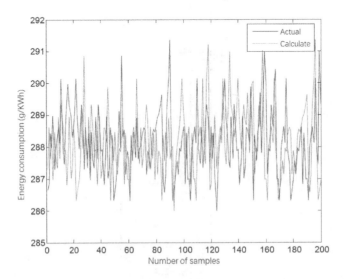

Fig. 1.   The comparison curves according to Eq. (6) and 66 modeling samples.

Table 3.   The data and the errors according to Eq. (6) and 200 test samples.

Number	1	2	3	⋯	99	100	101	⋯	⋯	⋯	⋯	198	199	200
Actual	286.62	286.87	288.49	⋯	288.36	288.69	286.83	⋯	⋯	⋯	⋯	287.49	291.00	289.08
Calculate	287.35	288.71	287.62	⋯	290.21	289.04	288.51	⋯	⋯	⋯	⋯	286.35	286.71	287.01
Error	0.73	1.84	0.87	⋯	1.85	0.35	1.68	⋯	⋯	⋯	⋯	1.14	4.29	2.07
Relative error	0.25%	0.64%	0.30%	⋯	0.64%	0.12%	0.59%	⋯	⋯	⋯	⋯	0.40%	1.47%	0.72%

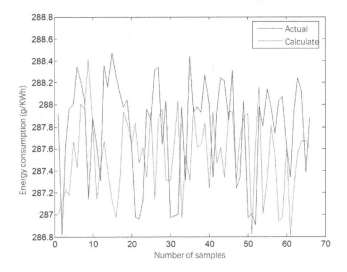

Fig. 2.   The comparison curves of the model verified according to 200 test samples.

The results show that actual energy consumption and calculated energy consumption vary with the number of modeling samples, and the maximum difference between them is 2.12 g/KWh and the absolute value of the error is less than 1%.

The data and the errors according to 200 test samples are shown in Table 3. The comparison curves are shown in Fig. 2.

The results show that the maximum difference between the actual energy consumption and the calculated energy consumption in the test samples is 4.29 g/KWh and the maximum absolute value of the error is 1.47%, indicating that the accuracy of the PLS model meets the production requirements.

In order to simplify the PLS model established above, characteristic variable extraction is performed on seven independent variables based on gray correlation algorithm. Table 4 shows the correlation degree of the slopes of the independent variable and the dependent variable calculated according to Eq. (5).

Table 4 shows that x_5 has the greatest impact on energy consumption. The distribution of the correlation degree of the slope of each variable is uniform, thus the average value is taken as the threshold value of the characteristic variable extraction, and the four variables x_1, x_5, x_6, and x_7 are selected to establish the PLS model as follows:

$$y = 12.08 - 19.13x_1 + 130.12x_5 + 73.04x_6 + 8.03x_7. \qquad (7)$$

Table 4.   Correlation degree of independent variable.

Independent variable	x_1	x_2	x_4	x_5	x_6	x_7	x_8
Correlation degree	0.84	0.75	0.69	0.90	0.88	0.83	0.80

128 *G. Yi et al.*

Table 5. The data and the errors according to Eq. (7) and 66 modeling samples.

Number	1	2	3	...	14	15	16	...	61	62	63
Actual	287.86	286.83	287.67	...	288.16	288.48	288.21	...	287.38	287.85	288.24
Calculate	287.01	287.13	287.23	...	287.38	287.09	286.98	...	286.81	287.23	287.56
Error	0.85	0.3	0.44	...	0.78	1.39	1.25	...	0.57	0.62	0.68
Relative error	0.30%	0.10%	0.15%	...	0.27%	0.48%	0.43%	...	0.20%	0.22%	0.24%

The data and the errors between the actual energy consumption of the steam turbine and the calculated energy consumption according to Eq. (7) and 66 modeling samples are shown in Table 5. The comparison curves are shown in Fig. 3.

Results show that the maximum difference between the actual energy consumption and the calculated energy consumption is 1.39 g/KWh and the absolute value of the error is still less than 1% when the four principal components are used for modeling.

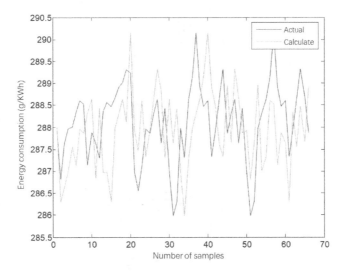

Fig. 3. The comparison and error curves according to Eq. (7) and 66 modeling samples.

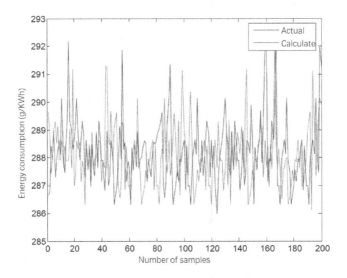

Fig. 4. The accuracy of the model verified according to 200 test samples.

Table 6.   The data and the errors according to Eq. (7) and 200 test samples.

Number	1	2	3	...	15	16	17	...	198	199	200
Actual	286.75	288.51	288.01	...	288.93	292.25	289.34	...	287.52	291.96	291.31
Calculate	289.61	287.46	288.03	...	287.91	287.93	289.02	...	289.63	290.11	289.93
Error	2.86	1.05	0.02	...	1.02	4.32	0.32	...	2.11	1.85	1.38
Relative error	1.00%	0.36%	0.01%	...	0.35%	1.48%	0.11%	...	0.73%	0.63%	0.47%

The data and the errors according to Eq. (7) and 200 test samples are shown in Table 6. The comparison curves are shown in Fig. 4. Figure 4 shows that the maximum difference between the actual energy consumption and the calculated energy consumption in the test samples is 4.32 g/KWh and the maximum relative error is 1.48%. Therefore, the model established by the four independent variables selected by the GRA method is simpler than the model established by the seven independent variables, but the accuracy is not reduced.

6. Conclusion

Aiming at the problem of equipment performance modeling and analysis, this paper proposes a data-driven reverse process modeling method for equipment. First, the performance-related factors are selected as independent variables and the specified performance is selected as the dependent variable based on professional knowledge and actual experience. Second, performance-related factors and characteristic variables are extracted and screened according to the PLS and GRA methods. Third, the accuracy of the model is verified by data simulation, and the performance is analyzed and calculated backwards from "result" to "cause". Finally, the energy consumption analysis of an industrial steam turbines is taken as the example, and the results show that the model established by the method studied in the paper is simpler and more accurate.

Acknowledgments

This research was funded by the National Key Research and Development Program of China, grant number 2018YFB1701600; the National Natural Science Foundation of China, grant number 51875515; the Key Research and Development Program of Zhejiang Province, grant number 2020C0409.

References

1. Zhang C. F. *et al.*, The variable load operation characteristic and energy-saving optimizing control system of power plant, *Int. Conf. Mach. Learn. Cybern.*, IEEE, Hong Kong, pp. 443–448, 2007.
2. Colonna P., van Putten H., Dynamic modeling of steam power cycles: Part I-Modeling paradigm and validation, *Appl. Therm. Eng.* **27**(2–3):467–480, 2007.
3. van Putten H., Colonna P., Dynamic modeling of steam power cycles: Part II - Simulation of a small simple Rankine cycle system, *Appl. Therm. Eng.* **27**(14–15):2566–2582, 2007.
4. Kulkowski K. *et al.*, Nuclear power plant steam turbine Modeling for model based control purposes, *Appl. Math. Model.* **48**:491–515, 2017.
5. Yu, J. X., Liu, P., Li Z., Hybrid modelling and digital twin development of a steam turbine control stage for online performance monitoring, *Renew. Sust. Energy Rev.* **133**:13, 2020.
6. Chaibakhsh A., Ghaffari A., Steam turbine model, *Simul. Model. Pract. Theory* **16**:1145–1162, 2008.

7. Morini G. L., Piva S., The simulation of transients in thermal plant Part I: Mathematical model, *Appl. Therm. Eng.* **27**(11–12):2138–2144, 2007.
8. Morini G. L., Piva S. The simulation of transients in thermal plant Part II: Applications, *Appl. Therm. Eng.* **28**(2–3):244–251, 2008.
9. Liu Z. Q., Zhao L., Du W. L., Qian F., Modeling and optimization of the steam turbine network of an ethylene plant, *Chin. J. Chem. Eng.* **21**(5):520–528, 2013.
10. Yu J. X. *et al.*, Modeling of steam turbine control stage under variable conditions based on operation data, *Dongli Gongcheng Xuebao* **39**(7):541–547, 2019.
11. Yan S. L. *et al.*, Research on the unified physical model and mathematic model of heat-economic analysis for the coal-fired power unit, *Zhongguo Dianji Gongcheng Xuebao* **28**(23):37–41, 2008.
12. Valero A., On the thermo-economic approach to the diagnosis of energy system malfunctions: Part 2. Malfunction definitions and assessment, *Energy* **29**(12–15):1889–1907, 2004.
13. Valero A., Exergy accounting: Capabilities and drawbacks, *Energy* **31**(1):164–180, 2006.
14. Penning F. M., De Lange H. C, Steam injection: Analysis of a typical application, *Appl. Therm. Eng.* **16**(2):115–125, 1996.
15. Mavromatis S. P., Kokossis A. C. Conceptual optimisation of utility networks for operational variations-I. Targets and level optimization, *Chem. Eng. Sci.* **53**(8):1585–1608, 1998.
16. Hubka L. Skolnik P., Steam turbine and steam reheating simulation model. 2013 *Int. Conf. IEEE Process Control* (PC), Strbske Pleso, Slovakia, pp. 31–36, 2013.
17. Zhang W.Q. *et al.*, Heat rate regression analysis based on partial least squares algorithm, *Xiandai Dianli* **26**(5):56–59, 2009.
18. Zhang Y. *et al.*, Variable selection by use of combining the genetic algorithms with simulated annealing algorithm, *Fenxi Huaxue* **27**(10):1131–1135, 1999.
19. Zhang C. *et al.*, A steam-water distribution matrix equation of the whole thermal system for coal-fired power plant and its general construction regulations, *Int. Joint Power Genereration Conf.*, Burlingame, CA (US), 1999.

Chapter 8

Simulation-oriented model reuse in cyber-physical systems: A method based on constrained directed graph

Wenzheng Liu[*,¶], Heming Zhang[*,‖], Chao Tang[†,**], Shuangfei Wu[‡,††]
and Hongguang Zhu[§,‡‡]

*National CIMS Engineering Research Center
Tsinghua University, Beijing 100084, P. R. China

†Gridsum Holding, Inc., Beijing 100086, P. R. China

‡Center of Intelligent Control and Telescience
Tsinghua Shenzhen International Graduate School
Shenzhen 518055, P. R. China

§Institute of Computing Technology
China Academy of Railway Sciences Corporation Limited
Beijing 100084, P. R. China

¶liu-wz19@mails.tsinghua.edu.cn
‖hmz@mail.tsinghua.edu.cn
**tider_tang@163.com
††WSF20@mails.tsinghua.edu.cn
‡‡zhu_hg@139.com

Abstract

Modeling and Simulation of Cyber-Physical Systems (MSCPS) is demanding in terms of immediate response to dynamic and complex changes of CPS. Simulation-oriented model reuse can be used to build a whole CPS model by reusing developed models in a new simulation application, which avoid repeated modeling and thus reduce the redevelopment of submodels. Model composition, one of the important methods, enables model reuse by selecting and adopting diversified integration solutions of simulation components to meet the requirements of simulation application systems. In this paper, a real-time model integration approach for global CPS modeling is proposed, which reuses developed submodels by compositing submodel nodes. Specifically, a constrained directed graph of submodels for the whole system which can meet the simulation requirements is constructed by reverse matching. Submodel properties, including co-simulation distance between submodel nodes, reuse benefit and simulation performance of model nodes, are quantified. Based on the properties, the model-integrated solution for the whole CPS simulation is retrieved throughout the model constrained digraph by the Genetic Algorithm (GA). In the experiment, the proposed method is applied to a typical model integrated computing scenario containing multiple model-integration solutions, among which the Pareto optimal solutions are retrieved. Results show that the effectiveness of the model integration method proposed in this paper is verified.

‖Corresponding author.

1. Introduction

Traditional complex systems are modeled and simulated in a virtual environment. Tremendous human and computing resources are spent to precisely describe their changes in mechanical structure, operating processes based on electro-hydraulic controlling principles, and kinematic and kinetic laws. To model and synthesize subsystems of a complex system, cross-disciplinary knowledge of mechanics, electrics, hydraulics, control, etc. is comprehensively applied, which requires professional modelers to carry out domain modeling in their own corresponding discipline software.

CPS improves the precision of the traditional virtual modeling by in-loop feedback of the physical system. It breaks down discipline barriers in traditional modeling through intelligent computing of information systems.[3] CPS combines digital and analog devices, interfaces, computers, and such with the man-made physical environment. It adapts to the flexible and personalized industrial needs through the integration of intelligent computing processes and physical processes. Common CPS such as intelligent cars, robots, intelligent factories, and intelligent power plants are characterized by multi-level structures, real-time data perception and dynamic application scenarios. Therefore, information system and physical system should be accurately mapped in real time when integrating submodules and Modeling-and-Simulation of Cyber-Physical Systems (MSCPS). Those characteristics of variability and complexity make their modeling cost of using traditional modeling techniques exponentially higher than that of ordinary complex systems.

Model reuse for simulation recycles a developed model in a new simulation application, which avoids repeated modeling and thus reduces modeling time. On this account, it provides an implementation paradigm for MSCPS. Modeling by reuse analysis of CPS involves interdisciplinary knowledge fusion and comprehensive reuse of corresponding domain models. Technical challenges including distributed collaborative modeling and integration of a large number of heterogeneous models need to be addressed, which can be enabled by service-oriented model composition technology.

Many scholars have studied the basic techniques such as modeling template and modeling framework, model composition, model base, etc.[1] In order to facilitate the construction of model templates for reusing, some scholars have studied the unified description technology of models such as meta-model technology,[2] component technology[4] and basic object model BOM.[5] On this basis, research on unified modeling framework supporting model reuse includes the high-level architecture (HLA),[6] model-driven architecture (MDA) technology,[7] specification of model portability (SMP),[8] modeling language (Modelica[9]), open-source simulation language (SML[10]), modeling environment and operating environment supporting model reuse (Simulink[11]), model reuse framework based on semantic web service,[12] etc.

Based on the unified description of subsystems, the reusability of a developed model for service encapsulation is studied. Model reusability includes its maturity, reusing cost and other simulation properties. Maturity mainly describes the completeness of simulation elements such as functional input and output of the simulation model, which is the premise and basis for quantifying reusability of the simulation model. Reusing cost studies cost and benefits[1] required for the application and development of the model in multiple simulation scenarios after a complete reuse process. Many research studies explored model reuse from the perspective of model composition.[13] Specifically, simulation application systems that meet the requirements are constructed by selecting and adopting diversified integrated simulation components for reusability analysis so as to provide more efficient model reuse services. With the development of cloud computing, service-oriented technology and cloud architecture are better integrated together. The cloud environment is upgrading its resource integration ability and the service platform. The combination of cloud computing architecture and simulation, which enables MSCPS in the form of services to provide a wider range of sharing and reuse, has gradually become the focus of academic attention in the field of simulation. Recently, with the development of modeling based on network and ontology technology, as well as service-oriented architecture (SOA) and other technologies, some new methods have emerged to composite sub-models, mainly including modeling language based on SOA (SOA ML[14]), modeling language based on DEVS (DEVSML[15]), ontology-based modeling language DEVSMO,[16,20] etc.

Koutsoukos[17] integrated cyber-attack models to address security issues to assure safety and resilience in cyber-physical systems.

The literature[18] puts forward the concept of modeling and simulation as a service (MSAAS) and points out that simulation services based on cloud computing framework have the advantages of cloud resource allocation on demand, high-speed network and fast response. SIMIO and MATLAB are combined to offer decision supporting service.[19] Structured simulation[21] is always regarded as real-time service for complex systems simulation, which is usually implemented in simulation software.[22]

On the basis of quantified reusabilities of models, researchers explored the methods of compositing models, constructing model libraries, establishing modeling templates, etc. to provide support for model reuse. Assuming the reusability of the model, model composition pays attention to whether the model can be meaningfully combined and the effectiveness after the combination. That is, it pays attention to the evaluation of model composition and the verification of model composition.

However, the current research on model reuse mostly stays in the essence of reuse theory and architecture, without the formation of supporting methodology to implement these architectures. Quantitative calculation of model reusability is rarely studied. Therefore, co-simulation distances of heterogeneous models and model reuse cost are first estimated in this paper based on reusing data of heterogeneous models in historical simulation scenarios. To search the optimal model composition scheme, a multi-objective genetic algorithm is tested. Finally, the effectiveness of the model composition method is verified by generated data in simulation experiments.

The remainder of this paper is organized as follows. In Sec. 2, a restricted digraph of simulation models is constructed to meet the demand of a particular simulation. Section 3 lays the groundwork for the basic theory of heterogeneous model integration method used in MSCPS, including estimation of co-simulation distance between heterogeneous models recorded in some cloud simulation application, quantitative calculation of model maturity and reuse cost used for collaborative simulation, and how to generate model composition solution based on a model node coder. Section 4 describes in detail how to search the optimal model composition solution based on multi-objective genetic algorithm in the restricted directed graph is proposed in Sec. 3. Section 5 verifies the model integration scheme based on model composition searching through experiments. Section 6 analyzes and summarizes the effectiveness of the algorithm according to the experimental results.

2. Concepts of Model Reuse and Composition for CPS

2.1. *Characteristics of model in CPS*

An important feature of CPS is dynamic change imposed in system structure and data perception. Therefore, to construct its system-wide model, real-time dynamic response is needed. In order to enable MSCPS, description of its sub-systems is necessary at the component level, the behavior-state level and the underlying implementation function level. In different simulation application scenarios, various sub-models in model base are composited and integrated. Model behavior description is different in resolution level,[23] perceptibility, etc. A white box model with high perceptual degree details the precise mechanism among input, output and intermediate state based on domain knowledge. Therefore, this kind of model is often difficult to simulate the real CPS application scene accurately. The black box model, which completely depends on perceived data, ignores the real discipline mechanism. This kind of model often has a high fitting accuracy for the input–output relationship in simulated scenes but is difficult to be extended to new simulation scenes. As for a grey box model,[24] the mechanism of the simulation scene is explored. This kind of model is driven by mathematical knowledge and perceived data. It not only approximates the behavior function of the real simulated system but also can be extended for unknown application at the same time. Therefore, to simulate a CPS application that meets the switching requirements of simulation scene, simulation precision and efficiency, it is needed to search for a nearly optimal model integration solution among various models with different resolutions and system perceptibility.

2.2. *Constrained directed graph of models*

Multiple models and their connections constitute the topology structure. There may be dependencies among the connection relations. As model nodes and edges of topology structure increase, the number of feasible paths increases. How to construct CPS simulation model relations and find a feasible path with better performances given models' topology structure is a problem worth studying. This section tries to build constrained directed graph of simulation sub-models to be integrated according to specific simulation requirements.

Constraint directed graph of simulation models provides many solutions for CPS to composite and integrate its sub-models with different functions. Constrained directed graphs refer to those digraphs with sufficient constraints, necessary constraints and XOR constraints between directed connections. In order to solve the model composition problem of CPS, it is necessary to study the optimization of model composition strategy so as to search the best model composition and integration solution that meets the simulation requirements. To this end, this paper attempts to give relevant definitions as follows:

Definition 2.1 (Model Node). In constrained directed graph of simulation model, node $M(\text{In}, \text{Out})$ represents a simulation model with certain simulation functions and input port In and out port Out. $M(\text{In}, \text{Out})$ can be a component model or a continuous, discrete behavior description model. Only solvable and executable model nodes with complete inputs and outputs are involved here.

Definition 2.2 (Preceding Node/Subsequent Node). If the output of node M_1 is connected to the input of M_2, M_1 is called the preceding node of M_2. In this way, M_2 is subsequent node of M_1, as shown in Fig. 1(a).

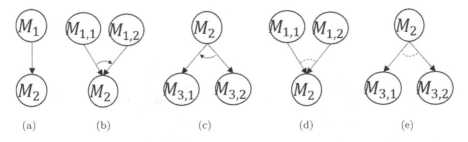

(a)   (b)   (c)   (d)   (e)

Fig. 1.   Constrains of model connections.

Definition 2.3 (Sufficient/Necessary Connection). While the out port of model $M_{1,1}$ is connected to the input of M_2, the out port of $M_{1,2}$ must be listed in the input vector of M_2. The connection of $M_{1,1}$ with M_2 is called the sufficient input connection of $M_{1,2}$ with M_2, as shown in Fig. 1(b). And vice versa, it is called necessary input connection. Similarly, a sufficient output connection and a necessary output connection can be defined. As shown in Fig. 1(c), the connection of M_2 with $M_{3,1}$ is the necessary output connection of M_2 with $M_{3,2}$. Sufficient connection as shown in Fig. 1(b) can be expressed as $\{M_{1,2}, M_2\}$ or $\{(M_{1,1}, M_{1,2}), M_2\}$.

Definition 2.4 (XOR Connection). The one and the only one out port of $M_{1,1}$ and $M_{1,2}$ is connected to the input of M_2. The connection of $M_{1,1}$ with M_2 or $M_{1,2}$ with M_2 is an XOR input connection of each other, same as the XOR output connection. XOR input and output connection are shown in Figs. 1(d) and 1(e), respectively.

Definition 2.5 (Digraph of Model Composition Solution). It is composed of a series of model nodes from the start node to the end node and their directed connections. A constrained directed graph for some specific simulation requirements is shown in Fig. 2(a). The two different models integration solution as shown in Figs. 2(b) and 2(c) correspond to $G_1 = (V_1, E_1) = (\{(M_1, M_2), M_3\}, \{(M_3, M_5), M_4\}, \{M_4, (M_7, M_5)\})$ and $G_2 = (V_2, E_2) = (\{(M_1, M_2, M_6), M_3\}, \{M_3, M_4\}, \{M_4, (M_7, M_6)\})$, respectively, in which V_1, E_1, V_2, E_2 are node set and connection set of composition solution G_1, node set and connection set of composition solution G_2, respectively.

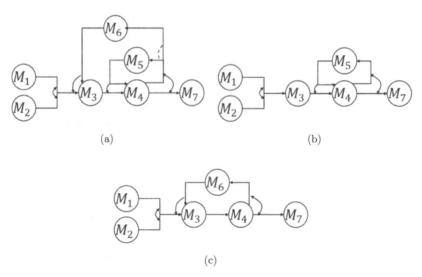

(a)   (b)

(c)

Fig. 2.   A case of constrained model directed graph (a) and its solutions (b) and (c).

3. Metrics for Model Composition in CPS

Resource costs such as time for CPS can be reduced by model reuse. Model composition is one effective implementation scheme due to the significant advantages of service encapsulation and heterogeneous integration. Searching for a model composition solution depends on the measures of model reusability and collaborative distance.

To this end, co-simulation distances between distributed and heterogeneous models, reuse cost and other simulation parameters are estimated. Based on quantitative performance indicators of simulation service, multi-objective optimization method is conducted to search simulation model integration solution.

3.1. *Co-simulation distance of heterogeneous models*

In intelligent manufacturing, the cloud architecture environment enables model sharing and simulation sharing. Therefore, to enable MSCPS, existing reusable models in different simulation scenarios can be recalled for integration. Model reuse in simulation as a service mode regards sub-models for whole system simulation as service nodes. It lacks necessary decision information for service composition when reusing existing models. Therefore, it is necessary to quantify the quality attributes of service nodes based on the historical data of experimental simulation. For simulation-oriented model integration, in addition to the simulation performance of model nodes, the collaborative interaction distance between model nodes should also be considered to quantify the difficulty and necessity of interaction between the two models during integration.

Models with basic functions often cooperate with other models frequently and appear in various simulation scenarios. Furthermore, a model with the same functional attributes with another but better compatibility and higher re-usability is easier to collaborate with other modules. It is reasonable to assume that this model has a high probability of being selected as a candidate for integration. Therefore, it is reasonable to estimate the distance between two models by the interaction frequency between two models.

A directed connection pointing from the upstream model to the downstream model if two models appear in the same simulation application is shown. This link, which only means close or distant interaction between the two models, is different from the direct connection of the models in the constrained directed graph. The more frequent the models pair appears in simulation scenarios, the easier or more necessary the link is, the more likely they will be integrated. Then, take Fig. 3 as an case to illustrate the estimation principle of the co-simulation distance of heterogeneous models. $M_1, M_2, M_3, M_4, M_5, M_6, M_7$ are sub-models from historical simulation scenarios stored in the model library. A directed graph is constructed to reflect their upstream and downstream relationships in historical simulation scenarios. $V = \{M_1, M_2, M_3, M_4, M_5, M_6, M_7\}$ is the node set. $\omega(i, j)$ denotes the connection strength of the directed edge, which in this paper is the number of simulation

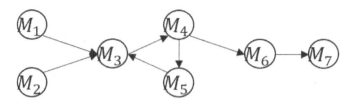

Fig. 3.   Interaction relation of models in model base.

scenes where node i acts as the upstream node of node j. Output probability $P_{i,j}^{\mathrm{out}}$, input probability $P_{i,j}^{\mathrm{in}}$ and model interaction probability $P(i,j)$ are closely related to this variable, which is detailed in the following definition. $d(i,j)$ representing the interaction distance of node i to j is defined as the expected steps from node i to node j in historical simulation library. The smaller $d(i,j)$ is, the more necessary and easier the interaction of node i to j is.

Definition 3.1 (Output Probability $P_{i,j}^{\mathrm{out}}$). For a node i with several output connections, any subsequent node can be selected as its output. According to the frustrated random walk algorithm,[25] the output probability of i to j is defined. $P_{i,j}^{\mathrm{out}} = \frac{\omega(i,j)}{\sum_{k \in S_i^{\mathrm{sub}}} \omega(i,k)}$, where S_i^{sub} denotes subsequent node set of i.

Definition 3.2 (Input Probability $P_{i,j}^{\mathrm{in}}$). For a node j with several input connections, any preceding node can be selected as its input. According to the frustrated random walk algorithm, the input probability $P_{i,j}^{\mathrm{in}}$ of j from i is defined. $P_{i,j}^{\mathrm{in}} = \frac{\omega(i,j)}{\sum_{h \in S_j^{\mathrm{pro}}} \omega(h,j)}$, in which S_j^{pro} denotes preceding node set of j.

Definition 3.3 (Model Interaction Probability $P_{(i,j)}$). It means the probability nodes i and j can interact successfully. According to the frustrated random walk algorithm, the output probability $P_{i,j}^{\mathrm{out}}$ of i to j and the input probability $P_{i,j}^{\mathrm{in}}$ of j from i are defined. $P(i,j) = P_{i,j}^{\mathrm{out}} \times P_{i,j}^{\mathrm{in}}$. It is worth reviewing that $\omega(i,j)$ is the number of simulation scenes in which i acted as the upstream node of j. In this way, $\omega(i,j) = 0$ if i never lead to j directly or indirectly.

The interaction probability $P(i,j)$ is defined in this way to take into account that there are different alternative model inputs and outputs to be composited and integrated. Randomness reflected by selecting alternative model nodes is in accordance with the weight quantified by their coexistence times. The expectation of node i first hitting node j can be used as a measure of their co-simulation distance, which is derived by the probability distribution of the steps required for the first interaction of i and j.

Estimating the co-simulation distance by Monte Carlo simulation is straightforward and easy to implement but needs repeated simulation. In this way, the result accuracy increases with simulation times which requires tremendous and nonnegligible computation. Therefore, this study explores the estimation of co-simulation distances between models by analytic calculation based on frustrated random walk.

For specific node i in the model library embedded in cloud architecture, feedback represented by model links enables it reaching node j after one or more steps.

The probability vector interacting with other nodes after n steps can be obtained by multiplying the one-step transition probability matrix with the interaction probability vector of $n-1$ steps.

$P(N_t^i = n)$ denotes the probability of node i interacting with node t for the first time after n steps.

$P(t)_n$ denotes the vector composed of $(P(N_t^i = n)), i \neq t$. $\mathrm{Sub}(i)$ denotes the set of successor node neighbors of i. $\mathrm{Pre}(i)$ denotes the set of preceding node neighbors of i.

T denotes the one-step transition probability matrix for direct interaction of model nodes. $T(i, j_i)$, $j_i \in \mathrm{Sub}(i)$ is the ith entry at the j_ith column of T, which means the probability of i first interacting with j_i after one step and can be calculated by (1). If $T(i, j_i) = 1$, then $d(i, j_i) = 1$. Thus, $T(i, j_i)$, $j_i \in Sub(i)$ is computed as Eq. (1), only those $T(i, j_i) < 1$ are considered.

$$
T_{i,j_i} = \begin{cases}
\dfrac{\omega_{i,j_i}}{\sum_{k\in\mathrm{Sub}(i)} \omega_{i,k}} \cdot \dfrac{\omega_{i,j_i}}{\sum_{m\in\mathrm{pre}(i)} \omega_{m,j_i}}, & t \neq j_i, \ i \neq j_i, \\[3ex]
0, & t = j_i, \ i \neq j_i, \\[2ex]
1 - \sum_{h\neq j_i} \dfrac{\omega_{i,h}}{\sum_{k\in\mathrm{Sub}(i)} \omega_{i,k}} \cdot \dfrac{\omega_{i,h}}{\sum_{m\in\mathrm{pre}(i)} \omega_{m,j_i}}, & i = j_i, \ i \notin \mathrm{Pre}(t), \\[3ex]
1 - \sum_{h\neq j_i} \dfrac{\omega_{i,h}}{\sum_{k\in\mathrm{Sub}(i)} \omega_{i,k}} \cdot \dfrac{\omega_{i,h}}{\sum_{m\in\mathrm{pre}(i)} \omega_{m,j_i}} \\[2ex]
\quad - \dfrac{\omega_{i,j_i}}{\sum_{k\in\mathrm{Sub}(i)} \omega_{i,k}} \cdot \dfrac{\omega_{i,j_i}}{\sum_{m\in\mathrm{pre}(i)} \omega_{m,j_i}}, & i = j_i, \ i \in \mathrm{Pre}(t).
\end{cases}
\tag{1}
$$

According to the transition relation, $P(N_t^i = n)$ is calculated by (2) and $P(t)_n$ by (3).

$$
P(N_t^i = n) = \sum_{j_i \in \mathrm{Sub}(i)} T_{i,j_i} P(N_t^{j_i} = n-1), \quad n \geq 2,
\tag{2}
$$

$$
P(t)_n = TP(t)_{n-1} = T^{n-1} P(t)_1, \quad n \geq 1,
\tag{3}
$$

$$
\sum_{h\neq j_i} T_{i,j_i} = \begin{cases}
1 - \dfrac{\omega_{i,j_i}}{\sum_{k\in\mathrm{Sub}(i)} \omega_{i,k}} \cdot \dfrac{\omega_{i,j_i}}{\sum_{m\in\mathrm{pre}(i)} \omega_{m,j_i}}, & i \in \mathrm{Pre}(j_i), \\[3ex]
1, & i \notin \mathrm{Pre}(j_i).
\end{cases}
\tag{4}
$$

From (4), according to the Gershgorin Circle Theorem, the maximum eigenvalues and the spectral radius of T are less than 1.

$P(t)_n$ can be easily obtained according to one-step transmission relation of model nodes. N_t denotes step vector required for other nodes first hitting the target node t, whose ith entry is N_t^i denoting the steps required for node i first hitting t.

Its mathematical expectation is computed as (5).

$$EN_t^i = \sum_{n=1}^{\infty} nP(N_t^i = n) := \sum_{n=1}^{\infty} nP(t)_n^i. \tag{5}$$

Equation (5) can be equivalently shown in the vector formula (6).

$$EN_t = \sum_{n=1}^{\infty} nP(N_t = n) := \sum_{n=1}^{\infty} nP(t)_n$$

$$= \sum_{n=2}^{\infty} nP(t)_n + P(t)_1$$

$$= \sum_{n=2}^{\infty} nTP(t)_{n-1} + P(t)_1$$

$$= T \sum_{n=2}^{\infty} nP(t)_{n-1} + P(t)_1$$

$$= T \sum_{n=2}^{\infty} (n-1)P(t)_{n-1} + T \sum_{n=2}^{\infty} P(t)_{n-1} + P(t)_1$$

$$= T \sum_{n=2}^{\infty} (n-1)P(t)_{n-1} + \sum_{n=1}^{\infty} P(t)_n$$

$$= TEN_t + 1. \tag{6}$$

Equation (6) is reduced to Eq. (7).

$$(I - T)EN_t = 1. \tag{7}$$

1 is the vector whose entries are 1. $(I - T)$ can be eliminated by multiply $(I - T)^{-1}$ on the left. According to Abel's theorem, spectral radius of T is less than 1. Thus, the power series $I + T^1 + T^2 + \cdots$ converge to $(I - T)^{-1}$.

$$EN_t = (I + T^1 + T^2 + \cdots)1 = \sum_{n=1}^{\infty} T^n 1. \tag{8}$$

EN_t can be solved by numerical (8), where 1 is the vector whose entries are 1.

In (8), T is often a sparse matrix. To avoid direct power calculation of T^n, T is repeatedly applied to the column vector 1. The summing result is recorded with another column vector. Sparsity of T can speed up the calculation and reduce memory. Thus, by applying the above calculation process to other target nodes in the model base, a preliminary estimation of the pair-to-pair interaction distance between all models can be obtained.

3.2. *Reusability of model node*

Model reusability measures the fitness of model nodes for reusable simulation scenarios referring to several key characteristics including model maturity, reuse cost, average simulation accuracy, computation efficiency and model perceptibility.

- *Model maturity.* It mainly describes the completeness of the functional input, output and other simulation elements of a simulation model. It is the premise to measure the reusability of a simulation model. The quantitative research is not the focus of this paper. In this paper, the preliminary measurement is simplified as (9). In this expression, $ifIn$, $ifOut$ and $ifEnv$ are boolean variables, respectively, which are used to measure whether the input signal, output signal and model operation, environments are fully specified. When $ifIn = 1$ and $ifOut = 1$ and $ifEnv = 1$ and $isSolver = 0$, it is reasonable to infer that the model could run initially. The model maturity is 0.6. $isSolver$ measures whether a solver is set for the model. The model failed to perform operations while no solver is specified. Therefore, it is reasonable to assume that on the basis of initial run, the maturity of the model executed according to the solver Settings is 1.

$$Mty = \begin{cases} 0, & ifIn = 0 \ or \ ifOut = 0 \ or \ ifEnv = 0, \\ 0.6, & ifIn = 1 \ and \ ifOut = 1 \ and \ ifEnv = 1 \ and \ isSolver = 0, \\ 1.0, & ifIn = 1 \ and \ ifOut = 1 \ and \ ifEnv = 1 \ and \ isSolver = 1. \end{cases}$$

$$(9)$$

- *Reuse cost.* It represents model reuse cost for new simulation application through a complete reuse process, which is calculated based on historical simulation data and is shown in (10).

$$K_N = (C + A(N - 1))/N, \tag{10}$$

where K_N means the average reuse cost, C denotes cost to develop the model for its first use, A denotes cost to adapt for reuse each time it is reused and N denotes number of times that the model is reused. These calculations draw on the theoretical basis of software reuse in.
- *Simulation accuracy.* $SimAc$ refers to the deviation of the model applied in historical simulation scenes from its simulated entity behavior parameters. Apparently, the smaller it is, the more accurate the simulation is.
- *Computation efficiency.* $ComEf$ measures the statistical time cost for the model to calculate the output result from the received input signal, which is usually obtained by averaging multiple iterations.
- *Perceptibility.* Per means the extent to which the computational execution mechanism of the model is interpretable. According to this feature, the models used in integrated simulation scenarios can be basically divided into three classes, wherein the calculation execution mechanism of the white box model from the

input signal to the output signal of the model can be fully perceived. Grey box models are those which can partially explain the inner principle of the models but have no complete theoretical details. A black box model hides all of the model implementation details and provides only input and output ports. Their perceptibilities can be quantified as 1, 0.5 and 0, respectively.

Various models and their interaction for CPS constitute a topological restricted directed graph. The models act as nodes. Their interaction connections act as edges. By searching a model combination solution with better node and edge attribute values, the model reuse scheme of CPS can be optimized.

3.3. *Initialization of constrained directed models graph*

Assume models as nodes and their connections as edges. There are all kinds of dependent relationships between some edges, such as sufficient, necessary, necessary and sufficient. To construct the constrained directed graph of models according to simulation requirements, node set including the starting node to the ending node, edge set, node weight, edge weight, and the dependency relationship between edges are recorded and set.

According to the connectivity of the model nodes, for the nonterminating node, the union of its possible next nodes is taken as the dependent model set of the current node. Once executed to the current node, at least one of the dependent model set should be selected as the subsequent node.

As described in Sec. 2, there exist the following dependencies between edges. While edge $Edge_1$ is selected to model composition path, $Edge_2$ must be added to the collection, which can be denoted as $Edge_1->Edge_2$; if $Edge_3$ is selected, either $Edge_4$ or $Edge_5$ must be added, which can be denoted as $Edge_3->(Edge_4 \cup Edge_5)$; without loss of generality, there may be multiple classes of constraints on one edge, for example, $Edge_1->(Edge_2) \cap (Edge_4 \cup Edge_5)$. To generate a feasible path, BFS is adopted to deal with the dependencies as follows:

(i) Adds $Edge_1$ to set S, which denotes the edge set making a path for model composition solution.
(ii) Initialize queue Q, which hosts the current visited edge that to act as the next component of the path.
(iii) Add $Edge_1$ to Q.
(iv) If Q is not empty, pop out the uppermost element A; If Q is empty, then exit.
(v) Deal with every A_{rely} in dependent edge set of A in turn. Namely, if it exists in Q, do nothing; otherwise, go to the next step.
(vi) If A_{rely} is not in Q and without XOR edge in dependent edge set of A, add A_{rely} to S and Q. If there exist XOR edges of A_{rely}, select one edge according to the priority of those XOR edges and add it to S and Q, which is detailed in the next section.
(vii) Return to step (iv), until Q is null.

Algorithm 1. Procedure to generate model integration solution.

Initialization: Graph edge info set E, node info set V and constraints info CE;

    Priority list: P recording the node priority

    Current edge to be handled: $E_s tart$

    List S is used to store path generated

    Empty queue Q which is used to store the current edge

Update:

  1: add $E_s tart$ to S

  2: add $E_s tart$ to Q

  3: **while** Q is not empty **do**

  4:    Pop out the uppermost element A from Q

  5:    Get all dependencies $AList_{rely}$ of A based on CE

  6:    **for** A_{rely} in $AList_{rely}$ **do**

  7:      **if** A_{rely} in S **then**

  8:        skip

  9:      **end if**

10:      **if** A_{rely} not in S **then**

11:        **if** XOR edges in A_{rely} **then**

12:          select one edge $e_t emp$ according to P add $e_t emp$ to S and Q

13:        **end if**

14:        **if** no XOR edges in A_{rely} **then**

15:          add A_{rely} to S and Q

16:        **end if**

17:      **end if**

18:    **end for**

19: **end while**

The procedure of generating model integration scheme based on a priority coder is detailed in Algorithm 1.

4. Model Composition Method Based on Multi-Objective Genetic Algorithm

To search and optimize the feasible model combination path in the constrained topology directed diagram composed of the CPS subsystem model and their interaction connections, the multi-objective genetic algorithm is introduced containing the following key points.

4.1. *Encoding and evolution*

To meet the simulation requirements, candidate models to be integrated are connected by their interaction links in the form of a constrained model diagram.

$V = \{M_1, \ldots, M_k\}$ is the model nodes set, in which $M_i =< M_i : Mty_i, K_{N,i} >$. $E = \{e_{i,j}, \ldots\}$, in which $e_{i,j} =< (M_i, M_j) : d_{i,j} >$, M_i denotes the upstream node of edge $e_{i,j}$, M_j denotes the downstream node of edge $e_{i,j}$, and $d_{i,j}$ denotes the collaboration distance of node i and j.

- *Encoding.* Chromosomal coding based on full permutation of $(1, \ldots, N)$ indicating the priority orders of the N model nodes are adopted. Each permutation coder can be mapped with a unique model composition scheme generated by Algorithm 1.
- *Crossover.* Select two codes $Coder_1$ and $Coder_2$. Change a certain continuous segment in $Coder_1$ with corresponding value and order in $Coder_2$. The crossover operator is implemented by a *Xovox* function embedded in a toolkit called *geatpy*.
- *Mutation.* Randomly select several elements in the coder and switch their positions. The mutation operator is implemented by a *Mutinv* function embedded in a toolkit called *geatpy*.
- *Fitness.* Define the number of optimization goals that each chromosome can dominate other chromosomes as the fitness function of a coder. Chromosomes that can dominate other chromosomes are selected and left to repeat *Crossover* and *Mutation*.

4.2. *Generating model composition path*

After obtaining the node priority, in the path generation process, if there are multiple alternative edges corresponding to the current node, select the edge with smaller coding value according to the priority of the corresponding node to join the path edge set. In the dependency processing part, BFS is used to solve the dependency problem of the newly added edge. Until the end node is reached.

In order to solve the partial coding loop problem in a sub-connected domain, the priority of each repeatedly selected edge is punished to a certain extent after selection so as to increase the exploration ability of path generation and prevent routing from falling into an infinite loop locally.

4.3. *Complexity analysis*

For searching the optimal model composition solution in the restricted directed graph of sub-models, K node priority sequence coders are generated. Length of each coder is n. n denotes the number of model nodes. BFS is adopted to search for the mapping model composition solution based on the priority coder. There exist at most $n(n-1)/2$ joining edges and at most $n(n-1)[n(n-1)/2-1]/4$ in the graph. Thus, in one single search, the complexity of time and space consuming accords to $O(n^4)$. M generation is iterated. The total time and space consuming accords to $O(KMn^4)$.

5. Experiment and Analysis

The following simulation model integration digraphs are used to verify the effectiveness of the proposed simulation-oriented model combination and reuse method. Case 1 as shown in Fig. 4 and case 2 as shown in Fig. 5 are typical model digraphs of CPS with more feedforward links and more feedback links, respectively. Wherein, nodes represent models to be integrated or combined and links between nodes represent directed signal transmissions.

First, the collaborative interaction distance between model nodes is estimated based on frustrated walk method introduced in Sec. 3.1. Some of the results of analytical estimates and Monte Carlo simulation results are compared in Table 1.

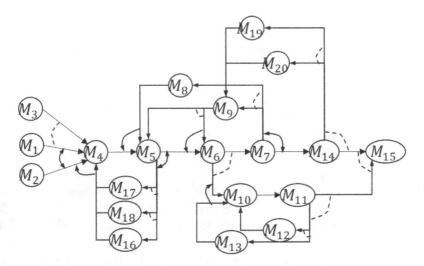

Fig. 4. Constrained model directed graph for case 1.

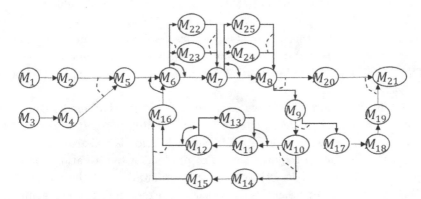

Fig. 5. Constrained model directed graph for case 2.

Table 1.   Comparison of distance estimation based on Monte Carlo and random walk.

Model node pair	Monte Carlo dist.	Random walk dist.
Case 1: M_1 and M_4	1.00	1.03
Case 1: M_4 and M_5	1.00	0.95
Case 1: M_5 and M_6	1.00	1.10
Case 1: M_6 and M_{11}	4.21	4.19
Case 2: M_6 and M_7	1.0	1.13
Case 1: M_6 and M_{23}	2.09	1.94

Table 2.   Parameters of the multi-objective search method.

Parameter	Value
Node number of case 1	20
Node number of case 2	25
Population size	6
Total generations	30
Converge generation of case 1	13
Converge generation of case 2	12

Then the model node attributes in the directed graph are quantified based on the simulation data as described in Sec. 3.2.

Finally, the model integration solution with better path fitness is explored based on the multi-objective optimization algorithm introduced in Sec. 4. The parameter setting in the experiment is shown in Table 2. The fitness function which measures the number of other dominated chromosomes is designed. Specifically, the population is optimally divided according to whether there is other absolutely dominant coder of a certain coder. If not, this coder belongs to the top subgroup. After that, the following subgroups are divided in the same way. In the same subgroup, individuals are ranked according to their sparsity[26] with their neighbors.

Simulation performances of case 1 and case 2 vary with iteration as shown in Fig. 6. The red dots are their Pareto Optimal front solutions of the 30th generation. Compared with the blue dots, the red ones show better performance parameters.

Their final model combination solutions are illustrated in Figs. 7 and 8, respectively.

It can be seen from the above experimental results that model composition performance tends to converge after the first few iterations. It is reasonable to infer that the corresponding model composition solution is a near-optimal solution satisfying the simulation requirements. The product of the iteration number and the population size is far less than the total permutations of the nodes number, which is inevitable after feasibility judgment of corresponding model composition solution is introduced during iteration.

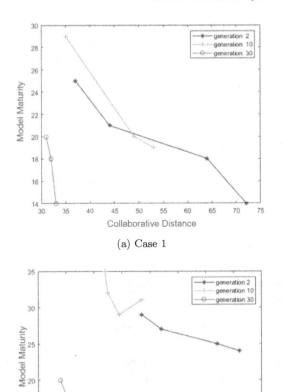

(a) Case 1

(b) Case 2

Fig. 6.   Pareto Optimal front solutions.

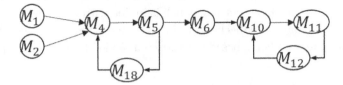

Fig. 7.   Model composition solution of case 1.

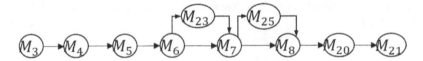

Fig. 8.   Model composition solution of case 2.

To fulfill specific simulation requirements, the collaborative interaction distance between each sub-model pair is first analytically estimated based on historical simulation data, which is within 1% gap with Monte Carlo simulation results. Therefore, it can be inferred that the analytical estimation method is effective.

6. Conclusion

The contributions of real-time modeling of CPS in this paper refer to reusing existing models in historical simulation scenarios rather than starting from scratch. This work does not focus on the searching step. Specifically, the models with integrated relationship constraints are aggregated as a constrained directed connection graph. Therefore, an approach of near-optimal model composition based on multi-objective optimization genetic algorithm is presented. The Genetic Algorithm is adopted to represent the feasibility of the reuse scheme and to prove that modeling starting from scratch can be avoided. In fact, due to the constrained relations, the optimal scheme can be obtained at the beginning several iterations of chromosomes. The main contribution of the paper is given as follows:

- An architecture supporting quantitative model reuse based on Constrained Directed Graph is proposed.
- Difficulty or necessity of model-pair interaction, named co-simulation distance of heterogeneous models, is estimated based on random walk algorithm.
- Multi-objective genetic algorithm (MGA) is applied to the Restricted Directed Graph to search model combination scheme.

Due to the difficulty in unifying different simulation performance of model nodes and their connecting edges, the multi-objective optimization genetic algorithm based on Pareto optimality is adopted. Gradient fitness is used as the fitness function to measure the model composition solution corresponding to nodes' code. The penalty term of cyclic segment is introduced in routing through the directed model graph. It not only reduces the waste of routing dead-loop but also reduces the nesting of multi-layer loop segments, which is in line with the strategy to avoid the dead-lock of multi-layer feedback easily in an actual CPS. Thus, the result shows that the model reuse scheme based on restricted model directed graph proposed in this paper is effective.

Acknowledgments

This work was supported by the National Key R&D Program of China (No. 2018YFB1701600).

References

1. Robinson S., Nance R. E., Paul R. J., Pidd M., Taylor S. J., Simulation model reuse: Definitions, benefits and obstacles, *Simul. Pract. Theory* **12**(7–8):479–494, 2004.

2. Hawryszkiewycz I. T., A metamodel for modeling collaborative systems, *J. Comput. Inform. Syst.* **45**(3):63–72, 2005.

3. Hehenberger P., Vogel-Heuser B., Bradley D., Eynard B., Tomiyama T., Achiche S., Design, modelling, simulation and integration of cyber physical systems: Methods and applications, *Comput. Indus.* **82**:273–289, 2016.

4. Wang J., Beu J., Yalamanchili S., Conte T., Designing configurable, modifiable and reusable components for simulation of multicore systems, *2012 SC Companion*: *High Performance Computing, Networking Storage and Analysis*, IEEE, pp. 472–476, 2012.

5. Peng G., Mao H., Wang H., Zhang H., BOM-based design knowledge representation and reasoning for collaborative product development, *J. Syst. Sci. Syst. Eng.* **25**(2):159–176, 2016.

6. Bruzzone A. G., Pereira D. C., Tremori A., Massei M., Scapparone M., Interoperability and performance analysis of a complex marine multidomain simulation based on high level architecture, *Int. Conf. Harbour, Marit. Multimodal Logist. Model. Simul.* 117, 2015.

7. Zhang R., Application pattern of RTI in MDA-based HLA simulation, *J. Theor. Appl. Inform. Technol.* **47**(3):1082–1086, 2013.

8. Nemeth S., Demarest P., Research and development in application of the simulation model portability standard, *SpaceOps 2010 Conf. Delivering on the Dream Hosted by NASA Marshall Space Flight Center and Organized by AIAA*, Huntsville, Alabama, AIAA 2010-2268, 2010.

9. Fritzson P., *Principles of Object-Oriented Modeling and Simulation with Modelica 3.3: A Cyber-Physical Approach*, John Wiley & Sons, 2014.

10. Kilgore R. A., Open source simulation modeling language (SML), *Proc. 2001 Winter Simulation Conf. (Cat. No. 01CH37304)*, Vol. 1, IEEE, pp. 607–613, 2001.

11. Whalen M. W., Murugesan A., Rayadurgam S., Heimdahl M. P., Structuring simulink models for verification and reuse, *Proc. 6th Int. Workshop on Modeling in Software Engineering*, ACM, pp. 19–24, 2014.

12. Bell D., de Cesare S., Lycett M., Mustafee N., Taylor S. J., Semantic web service architecture for simulation model reuse, *11th IEEE Int. Symp. Distributed Simulation and Real-Time Applications (DS-RT'07)*, IEEE, pp. 129–136, 2007.

13. Cai Y., Service-oriented simulation supports key environmental technology research, Dissertation for Ph.D. Degree, National University of Defense Technology, Changsha, 2014 (in Chinese).

14. Tounsi I., Zied H., Kacem M. H., Kacem A. H., Drira K., Using SoaML models and event-B specifications for modeling SOA design patterns, *Int. Conf. Enterprise Information Systems (ICEIS)*, Angers, France, 11 pp., 2013.

15. Hu J., Huang L., Cao B., Chang X., Executable modeling approach to service oriented architecture using SoaML in conjunction with extended DEVSML, *2014 IEEE Int. Conf. Services Computing*, IEEE, pp. 243–250, 2014.

16. Hu Y., Xiao J., Zhao H., Rong G., DEVSMO: An ontology of DEVS model representation for model reuse, *Proc. 2013 Winter Simulation Conf.: Simulation: Making Decisions in a Complex World*, pp. 4002–4003, 2013.

17. Koutsoukos X. *et al.*, SURE: A modeling and simulation integration platform for evaluation of secure and resilient cyber-physical systems, *Proc. IEEE* **106**(1):93–112, 2017.

18. Cayirci E., Configuration schemes for modeling and simulation as a service federation, *Simulation* **89**:1388–1399, 2013.

19. Dehghanimohammadabadi M., Keyser T. K., Intelligent simulation: Integration of SIMIO and MATLAB to deploy decision support systems to simulation environment, *Simul. Model. Pract. Theory* **71**:45–60, 2017.

20. Karhela T., Villberg A., Niemistö H., Open ontology-based integration platform for modeling and simulation in engineering, *Int. J. Model. Simul. Sci. Comput.* **3**(02):1250004, 2012.
21. Kaufmann D., Rossmann J., Integration of structural simulations into a real-time capable Overall System Simulation for complex mechatronic systems, *Int. J. Model. Simul. Sci. Comput.* **10**(2):1940002, 2019.
22. Li W., Lu L., Liu Z., Ma P., Yang M., HIT-SEDAES: An integrated software environment for simulation experiment design, analysis and evaluation, *Int. J. Model. Simul. Sci. Comput.* **7**(3):1650027, 2016.
23. Steiniger A., Uhrmacher A. M., Intensional couplings in variable-structure models: An exploration based on multilevel-DEVs, *ACM Trans. Model. Comput. Simul.* **26**(2):1–27, 2016.
24. Zhao J., Wang H., Liu W., Zhang H., A learning-based multiscale modelling approach to real-time serial manipulator kinematics simulation, *Neurocomputing* **390**:280–293, 2020.
25. Li E., Le Z., Frustrated random walks: A faster algorithm to evaluate node distances on connected and undirected graphs, *Phys. Rev. E* **102**(5):052135, 2020.
26. Deb K., Pratap A., Agarwal S., Meyarivan T. A. M. T., A fast and elitist multiobjective genetic algorithm: NSGA-II, *IEEE Trans. Evol. Comput.* **6**(2):182–197, 2002.

Chapter 9

Model maturity towards modeling and simulation: Concepts, index system framework and evaluation method

Lin Zhang[*,†,‡], Ying Liu[*], Yuanjun Laili[*] and Weicun Zhang[†]

*School of Automation Science and Electrical Engineering
Beihang University (BUAA), Engineering Research
Center of Complex Product Advanced Manufacturing Systems
Systems, Ministry of Education, Beijing Advanced
Innovation Center for Big Data-Based Precision Medicine
Beijing 100191, P. R. China

†School of Automation and Electrical Engineering
University of Science and Technology Beijing
Beijing 100083, P. R. China
‡johnlin9999@163.com

Abstract

Simulation has become an essential way and sometimes the only way to study complex systems (e.g. system of systems, SoS). Simulation is the model based activity. How to build a high-quality model is the first consideration in simulation. Fidelity and credibility are the two mostly used metrices to evaluate the quality of a model. However, the definitions and evaluation methods of fidelity and credibility vary from one research to another and it's hard to evaluate the metrics precisely. More importantly, the evolution process of a model in use cannot be directly reflected by the two metrics. Therefore, this paper introduces the model maturity to track the status of a model during its life cycle, especially in the use and management phases, which will be an important supplement to the quality evaluation system of models. The concept of model maturity is given and a framework of index system for model maturity evaluation is established. Then, a hierarchical evaluation method based on qualitative and quantitative analysis (HEQQ) for model maturity is proposed. Finally, a case study is used to validate the feasibility and effectiveness of the proposed method.

1. Introduction

Model is the basis of simulation. The effectiveness of a simulation relies heavily on the quality of the model. At present, the evaluation of model quality mainly uses two metrics, namely, fidelity[1–3] and credibility.[4–6] However, the two metrics mainly focus on the static status or performance of a model at a specific stage or condition, and cannot directly reflect the changes of the model in its use and management process. Actually, the status or performance of a model in its use and management

---

‡Corresponding author.

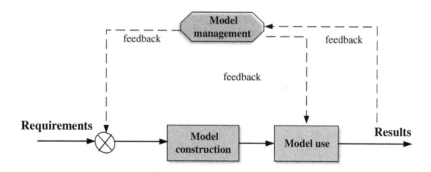

Fig. 1.   The process of model maturing.

processes is also an important aspect of its quality, which has a significant impact on whether the model can be reused. However, there is no corresponding metrics for evaluating the model in its use and management processes. This paper proposes to use "model maturity" to evaluate the performance after the model is constructed.

The cyclic feedback relationship in the lifecycle of the model is shown in Fig. 1. The lifecycle of a model can be roughly divided into three phases, i.e., model construction, model use (model implementation, execution, interoperation, etc.), and model management (storage, modification, reconfiguration, optimization, integration, etc.). Feedbacks between the processes keep the model involved and optimized. This is also the process by which the model gradually matures.

The purpose of this paper is to propose the concept of model maturity for simulation, give its definition, an index system framework and an evaluation method. The introduction of model maturity will be conducive to the standardized development and management of models and will provide guidance to model evaluation, optimization and reuse.

The rest of this paper is organized as follows. In Sec. 2, the concept of model maturity is proposed. The levels of model maturity are described in Sec. 3. A framework of evaluation indexes system for model maturity is established in Sec. 4. Then a hierarchical evaluation method based on qualitative and quantitative (HEQQ) analysis for model maturity is proposed in Sec. 5. A case study is presented in Sec. 6. The conclusions and some suggestions for future work are given in Sec. 7.

2. The Concept of Model Maturity

2.1. *Definition*

Models for simulation generally include requirement models (also known as requirement specifications), conceptual models, mathematical models, and simulation models.[7] The maturity we studied in this paper covers all these types of models and is relative to the whole lifecycle of the models, as shown in Fig. 2. In the

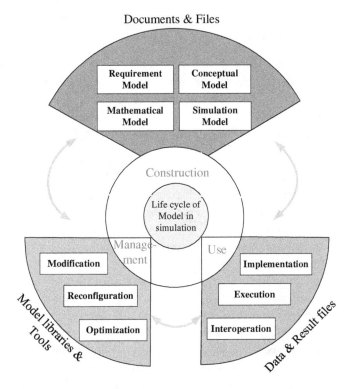

Fig. 2.   Schematic diagram of the model life cycle.

phase of model construction, various types of models are produced in the form of documents or model files. In the phase of model use, executable models are implemented and run in a simulation environment to fulfill simulation tasks, e.g., analyses, predictions, or decision making. In the phase of model management, models will be modified, reconfigured or optimized according to changes of requirements and feedback information from use phase.

There are many studies on maturity in different areas.[8–10] The concept of maturity is seldom discussed individually, its generally related to a specific application area, such as technology maturity,[11] product maturity,[12] manufacturing maturity,[13] system maturity, software development capability maturity CMMI,[14] and other maturity models (process maturity, knowledge maturity, data maturity, etc.).[15–20] Some common characteristics of maturity can be summarized as follows: (a) The maturity is mainly concerned about the degree of satisfaction, completeness, stability and repeatability in applications. (b) The maturity is usually divided into different levels to represent the status of the object being evaluated. Each level has its own criteria. (c) The level gradually increases, which reflect the trend of continuous improvement and optimization of the object.

Drawing on the ideas of various maturity models, this paper gives the definition of model maturity for simulation.

Definition 1. Model maturity is a measure of how well a model meets the expected effects and application requirements as time and frequency of using the model increases, which describes the developing status of the model compared with the actual object being modeled. The process of model maturing is the process that the model's performance gradually stabilizes and meets the requirements.

Model maturity reflects the practicability of the model itself. The model is continuously improved and revised during the use and evolution process. While the maturity of the model will gradually increase. Especially in the process of model reuse, mature models have higher priority and low risks than immature models or newly developed models.

In order to further understand the concept of model maturity, some characteristics of mature and immature models are given as follows:

(1) *The immature* model: (a) The model has bad properties (e.g., standardization, scalability and portability). (b) The processes of model use and model management are disordered and poorly documented. (c) There are many uncertainties in the simulation results with the model. (d) There are many errors or failures in the process of model execution; (e) The model is difficult to be reused.

(2) *The mature* model: (a) The model has good properties. The model is clearly defined and the related documents are standardized. (b) The processes of model use and model management are well controlled and documented. (c) There is no uncertainty in simulation results with the model. (d) There are no errors or failures in the process of model execution. (e) The model is easy to be reused.

The maturity of a model can be divided into five levels that will be described in details in Sec. 3.

2.2. *Features of model maturity compared with other metrics*

In the field of modeling and simulation (M&S), fidelity and credibility are two most important metrics used to evaluate the quality of a model.

The fidelity of the model emphasizes the similarity between the model and the corresponding entity on a certain side, which reflects the essential attributes of the entity, and is an objective and ideal evaluation metric. The fidelity of the model does not change as simulation requirements change. However, it is difficult to accurately describe the internal characteristics of many systems, especially for complex systems whose mechanism is unclear, which makes it difficult or impossible to calculate the fidelity of a model versus the entity being modeled. Therefore, for the evaluation of model fidelity, external features, such as inputs and outputs, are often used to indirectly verify the fidelity of the model. However, this verification can only be based on a limited number of data sets. In the case of insufficient data, even if the model and the corresponding entity have similar or identical external features, it does not mean that the internal structure and attributes of the two are similar or identical. For those models used for visualization, their fidelities are often judged by user's experiences and senses.

Model credibility reflects the degree of user's confidence in the correctness of the model, that is, the accuracy of certain characteristics of the corresponding entity reflected by the model under specific requirements. Model credibility is a measure of model's usability from another perspective when fidelity cannot be accurately calculated. Due to the complexity of the real world, it is difficult to construct a model that is "exactly the same" as the entity being modeled. In fact, the same entity will show different characteristics in completing different tasks, and each simulation task is performed for a specific requirement, as a result, the credibility of the corresponding model may be different with respect to different simulation requirements. Therefore, for most simulation systems, credibility is used more often in practice than fidelity. Since the credibility of the model is closely related to the requirements, there are some subjective factors in its evaluation, which bring considerable difficulties to the credibility evaluation.

Essentially, both fidelity and credibility are measurements of similarity between the model and the corresponding entity, while similarity measurements are usually not unique and vague, so there are still great challenges in the evaluation of the two metrics. Although some basic principles are given in the VV & A methodologies, most of them are qualitative rules and procedures, and lack quantitative and authoritative evaluation methods. In addition, these two metrics do not take into account the model standardization, portability, scalability, and other characteristics that have an important impact on model use and reuse. In fact, after the model is developed, it will be continuously improved and optimized in the process of use. The maturity of a model focuses on the performance of the model in its use and management process. A model with high maturity will have a high degree of credibility or fidelity, but a model with high credibility or fidelity does not necessarily have a high degree of maturity. Of course, fidelity and credibility will have some impact on maturity to some extent. In summary, the maturity will make up for the limitations of fidelity and credibility on model evaluation.

2.3. *Evaluation of model maturity*

Regarding the evaluation of maturity, there are some related works in different fields, such as information maturity evaluation,[21] technology maturity evaluation,[22] innovation capability and industry maturity evaluation,[23] and software development capability maturity evaluation.[24] All of these can provide references for model maturity evaluation.

Due to the diversity and heterogeneity of models, different application requirements, and different understandings of the model by different users, the evaluation of model maturity is very challenging. At present, the evaluation methods of various maturities are usually based on the experience of domain experts for qualitative evaluation, which are subjective. It is necessary to find an objective evaluation method, which transforms the relevant factors of model maturity into quantifiable indexes and evaluates the model maturity with rigorous process and standardized operations. The method will take advantages of both qualitative and quantitative methods. The reliable evaluation of model maturity will help to improve and optimize the quality of a model so as to meet the application demands perfectly.

3. Five Levels of Model Maturity

Referring to the maturity level classification method in other fields, the model maturity can be divided into five levels, as shown in Fig. 3. The five levels are described as follows:

Level 0: Initial level. The modeling process is unnormalized. There are no or few model documents. The model is not verified and validated. There are many errors that result in failures of simulation with the model. There are many uncertainties in the use of the model. There are no management tools and the model is not managed.

Level 1: Verified level. Low level of normalization of modeling process. Model documents are incomplete and not standard. The model has been primarily verified and validated by the internal personnel of the model developer. There are few errors that result in failures of simulation with the model, but still many problems that lead to malfunctioning of the simulation. There are few uncertainties in the use of the model. There are few management tools and the model is not well managed.

Level 2: Reusable level. The modeling process is well organized. Model documents are complete and standardized. The model has been professionally verified, validated and accredited and has an acceptable credibility. There is no error or problem that lead to failures or malfunctioning. The model has friendly interfaces. The model can be reconfigured without degrading its performance. The model is managed with a model library.

Level 3: Collaboration level. The modeling process has a high degree of standardization. The model has been verified, validated and accredited by professional agencies and has a high credibility. The model has friendly interfaces that meet the interoperability standards of specific fields. The model has certain adaptability to heterogeneous environments. There are few trivial problems during the use of the model. The model can be easily reconfigured to meet different requirements without degrading its performance. The model is well managed with an engineering level model library.

Level 4: Optimal level. The modeling process has a very high degree of standardization. The model has been completely verified, validated and accredited by professional third-party agencies and has a high credibility and fidelity. The interfaces of the model are very friendly and are adaptable to different interoperability standards. The model has strong adaptability to heterogeneous environments. There are no problems during the use of the model. The model can be easily reconfigured and

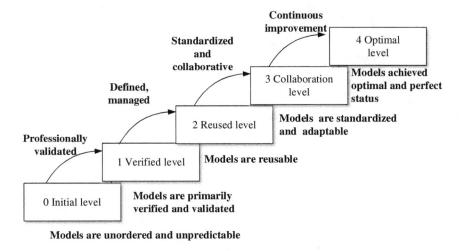

Fig. 3. The five levels of model maturity.

reconstructed to meet different requirements without degrading its performance. The model is professionally managed with a commercial level model library and supporting tools.

4. Construction of the Model Maturity Index System

4.1. *Principles*

In addition to the common principles of evaluation index systems, characteristics of simulation systems should be considered in the construction of the index system of model maturity for simulation. Domain-independent indexes will be selected as many as possible, which can objectively evaluate the performance of models in cross-domain reuse and scalability. More importantly, indexes that change with time, model use, and management will play key roles in the index system so as to highlight the evolution process of the models. In summary, the construction of the index system for model maturity evaluation should follow the principles:

(a) The basic principle. It includes the completeness, computability, nonredundancy and objectivity, etc.
(b) Use and time relative principle. To select indexes that change with use and time to reflect the status in the process of a model being used and managed.
(c) Domain-independent principle. To select domain-independent indexes as far as possible, which can guarantee the generality and scalability of the index system.

4.2. *A framework of index system for model maturity evaluation*

Influence factors of model maturity are involved in the three phases of the model life cycle, i.e., model construction, model use and model management. Hence, the index

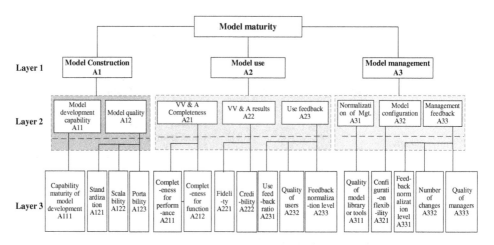

Fig. 4.   The framework of index system for model maturity.

system will be established in multiple layers, as shown in Fig. 4. The first layer is the phases of the model lifecycle, the middle layer gives factors that have impacts on the model maturity in the corresponding phases, and the bottom layer gives the indexes corresponding to each factor. In some cases, there may have multiple middle layers.

(1) Model construction: As mentioned above, there are different types of models relative to simulation, e.g., requirement models, conceptual models, mathematical models and simulation models. Various indexes that may influence the use or reuse of these models can be defined, such as the level of standardization, portability, scalability, etc. Another important factor that has an important impact on the quality of a model is the capability of modeling organizations (model developers), which is seldom considered in current research. The developer is generally an organization for building a complex model. They need to be well organized and follow normalized processes to guarantee the correctness and quality of models. The capability maturity model integration (CMMI) originated in software engineering is used for evaluating the capability of a software development organization. However, in the field of M&S, there is no such standardized and systematic evaluation methodology developed for modeling processes.[25] Because the development of many models, especially simulation models, has certain similarities with the software development process, the CMMI can be used as a reference. Of course, the model development process is more complicated than ordinary software development, so it is necessary to develop capability maturity for M&S in the future. Four indexes, capability maturity of model development, standardization, portability, scalability are listed in Fig. 4 as examples.

(2) Model use: As mentioned above, the model use phase includes model implementation, execution, verification, validation and accreditation (VV&A), interoperation, etc. Participants in this phase are people or organizations (model users) that

use the model to perform various simulation activities. The model users conduct these activities and send problems they met to the model management phase, in the meantime, receive modification and update information from the management phase (see Fig. 1). Many factors involved in these activities influence the degree of model maturity. For example, VV&A is indispensable to guarantee the correctness of a model. Even if it is needed in almost every phase of the model lifecycle, many VV&A activities can only be conducted when the model runs. Hence, we choose VV&A related factors to be included in the model use phase. Theoretically, every part and every function point should be verified and validated with a normalized process, but in reality there are always some parts or functions are missing, and the VV&A is not will organized. This is especially true for complex systems. So, the completeness of VV&A can be taken as a factor, and the completeness of VV&A for performance, completeness of VV&A for functions and the normalization level of the VV&A progress, can be chosen as the indexes of the factor. The VV&A results tell if the model is correct or meet the requirements, which can be presented in different forms. Some quantifiable measures, such as fidelity, credibility, are preferred to be indexes of the VV&A results. The use feedback includes two kinds of activities, one is to receive feedback information about model modifications and updates from the model management phase and apply the information to improve or optimize the use of the model, the other is to send the information of errors and problems collected in the use process back to the management phase. The quality of model users and whether the feedback information from management phase is well documented or not will also have impact on the effect of the improvement. As a result, the use feedback ratio, quality of users, and the feedback normalization level can be taken as indexes.

(3) Model management: This phase manages and maintains the models constructed by different developers. Participants include model managers, maintainers, and developers may also participate in the model management in some cases. They are called model managers here. Model management include the activities such as model storage, model modification, model reconfiguration, model modification, model optimization, model integration, etc. Many factors have impact on the effect of model management. Some examples are (1) if the models are managed in a normalized way, (2) if the model parameters are easy reconfigured to meet different requirements, and (3) if feedback information from model users is sufficiently applied to modify or optimized the models. Indexes relative to each factor can be defined according to characteristics of the factor. For the normalization of management, there are many aspects related to model management, e.g., model representation and model storage, model search, and documentation. A high-quality model library is the guarantee of model management. We use the quality of the model library as the index to represent the level of management normalization. The configuration flexibility can be taken as the index for model reconfiguration, which indicates how easy the model parameters can be reconfigured. Similar to the use feedback, the management feedback has two kinds of activities, i.e., receive the

feedback information from model users and send modified and updated information back to model users. Some indexes can be chosen to reflect the level of handling the feedback, such as feedback normalization level, the number of changes to the model guided by the feedback, and the quality of the model managers.

What needs to be pointed out is that the framework of index system is open. The factors and indexes given in Fig. 4 are just examples, which can be adjusted according to characteristics of the models in specific application domains.

4.3. *Further explanation of model maturity indexes*

To get a quantitative evaluation of the maturity of a model, each index in Fig. 4 need to be set a value with different methods.

(1) Model development capability: There is one index for this factor, i.e., the capability maturity of model development. As mentioned above, there is no such an index and method to evaluate the capability of a model developer. Referring to the CMMI for software, the capability maturity can be divided into five levels. It can be evaluated by CMMI evaluation agency if the model is software intensive. In other cases, it can be roughly evaluated by domain experts based on their expertise. The domain expert here refers to the people who has specialized knowledge on model development, evaluation or management.

(2) Model quality: Three indexes are listed, they are standardization, scalability and portability. All of them are qualitative indexes, which can be evaluated and scored by domain experts.

(3) VV&A completeness: It contains two parts at least, i.e., the VV&A completeness of performance and the VV&A completeness of function of the model. Both the two indexes can be scored by domain experts based on the VV&A documentation.

(4) The VV&A result: Credibility and fidelity are chosen to be the indexes. Some methods can give quantitative values for the two indexes. Due to different evaluation methods may give different values for the same model, we need to choose an appropriate one with respect the characteristics of the model. Expertise of domain experts are needed to make such a choice.

(5) Use feedback: The use feedback ratio reflects the proportion of feedback problems from model managers that have been handled successfully. It can be calculated by dividing the number of handled feedback problems by the total number of feedback problems in a given time period. Feedback normalization level can be scored by domain experts based on the documentation provided by model managers. The quality of users that indicate whether the professional ability of the users reaches the standard, which can be evaluated and scored by the human resource department.

(6) Normalization of management: A professional model library will provide strong support to model management. Based on the information including the model library's developer, popularity, documentation normalization level, etc., the

quality of the library can be evaluated and scored by domain experts or a third party agency.

(7) Model configuration: The parameter configuration can change the performance of a model and enable the model to meet changed requirements, which will also affect the maturity of the model. The more convenient and flexible the parameter configuration is, the easier the model can be reused, and therefore the more mature the model becomes. Parameter configuration flexibility can be evaluated by model users and/or managers.

(8) Management feedback: The feedback information that comes from the model users can guide managers to modify and optimize the model. The feedback normalization level can be scored by domain experts based on the feedback documents provided by model users. The quality of managers can be evaluated and scored by the human resource department. The number of changes to the model is a quantitative index. With the continuous improvement of the model, the number of changes will gradually decrease.

5. A HEQQ Analysis for Model Maturity

5.1. *Main idea of HEQQ*

According to the framework of the index system in Fig. 4, a HEQQ analysis method for model maturity is proposed in this paper.

For a given model, only the indexes in the lowest layer can be assigned values. According to common evaluation methods, the values of these indexes can be scored by domain experts or evaluated based on historical data. These index values are integrated (such as weighted sum) to define the maturity of the model. A lot of research has focused on how to determine the weights more reasonably. However, these methods do not take into account the factor in the higher layer to which each index belongs and the life cycle phase to which the corresponding factor belongs. In fact, different phases have different effects on model maturity, and different factors have different importance in the same phase. Therefore, treating all indexes as equal cannot accurately reflect the actual impact of each index on model maturity.

The basic idea of the HEQQ is to hierarchically determine the weight of each index. First, "quantify" the factors in the first layer, and phases in the second layer by defining an "abstract index" to each factor and phase (the abstract index is a kind of virtual index whose value is not directly from real data), then use different methods for each layer to determine the weight of each abstract index, and the abstract index values in each layer are obtained from the lower layer, the index values in the bottom layer are obtained from real data, e.g., scores of domain experts or calculated based on historical data.

Usually, the weights of abstract indexes in the first layer can be set using expert experience. Because for a specific type of model, there is a certain consensus among domain experts about the impact of each phase of the model maturity. The weights of the middle layer can be determined by a combination of qualitative and quantitative methods, such as analytic hierarchy process (AHP[26]) or fuzzy analytic hierarchy process (FAHP[27]). The weights of the bottom layer need to be determined by different quantitative methods (such as entropy weight method, neural network, etc.) according to the data.

This hierarchical evaluation method considers the influences of phases and factors in different layers and can also reduce the impact of the uncertainty of computation of the indexes in the bottom layer on the overall maturity evaluation results due to incomplete or inaccurate data. The HEQQ method is especially suitable for the evaluation of model maturity with a complex index system and multiple layers.

5.2. *Mathematical description of HEQQ*

It is assumed that the final maturity is calculated by the comprehensive evaluation function $F(\bullet)$. The index system has m layers (m is set to 3 in this paper). Except that the lowest layer index values are real data, other layers only have abstract indexes. The upper layer abstract index is the parent index, and the lower-layer index is the child one. If the function $F(\bullet)$ is linearly weighted, the formula for maturity is given as follows:

Layer 1:

$$F(\bullet) = \sum_{i=1}^{n} w_i E_i, \tag{1}$$

where $n(n \geq 1)$ is the number of life cycle phases of the first layer, w_i is the weight of the ith abstract index corresponding to the ith phase at this layer, and E_i is the value of the ith abstract index;

Layer 2:

$$E_i = \sum_{j=1}^{h_i} w_{ij} \, E_{ij}, \tag{2}$$

where h_i is the number of factors in the second layer under the ith phase, w_{ij} is the weight of the jth factor in this layer, and E_{ij} is the jth abstract index value;

Layer m:

$$E_{\underbrace{ij\ldots u}_{m-1}} = \sum_{v=1}^{\overbrace{y_{ij\ldots u}}^{m-1}} w_{\underbrace{ij\ldots uv}_{m}} E_{\underbrace{ij\ldots uv}_{m}}, \tag{3}$$

where $y_{\underbrace{ij\ldots u}_{m-1}}$ is the number of abstract indexes $E_{\underbrace{ij\ldots u}_{m-1}}$ in the mth layer under the corresponding factors in the upper layer, $w_{\underbrace{ij\ldots uv}_{m}}$ is the weight of the vth

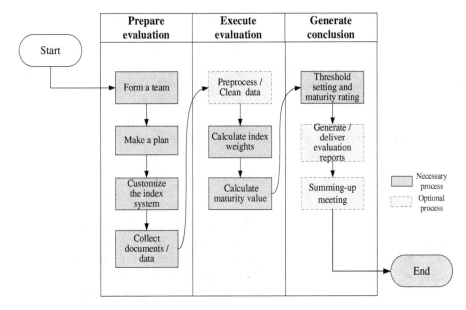

Fig. 5.   A general process of model maturity evaluation.

abstract index of $E_{ij\ldots u}$ at this layer, and $E_{ij\ldots uv}$ is the vth abstract index
$\underbrace{\phantom{E_{ij\ldots u}}}_{m-1}$ $\underbrace{\phantom{E_{ij\ldots uv}}}_{m}$

value of $E_{ij\ldots u}$. (The abstract index will be the real index for the bottom layer).
$\underbrace{\phantom{E_{ij\ldots u}}}_{m-1}$

The final model maturity value is the result of function $F(\bullet)$. In the equations
above, the values of indexes are normalized, and the final maturity value ranges
from $[0, 1]$.

5.3. *The evaluation process of model maturity based on HEQQ*

Referring to the general process of multi-index comprehensive evaluation, we give
a general process of model maturity evaluation, as shown in Fig. 5. The evaluation
process is described as follows:

(1) Form a team. The maturity can be evaluated by either the model user or the
model manager or a third-party organization. A team usually consists of evaluation
engineers in the field of M&S and industry experts in the field to which the model
belongs.

(2) Make a plan. To make a detailed plan and millstones for evaluation based
on the complexity and size of the model being evaluated, capability and constraints
of the evaluation team.

(3) Customize the index system. Refer to the framework of the model maturity evaluation index system shown in Fig. 4, select or add new factors or indexes
according to the properties of the model and the feasibility of the evaluation work.

(4) Collect documents/data related to indexes in the bottom layer. According to the definition of each index, collect all documents/data to ensure that every index has a value. The data may need preprocessing or cleaning based on the quality.

(5) Determine the index weights. The weight value of each layer can be determined by a combination of qualitative and quantitative methods. The weight values of the upper layer can rely more on the experiences of experts, and the weight value of the lower layer will depend more on computation based on data. The methods to determine the index weight can be divided into three categories, subjective weighting methods, objective weighting methods, and combination weighting methods.

(6) Calculate the model maturity. The final maturity of the model can be obtained according to Eqs. (1)–(3). The function $F(\bullet)$ can have other forms that are different from Eq. (1).

(7) Threshold setting and maturity rating. Based on the maturity value obtained, the maturity can be divided into 5 levels that is presented in Sec. 3 by defining thresholds. This paper suggests that the thresholds are $(0, 0.15], (0.15, 0.3],$ $(0.3, 0.5], (0.5, 0.75], (0.75, 1)$, which correspond to the 0–4 level of model maturity as shown in Fig. 3. The thresholds can be adjusted according to the characteristics of models.

After the evaluation, a technical report can be provided as per the request and the experiences about the evaluation can be summarized.

5.4. *Analysis for weight determining methods*

As mentioned above, there are different methods to determine the weights. These methods will lead to different evaluation results. Generally, the evaluation methods include subjective evaluation methods, objective evaluation methods, and integrated evaluation method. We summarize the characteristics of the three kinds of methods from the aspects including the required sample size, the objectivity, how

Table 1.   Comparison of weight determination methods.

	Sample size	Objectivity	Number indexes	Calculation complexity	Information duplication	Uniqueness of results
Fuzzy comprehensive evaluation (FCE)[28]	★	★	★	★★★	★	★★★
AHP[26]	★	★★	★★	★★★	★★	★
Technique for order preference by similarity to an ideal solution (TOPSIS)[29]	★	★★★	★★★	★	★	★★
Principal component analysis (PCA)[30]	★★★	★★	★★★★	★★	★★★	★
Entropy weight method (EW)[31]	★★★	★★★★	★★★★	★	★★★	★★★
Grey Relation analysis (GRA)[32]	★	★★★★	★★★	★	★	★★★

many indexes can be dealt with, the calculation complexity, the information dupli-cation, and the uniqueness of results. One to four stars correspond to four grades are used to compare some of the methods, as shown in Table 1, the more stars assigned, the higher the corresponding attribute value is, but that does not mean the better the corresponding method is, it depends on the attribute description.

On the basis of above comparison, we use AHP to determine the weights for the second layer abstract indexes, and use entropy weight method to determine the weights for the third layer indexes. While the first layer abstract indexes will be given be experts.

5.5. *Determining index weights based on entropy weight method*

According to the characteristics of entropy in information theory, the entropy value can be used to judge the dispersion degree of an index. The smaller the entropy value of an index, the higher the degree of its dispersion, and therefore the greater its influence (weight) on the evaluation result. The general formula for calculating entropy is as follows[31]:

$$H = \frac{-\sum_{i=1}^{n} f_i \ln(f_i)}{\ln n}. \tag{4}$$

Among them,

$$fi = \frac{X_i}{\sum_{i=1}^{n} X_i}, \tag{5}$$

where n is the total sample number of a model, and X_i is the index value at the ith sampling point. Based on the classic entropy expression, we give the formula for calculating the weights as follows:

$$w_i = \frac{(1 - \alpha H_i)}{\sum_{i=1}^{m} (1 - \alpha H_i)}, \tag{6}$$

where H_i is the entropy of the ith index, m is the total number of indexes, and α is the adjustment coefficient of the entropy weight. In order to prevent the large divergence of index values given by different qualitative or quantitative methods, α is set to adjust the excessive difference in entropy weight of each index.

The entropy weight calculation process is as follows:

(1) Clean index extremums. The purpose is to reduce the influence of extremums on the entropy of the index. The usual way is to eliminate the maximum or minimum values in each index, and replace them with reasonable upper and lower bound values. The principle is to exclude extreme value samples that account for less than 1–2% of the total number of samples.

(2) Normalize the index. Most often used methods are the critical value method (CVM) and the Z-score (ZS) method. Either way, the index needs to be finally converted into a positive interval.

(3) Calculate the entropy values and weight values. To calculate the entropy and weight values of the indexes according to formulas (4)–(6).

(4) Calculate the abstract index. The abstract index value of the factor in the upper layer to which the indexes belong cab be calculated based on the principle of addition and multiplication. Commonly used is additive synthesis, i.e.,

$$S_i = \sum_{i=1}^{m} w_i X_i \qquad (7)$$

where X_i is the index value and w_i is the weight of the index i.

By using the entropy weight method repeatedly, the abstract index value of each factor in the upper layer can be calculated.

6. Case Study

6.1. *Data acquisition*

The original data used for experiments are obtained from the documents and information provided by a simulation company in China, and give the values of 11 indexes out of the 16 ones in Fig. 4 for 20 models. Two of them are calculated quantitatively and the 9 others are scored by domain experts or third-party agencies. The original samples include data about the evolution of the same model at different time points, as well as data of different models at different time points. Every model is marked with labels showing the maturity status at different time points. The labels are evaluated by domain experts based on the historical performance the model, which can be regarded as a standard value for the model maturity. Sampling data in 30 months of 50 models are used in the experiments.

6.2. *Comparative experiments*

To verify the feasibility of the proposed hierarchical method HEQQ, experiments will be conducted to compare the HEQQ with the traditional method, i.e., the one that treat all indexes in the last layer equally and obtained the weights with entropy weight method at one time without considering the influences of factors and phases, we call it the traditional entropy weight method (TEWM).

According to the HEQQ method, data are needed to be normalized and adjustment coefficients (AC) is needed to be set before calculating the weights with the entropy weight method. The ZS method and CVM are two typical normalization methods (NM). Different normalization method and adjustment coefficient will lead to different weight for the same index. The obtained weights of some indexes that belong to two factors of a model are listed in Table 2, where W(ZS, 1) represents the weight by using z-score normalization method and adjustment coefficient is set to 1 and so on.

It can be seen from Table 2 that the weights of the index A231 (use feedback ratio) and the inverse of the index A332 (numbers of feedback) are larger than others. This is more in line with the actual situation and reflects the impact of the two indexes on the model maturity. In the later experiments, the CVM will be used for normalization of indexes and the adjustment coefficient a is set to 1.

Table 2. Weight values of index under different NM and adjustment coefficients.

W (NM, AC)	A231	A232	A233	A331	A332	A333
W (ZS, 1)	0.5365	0.1994	0.2641	0.2797	0.4641	0.2562
W (ZS, 0.9)	0.4095	0.2831	0.3074	0.3122	0.3848	0.3030
W (CVM, 1)	0.6227	0.2637	0.1136	0.2220	0.5699	0.2081
W (CVM, 0.9)	0.4891	0.2958	0.2151	0.2812	0.4441	0.2747

Now, let us compare the performance of TEWM and the HEQQ method proposed in this paper. The weights of the indexes/abstract indexes can be obtained according to the HEQQ method as follows:

The third-layer index weights are calculated first based on the original data with the entropy weight method. The values in the row of W (CVM, 1) in Table 2 are some examples.

The weights of abstract indexes in the second layer are determined using the AHP method. The pairwise comparison matrix of the three factors in each of model use and model management phases is as follows:

$$A2 = [1 \ 1/2 \ 1/3; \ 2 \ 1 \ 1/2; \ 3 \ 2 \ 1],$$

$$A3 = [1 \ 3 \ 1/2; \ 1/3 \ 1 \ 1/2; \ 2 \ 5 \ 1].$$

The weights of the abstract indexes of the three factors under the use phase can be obtained with AHP, they are:

$$w_{21} = 0.1634, \quad w_{22} = 0.2970, \quad w_{23} = 0.5396.$$

The weights of the abstract indexes of the three factors under management phase are

$$w_{31} = 0.2973, \quad w_{32} = 0.1521, \quad w_{33} = 0.5506.$$

For the first layer, the weights of the abstract indexes of the three phases (model construction, model use and model management) are given based on knowledge of experts from the data provider, i.e., $w_1 = 0.25$, $w_2 = 0.4$, $w_3 = 0.35$. The model use phase has the biggest impact on model maturity, followed by the model management phase, and the model construction phase is less important compared with the other two.

Figure 6 shows that the trends of the maturity curve obtained by the two methods are basically the same. But the fluctuations of the curve (the blue line) obtained by HEQQ are smaller than the one obtained by the TEWM, which is more consistent with the actual situation of the sample data.

Another experiment is to compare the maturities of one model separately obtained by TEWM and HEQQ at different time points within 30 months. There are 27 sets of sample data available.

Using the HEQQ method, the maturity value of the model M1 at different periods is calculated, as shown in Fig. 7. The blue curve represents the maturity value

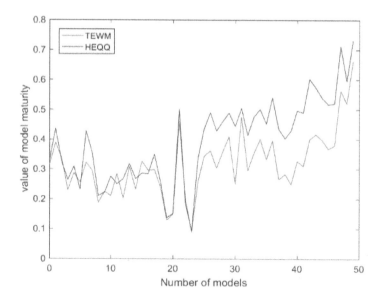

Fig. 6.   Maturity curves of different models using two methods.

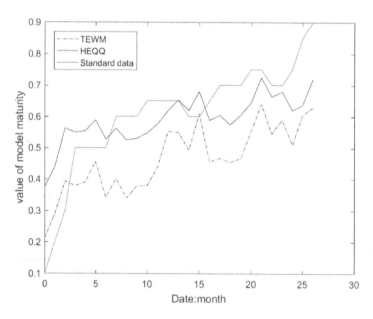

Fig. 7.   Comparison of maturity value curve of one model using different methods.

calculated by the HEQQ, the black curve represents the maturity value calculated by TEWM, and the red curve represents the standard value.

Figure 7 shows that the results obtained by both the HEQQ and TEWM have the same trend, but the blue curve is closer to the red one, which means that the

HEQQ proposed in this paper can get a better evaluation result of model maturity than the TEWM.

7. Conclusions and Future Work

Aiming at the evaluation of the performance of a model in its use and management phase of the lifecycle, this paper proposes the concept of model maturity, builds an index system for model maturity evaluation, and introduces a 5-level model of model maturity. On these bases, a HEQQ analysis for model maturity is given. The introduction of model maturity is an important complement to the model evaluation system, and especially provides a guidance for model reuse and optimization. Moreover, the index system of model maturity provides a reference for what data should be recorded in the model management process in order to improve the level of model management and optimize the performance of the model.

Nevertheless, this paper is only a preliminary study on the model maturity. There is a lot of work to do in the future. For example (1) This paper only provides the framework of the index system. For models in specific fields, the index system need to be customized according to the characteristics and needs of the fields; (2) In the current index system, only the number of feedback problems is considered and the contents of feedback are not considered. In fact, the contents of problems have more important impact on model modification and optimization; (3) The data used in the experiments is still not enough, and qualitative methods such as expert scoring still account for a large proportion in the process of determining the values of indexes and weights; (4) Only the entropy method, AHP and expert scoring are used in the evaluate method. Many other theories and techniques, e.g., neural networks, rough sets, fuzzy mathematics or new developed technology, can be used to improve the evaluation.

Acknowledgments

The research is supported by the National Key R&D Program of China under Grant No. 2018YFB1701600.

And thanks Beijing Huaru Technology Company for the original information about the data and helpful discussions with Mr. Xiong Tan on model indexes.

References

1. Kim H., McGinnis L. F., Chen Z., On fidelity and model selection for discrete event simulation, *Int. J. Simulation: Trans. Soc. Model. Simul. Int. (S0037-5497)* **1**:97–109, 2012.
2. Ping J. *et al.*, A space mapping method based on Gaussian process model for variable fidelity metamodeling, *Int. J. Simul. Model. Practice Theory* **81**:64–84, 2018.
3. Peng L. *et al.*, High fidelity modeling method of high performance electromechanical actuator, *J. Northwestern Polytech. Univ.* **1**:7–12, 2018.
4. Defense Modeling and Simulation Office, Verification, Validation and Accreditation Recommended Practice Guide, *Department of Defense*, Washington, USA, 2000.

5. Ahn J., De Weck O. L., Steele M., Credibility assessment of models and simulations based on NASA's models and simulation standard using the delphi method, *Int. J. Syst. Eng.* **2**:237–248, 2014.
6. Rider W. J., Witkowski W. R., Vincent A. M., Uncertainty quantification's role in modeling and simulation planning, and credibility assessment through the predictive capability maturity model, in *Handbook of Uncertainty Quantification*, Springer, Singapore, 2015, pp. 1–23.
7. Zeng Q. H., Yu A. B., Lu G. Q., Multiscale modeling and simulation of polymer nanocomposites, *Int. J. Progress in Polymer Sci.* **2**:191–269, 2008.
8. Spruit M., Pietzka K., MD3M: The master data management maturity model, *Int. J. Computers in Human Behavior* **51**PB(OCT.):1068–1076, 2015.
9. Aggestam L., Towards a maturity model for learning organizations-the role of knowledge management, *International Workshop on Database & Expert Systems Applications. IEEE Xplore*, Krakow, Poland, pp. 1–5, 2006.
10. Pereira R. and Silva M. M. D., A maturity model for implementing ITIL V3 in practice, *Int. Conf. Enterprise Distributed Object Computing Conference Workshops (EDOCW)*, 2011 15th IEEE International IEEE, Helsinki, Finland, pp. 259–268, 2011.
11. Taner A., Tanyel C., A technology readiness levels (TRLs) calculator software for systems engineering and technology management tool, *Int. J. Advances in Engineering Software* **5**:769–778, 2010.
12. Alexandra K. *et al.*, A new model to ascertain product maturity in product development processes, *Int. J. Procedia Cirp.* **50**:173–178, 2016.
13. Bikramjit B., Sourabh G., Assessment of technology and manufacturing readiness levels, in *Biomaterials for Musculoskeletal Regeneration*, Springer, Singapore, 2017, pp. 235–246.
14. Kujawski E., Analysis and critique of the system readiness level, *Int. J. IEEE Trans. Syst. Man Cybernetics Syst.* **43.4**:979–987, 2013.
15. Chrissis M. B., Konrad M., Shrum S., CMMI for Development: Guidelines for Process Integration and Product Improvement, in *Addison-Wesley Professional*, SEI Series in Software Engineering, 2011, p. 688.
16. Wang H., Chen K., Xu D., A maturity model for blockchain adoption, *Int. J. Financial Innovation* **12**:1–5, 2016.
17. Comuzzi M., Patel A., How organisations leverage: Big Data: A maturity model, *Int. J. Industrial Management Data Syst.* **8**:1468–1492, 2016.
18. Weber C. *et al.*, M2DDM-A maturity model for data-driven manufacturing, *Int. J. Procedia Cirp*, **63**:173–178, 2017.
19. Rapaccini M. *et al.*, Service development in product-service systems: A maturity model, *The Service industries J.* **33**:300–319, 2013.
20. Carvalho J. V. *et al.*, A Maturity model for hospital information systems, *J. Business Research* **94**:388–399, 2017.
21. Xiao-Yan G. *et al.*, An information security maturity evaluation mode, *Int. Conf. Advances in Engineering*, Bangkok, Thailand, pp. 335–339, 2011.
22. Kendoul F., Towards a unified framework for UAS Autonomy and Technology Readiness Assessment (ATRA), in *Autonomous Control Systems and Vehicles*, Springer, Japan, 2013, pp. 55–71.
23. Corsi P., Neau E., *Innovation Capability Maturity Model (Corsi/Innovation Capability Maturity Model)‖ Evaluating the Ability to Innovate*, John Wiley & Sons, 2015.

24. Juan P. C., Xavier F., Carme Q., Supporting CMMI Level 2 SAM PA with non-technical features catalogues, *Int. J. Software Process Improvement Practice* **2**:171–182, 2010.
25. Richard F. *et al.*, *Research Challenges in Modeling & Simulation for Engineering Complex Systems*, Springer, 2017.
26. Izadpanah S., Vahdat-Nejad H., Saadatfar H., A Framework for ranking ubiquitous computing services by AHP analysis, *Int. J. Model. Simul. Scientific Comput.* **9**(4):1850023.1–1850023.25, 2017.
27. Marzieh M., Majid H., Ali S., Application of Dempster–Shafer theory and fuzzy analytic hierarchy process for evaluating the effects of geological formation units on groundwater quality, *Int. J. Environmental Science and Pollution Research*, **4**:1–21, 2019.
28. Xiaoxiao W. *et al.*, Fuzzy comprehensive evaluation of the disaster reduction ability of an ethnic minority accumulation area on an analytic hierarchy process, *Int. J. Environmental and Ecological Statistics* **5**:1–12, 2019.
29. Monalisa P., Alok K. J., TOPSIS in Multi-Criteria Decision Making: A Survey, *2018 2nd Int. Conf. Data Science Business Analytics (ICDSBA)*, IEEE Computer Society, pp. 51–54, 2018.
30. Xiaogang D. *et al.*, Nonlinear process fault diagnosis based on serial principal component analysis, *IEEE Trans. Neural Networks Learn. Syst.* **3**:560–572, 2018.
31. Zhi-Hong Z., Yi Y., Jing-Nan S., Entropy method for determination of weight of evaluating indicators in fuzzy synthetic evaluation for water quality assessment, *J. Environmental Sci.* **5**:1020–1023, 2006.
32. Yang P., Xu G., Chen H., Multi-attribute ranking method for identifying key nodes in complex networks based on GRA, *Int. J. Mod. Phys. B* **32**:647–658, 2018.

Chapter 10

FPGA-based edge computing: Task modeling for cloud-edge collaboration

Chuan Xiao* and Chun Zhao[†]

School of Computer
Beijing Information Science and Technology University
Beijing 100101, China
*xiaochuan@bistu.edu.cn
†zhaochun@bistu.edu.cn

Abstract

With the development of the Internet of Things and devices continuing to scale, using cloud computing resources to process data in real-time is challenging. Edge computing technologies can improve real-time performance in processing data. By introducing the FPGA into the computing node and using the dynamic reconfigurability of the FPGA, the FPGA-based edge node can increase the edge node capability. In this paper, a task-based collaborative method for an FPGA-based edge computing system is proposed in order to meet the collaboration among FPGA-based edge nodes, edge nodes, and the cloud. The modeling of the task includes two parts, task information and task-dependent file. Task information is used to describe the running information and dependency information required for the task execution. Task-dependent file contains the configuration bit-stream of FPGA in running of the task. By analyzing the task behavior, this paper builds four basic behaviors, analyzes the critical attributes of each behavior, and summarizes the task model suitable for FPGA-based edge nodes. Tasks with specific functions can be created by modifying different attributes of model nodes. Finally, the availability of the model and the task-based collaborative method are verified by simulation experiments. The experimental results that the task model proposed in this paper can meet cloud-edge collaboration in the FPGA-based edge computing environment.

1. Introduce

With the continuous progress of hardware and software, more and more devices are connected to the Internet of Things (IoT).[1] The IoT receives widespread attention in applications such as smart grids,[2] intelligent homes,[3] buildings,[4] and smart cities.[5] As the IoT is the key technology to meet the interconnection of devices and the cloud, the growth of IoT devices also makes massive data to be processed in the cloud.[6] Using cloud computing resources can process massive device data, which rapidly increases the cloud's energy consumption cost and makes the cloud face

---

[†]Corresponding author.

the problem of network bandwidth.[7] Addressing the real-time requirements of the device by using cloud computing is a challenge.[8,9] Especially for specific industrial environments, network delays can cause serious security risks, and cloud computing is challenging to meet the real-time requirements.[10] In addition, applications such as intelligent transportation, intelligent medical care, and augmented reality require a lot of computing while requiring stricter real-time computing.[11] In order to improve the real-time performance of data processing, the device data at the edge should be processed at the source as far as possible.[12]

Edge computing is a new pattern of computing model that transfers some computing power from the cloud to the edge, which can process data from the data source faster.[13] Because of proximity to the data source, classification, clustering, and correlation analysis of data at the edge can significantly reduce transmission delay and improve reliability.[14] Linthicum builds applications on edge, which can collect and process most of the data, to avoid the delay caused by sending the data to the cloud.[15] Using FPGA to process streaming data can improve the real-time performance of data processing.[16] FPGA computing has the characteristics of parallelism and low latency. At present, many algorithms are trying to hardware-based implement and run on FPGA.[17,18] Using the low latency characteristics of hardware algorithms can significantly improve the computing power at the edge.[19]

Data processing using edge computing is similar to the distributed computing system, which needs to reasonably allocate tasks to suitable computing nodes to improve data processing efficiency.[20] The process of task allocation can be regarded as the process of task scheduling. The performance of the scheduling algorithm determines the performance of the system and the quality of service.[21] In order to schedule tasks effectively, various constraints and load balance between nodes need to be considered.[22,23] To meet task collaboration, Deng et al. create constraints such as sub-tasks, task arrival time, task execution time, deadline, and waiting time.[24] Tran et al. create limitations on response time, link delay, memory requirements, task execution deadline, deployment time, and task execution time.[25] Li et al. also focus on the size of the CPU used and storage space used during tasks processing.[26] Ma et al. focus on the node utilization rate, the qualified rate of the node output, and the failure rate of the node.[27] The constraints of Fan et al. increate the estimated execution time of the task.[28] Sahni et al. believe that there is a priority in task execution. Focus is established in the constraints.[29] The constraints set by Vijayalakshmi et al. are first minimum completion time of task and second minimum completion time.[30]

FPGA computing has the characteristics of parallelism and low latency. FPGA-based edge nodes can efficiently process data with high concurrency and high bandwidth properties, such as video processing, machine learning, etc. Compared with other patterns in edge computing, FPGA-based edge nodes have more computing resources provided by FPGAs. As computing resources such as FPGAs need to be reconfiguration in advance, the delivery of computing tasks to FPGA-based edge nodes is different from conventional methods. This paper uses communication-oriented tasks as the communication unit between FPGA-based edge nodes and the cloud to conveniently use the computing resources provided by FPGA-based edge nodes. The modeling of the task includes two parts, task information and task-dependent file. By analyzing the task behavior, this paper summarizes four basic behaviors, analyzes the critical attributes of each behavior, and builds the task model suitable for FPGA-based edge nodes. Tasks with specific functions can be created by modifying different attributes of model nodes. Finally, the availability of the model and the task-based collaborative method are verified by simulation experiments. The experimental results verify the usability of the model and prove the usability of the task-based collaborative method.

The structure of this paper is as follows. In Sec. 1, the task of the FPGA-based edge node is decomposed according to reusability, and the task collaboration method is designed. Section 2 analyzes and summarizes the behavior of the task. Section 3 explores the critical attributes of each behavior and creates the corresponding behavior model. Section 4 uses the behavior model to construct the task model. Section 5 verifies the usability of the task model and the task-based collaboration method through experiments, and the conclusion introduces this paper's contribution.

2. Task-Based Edge Node Collaboration Method

A cloud-edge collaboration framework based on FPGA in cloud manufacturing is introduced.[31] The framework consists of three parts: cloud layer, edge layer, device layer. The edge layer is composed of gateways and FPGA-based edge nodes. FPGA-based edge nodes can be connected to form a local edge computing network, and multiple local edge computing networks can be connected through a gateway. The edge nodes in this framework are composed of an FPGA module and embedded system module based on Linux. Because FPGA has reconfigurable characteristics, using this characteristic can meet the hardware of software algorithm on FPGA. The hardware algorithm has the features of natural parallelism and low latency. The FPGA module can significantly improve the computing power of edge nodes. The embedded system module based on Linux provides the running environment of a general program to provide communication service for edge nodes. The communication service program runs on the embedded system module, which exchanges information with the cloud and other nodes. At the same time, the embedded system module dynamically configures the FPGA module according to the received tasks. In addition, the embedded system module can also provide some computing power. The FPGA-based edge node's two computing resources are located in the FPGA and embedded system modules. FPGA module is reconfigurable, which can change the running algorithm according to the needs of users.

In order to make users get or modify the running state of the node, the communication-oriented task is used as the communication unit of the edge node. The communication-oriented task consists of two parts: including task information and task-dependent file. Task information is a structural text in XML used to describe the operation information and dependency information needed in the process of task execution. Task-dependent file includes a series of files, which is the entity of dependency information related to task information, such as FPGA reconfiguration file (e.g., Bit-stream file), application program coding by users, data file generated by the device, Dynamically Link Library (DLL), etc. Such files are independent of each other and not necessarily designed for a specific task. Therefore, building tasks can be seen as using task information to connect a series of files into a whole and finally describe users' particular needs through this whole. In the design of the task model, task information is lightweight and can be received, sent, and analyzed quickly. Task-dependent file is heavy-duty, which is not convenient for frequent exchange operations. However, because the monomer of a task-dependent file is independent of a specific task, the content of the task-dependent file can be stored and forwarded. Utilizing the feature of reuse can alleviate the export bandwidth pressure of the cloud. Therefore, while a task is distributed, only the task information is sent, and the task receiver checks whether the file required by the task exists in the current node. Suppose the receiver does not receive the file, or the file is incomplete, he receiver requests the file from the task sender.

In the face of the differences in data processing of different devices, the flexible configuration characteristics of FPGA-based edge nodes are used to send appropriate data processing algorithms to edge nodes through the cloud. While the computing power of a single edge node is limited, the data processing work is completed by collaborating with other edge nodes. Therefore, edge nodes need to communicate with the cloud and other edge nodes at runtime. According to the characteristics of each part of the task, a task-based edge node collaborating method is established, as shown in Fig. 1.

The process of using the cloud to configure edge nodes is shown on the right side of the figure. The task host in the cloud sends tasks (task information) to the edge node, and then the edge node checks whether the current node has task-dependent files. While the node does find task-dependent files, and the node requests the runtime library in the cloud. The runtime library in the cloud issues specific files according to the request. After the edge node obtains all the task-dependent files, the node enters the execution state. After the task is executed, the feedback information of task execution is sent to the cloud. While the cloud needs to store the data generated by the edge device, the edge node sends the device data to the cloud according to the data storage address described in the task information.

The process of data processing between edge nodes is shown on the left side of the figure. While the speed of data generation is faster than the speed of node

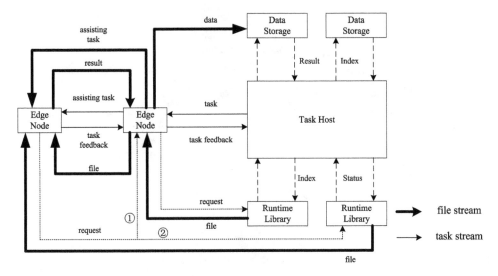

Fig. 1. Task-based collaborative method.

processing, the edge node asks the surrounding nodes for help to process the data and select the appropriate node through feedback information. The edge node sends the request to the assistant node to assist in the computing task, and then the associate node checks whether the current node has the files needed for the task according to the task information. While the assistance node does not have the required task-dependent files, the assistance node first requests the task-dependent files from the assistance sender. While the assistance node cannot obtain the task-dependent files from the task sender, the assistance node requests these task-dependent files from the cloud. After the assistance node gets the files needed for task execution, the node sends the feedback of task preparation to the assistance sender. Next, the assistance sender sends the data to the assistance node. After processing the data, the assistance node sends the processing result back to the assistance request node.

3. Behavior Analysis of Task

By analyzing the collaborative method of edge nodes, the task as a communication unit is responsible for transmitting user programs and equipment data, which is used to meet the flexible configuration function of the FPGA-based edge node. In addition, the task also needs to be responsible for guiding the user program running, setting the running status of the node, obtaining the running results of the node, etc. Therefore, the function of the task can be divided into two types, namely the exchange of information and the delivery of procedures. The information exchanged can be subdivided into the attribute information of the node and the data information associated with the node. The delivered program can be subdivided into instructions that execute pre-defined behaviors and programs that execute

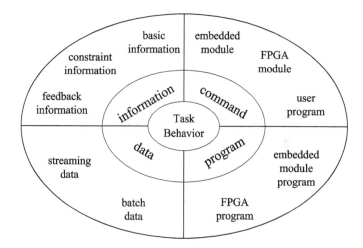

Fig. 2.   Four basic behaviors of the task.

user-defined behaviors. After further analyzing and summarizing the task behavior, the task behavior analysis tree, as shown in Fig. 2, is established by extracting task behavior and merging the common behavior of tasks. The task behavior is divided into four categories: information on transfer behavior, command transfer behavior, data transfer behavior, and program transfer behavior. Each behavior corresponds to different target objects.

The information in transferring data can be divided into three categories: the basic information needed for task communicating, the constraint conditions for task execution, and the feedback information used for various modules, instructions, or programs. The basic information describes the information required for task transfer, such as task ID and task source information. Constraints condition describes the conditions required for the current task's execution such as the information that the task depends on resources. The feedback information comes from the node's module, instruction result, or running program. The feedback information describes the available resources of the current node and the impact of instruction behavior on the module. Users can customize the information to be feedback in the application.

The objects that transfer command behavior are embedded system modules, FPGA modules, and user programs. Commands are used to run pre-defined actions. For example, all the device information connected by the current node can be obtained by sending a command to the node to get the device details without writing a program. Because the embedded system module runs the edge node system, which controls all kinds of system sub-modules and devices connected with the node, the module can pass commands to all kinds of sub-modules. The hardware algorithm and user program run by the FPGA module are used to process specific data. The function can be prefabricated in the algorithm program, and the particular activity can be run by external parameter transfer. For example, the program running in the FPGA module can receive commands from outside to get the inters remediate results of a program running. While users write programs, they can set external parameters and change the program's running by passing different parameters to the user program. Therefore, the FPGA module and user program need to use command behavior to allow users to use external parameters to obtain or change program operation.

Storing node device data in the cloud or using idle nodes to process data cooperatively causes the node to transmit data. Because the energy consumption of edge nodes is positively related to the communication frequency, the streaming data of transmission equipment means more frequent communication, which inevitably increases the energy consumption of nodes and affects the computing performance of nodes. By packing and compressing the streaming data of multiple periods to form batch data, energy-saving effect can be achieved by reducing the sending frequency, but the data lacks real-time. The two data types have their advantages and disadvantages. The characteristics of different scenarios and choosing the appropriate data type for transmission need to be considered. For example, while data from node devices is stored in the cloud, batch data is more likely to be used. While assisting other nodes in processing data, streaming data is more likely to be used. Streaming data is litter, can be sent by task information, and can be received faster, while the batch data is more extensive, which is more suitable for sending through task-dependent mode. While sending data, distinguishing the types of data sent is necessary.

The FPGA-based edge node has two different computing resources, located on the embedded system and FPGA modules. There are significant differences in the use of data processing programs located in separate modules. The embedded system calls the program of an embedded module in the form of a process or thread. The method of using FPGA modules is complex. First, the embedded system module sends the bits file to the FPGA module, and the FPGA module is reconfigured through the embedded system module. Second, the embedded system module sends the data to be processed to the FPGA module through the specified input port and obtains the processed data from the specified output port. The whole process is the procedure of calling the FPGA module. The different usage of the two computing resources leads to the various parameters carried by the task. Therefore, while moving the user program, distinguishing which user program is sent is necessary.

4. Task Critical Attribute Analysis

By analyzing the behavior of tasks, four types of tasks are summarized. In task modeling, four behaviors are built separately, including transfer information model (M_{TI}), transfer command model (M_{TC}), transfer data model (M_{TD}), and transfer program model (M_{TP}). Due to the different functions and objects of different modules, different modules have their critical attributes.

$$M_{TI} = \langle M_{BI}, M_{CI}, M_{FI} \rangle. \tag{1}$$

The information sent is subdivided into basic information, constraint conditions, and feedback information. Therefore, there are three sub-models for the information transfer model, including the basic information model (M_{BI}), the constraint information model (M_{CI}), and the feedback information model (M_{FI}). The critical attribute can be expressed as (1).

$$M_{\mathrm{BI}} = \langle \mathrm{BI}_{\mathrm{source}}, \mathrm{BI}_{\mathrm{id}}, \mathrm{BI}_{\mathrm{preference}}, \mathrm{BI}_{\mathrm{time}}, \mathrm{BI}_{\mathrm{deadline}} \rangle, \tag{2}$$

where M_{BI} describes the basic information of the current task, and the critical attribute can be expressed as (2). $\mathrm{BI}_{\mathrm{source}}$ means the task source. The task source is used to distinguish whether the task is a straightforward task from the cloud or a collaborative task from other edge nodes. $\mathrm{BI}_{\mathrm{id}}$ means the task id. The task id is the unique identification of a task. Tasks with the same id in different nodes are considered to perform the same task. $\mathrm{BI}_{\mathrm{preference}}$ is used to identify the priority level of the current task. Tasks with higher priority enter the running queue earlier than ordinary tasks at they meet the constraints. $\mathrm{BI}_{\mathrm{time}}$ means the time at the task is sent. $\mathrm{BI}_{\mathrm{deadline}}$ means the task deadline. The task deadline represents the survival time of a task. Each task has a predetermined deadline for execution. The task is not executed before the deadline, which means that the task has expired and no longer has execution value.

$$M_{\mathrm{CI}} = \langle \mathrm{CI}_{\mathrm{estimate}}, \mathrm{CI}_{\mathrm{tmax}}, \mathrm{CI}_{\mathrm{cpu}}, \mathrm{CI}_{\mathrm{mem}}, \mathrm{CI}_{\mathrm{sapce}}, \mathrm{CI}_{\mathrm{devices}} \rangle, \tag{3}$$

where M_{CI} describes the necessary conditions for the execution of the current task, and the critical attributes can be expressed as (3). $\mathrm{CI}_{\mathrm{estimated}}$ means the estimated execution time. The estimated execution time is the time taken by the standard edge node to execute the current task. This attribute provides the estimated execution time of the current task and determines whether the current node can run the task. $\mathrm{CI}_{\mathrm{tmax}}$ means the maximum tolerable communication delay. The maximum tolerable communication delay is used to constrain the feedback rate of the task, which requires that the node executing the task can complete the data processing and feedback the data processing results within the specified time. $\mathrm{CI}_{\mathrm{cpu}}$ means the CPU requirement of task execution. The CPU requirement of task execution indicates the CPU utilization of the task at the task is executed in the standard node. The current node can obtain the CPU utilization of the task through conversion. $\mathrm{CI}_{\mathrm{mem}}$ means the memory requirement of task execution. The memory requirement of task execution indicates the memory occupation of the task while the task is executed under the standard node. The current node can judge whether it can meet the memory requirements of the task through this attribute. $\mathrm{CI}_{\mathrm{space}}$ means the storage space requirement of task execution. The storage space requirement of task execution indicates that the task needs to occupy additional storage space during the performance. The required storage space is declared to the node executing the task through this attribute, and the node judges whether it can meet its storage space requirement during task execution. $\mathrm{CI}_{\mathrm{devices}}$ means the device requirement of task execution. The device requirement of a task indicates that the execution of the task depends on a specific device. This attribute is a necessary condition for the execution of a particular task.

$$M_{\text{FI}} = \langle \text{FI}_{\text{type}}, \text{FI}_{\text{source}}, \text{FI}_{\text{result}} \rangle. \tag{4}$$

The feedback information generated mainly comes from the internal modules, commands, or various user programs in operation. Therefore, a critical attribute at building a feedback information model is the type of feedback. This attribute identifies which part of the object generates the feedback information. Another critical attribute is needed, the source of feedback. The feedback type identifies which part of the feedback attribute belongs, but the feedback type does not indicate which object is generated. Therefore, the feedback source needs to indicate the object of the feedback. For example, while the feedback type indicates that the feedback information comes from a user-defined program, the feedback source shows the id of the program generating the feedback information. Another critical attribute is feedback result, which identifies the specific content of the feedback information. The expression of the model is as follows (4), FI_{type} means the feedback type, $\text{FI}_{\text{source}}$ means the feedback source, $\text{FI}_{\text{result}}$ means the feedback result.

$$M_{\text{TC}} = \langle C_{\text{object}}, C_{\text{command}}, C_{\text{args}} \rangle. \tag{5}$$

An embedded module, FPGA module, and user program receive a command. One of the critical attributes in establishing a command transfer model is to specify the command object. The embedded module is the default object of command. While the object is the FPGA model, the number of the FPGA module that the command acts on should be indicated. While the object is a running program, the program id indicates the action object of the command. In addition to the command object, the command's name and the command parameters are also critical attributes in the modeling. In addition to the command object, the command's name and the command parameters are also the critical attributes to be considered in the modeling. The expression of the model is as follows (5), C_{object} means the object of command, C_{command} implies the name of a command, C_{args} means the parameters of the command.

$$M_{\text{TD}} = \langle D_{\text{type}}, D_{\text{content}}, D_{\text{compression}}, D_{\text{verification}} \rangle. \tag{6}$$

While building the T_{DM}, whether the model object is streaming data or batch data needs to be considered. Due to the small size of streaming data, the data can be sent by task information, while the large size of batch data needs to be moved by task-dependent file, the critical attributes of different objects vary greatly. While the thing is streaming data, the data is directly filled into the task. The data content itself is the critical attribute. While the object is batch data, the task information carries the data storage address rather than the data itself. The data storage address replaces the data content as the critical attribute. To improve the transfer efficiency of batch data, pack and compressing the data is an excellent way. Therefore, the data compression method is also a critical attribute while sending batch data. At the same time, the data verification attribute should be set to avoid errors in the transmission process of the data compression package. There is no data validation attribute set for streaming data because the validation result of streaming data can be regarded as a part of data content. However, streaming data setting verification aims not to retrieve the error fragments but to identify the error data and discard them. Since streaming data is mainly used for real-time processing, reacquiring error fragments loses the significance of real-time. After the above analysis, the established T_{DM} can be expressed as (6). D_{type} means the date type. The data type attribute identifies whether the current transfer data is stream data or batch data. D_{content} means data content while streaming data and indicates data address during batch data. $D_{\text{compression}}$ means the data compression method. $D_{\text{verification}}$ means the data verification method.

While building the T_{PM}, whether the object of the model is an embedded system module or FPGA program needs to be considered. While the thing is an embedded system module, the input and output variables need to be considered. The input variable is used to pass in the node running preset parameters or the processed data results given by the program running in the node. The output variable transfers the data processing result of the program to the outside. While the object is an FPGA module, the critical attribute to be considered is the number of the target FPGA module. Because the FPGA module is regarded as a kind of device in designing an FPGA-based edge node, multiple FPGA modules can be connected at the edge node. While using the program to reconfiguration the FPGA module, the specific FPGA module is specified by the FPGA number. While reconfiguring the FPGA module, the interface provided by the embedded system module is needed to reconfiguration the FPGA module. While communicating with the FPGA module, the embedded system module is also used as an intermediary to exchange information between the FPGA module and external. Therefore, transferring a program to an FPGA module can be regarded as moving the program to an embedded system module. While the attribute of the FPGA number in the model is not empty, the embedded system module starts the reconfiguration program to reconfiguration the specified FPGA according to the number.

$$M_{\text{TP}} = \langle P_{\text{id}}, P_{\text{addr}}, P_{\text{fpga}}, P_{\text{in}}, P_{\text{out}} \rangle. \tag{7}$$

Through the above, the T_{PM} can be expressed as (7). P_{id} means the program id, P_{addr} means the program address, P_{fpga} means the number of target FPGA module, P_{in} means the input variables, P_{out} means the output variables. As the unique identification of the program, the program id is used for nodes to quickly retrieve whether the same program exists locally and reduce the number of times for nodes to obtain task-dependent files. The program address indicates the address where the current program is stored. While the node does not find the corresponding program locally, the specific program is obtained by using the address pointed by the attribute.

5. Task Modeling

Through the analysis of task behavior, the task behavior is divided into four basic behaviors: information transfer behavior, instruction transfer behavior, data transfer behavior, and program transfer behavior. By analyzing the critical attributes of each basic behavior, the corresponding behavior models are established: the information transfer model, instruction transfer model, data transfer model, and program transfer model. As can be seen from Fig. 1, the characteristics of task communication between edge nodes and the cloud and between edge nodes are that in the task request phase, tasks always carry relevant data and programs. In contrast, in the task feedback phase, tasks only carry data. The type of information carried by the task is asymmetric between the sender and the receiver. While building a task model, whether the current task belongs to the send stage or the feedback stage needs to be considered. Therefore, the task model is also divided into the task send model (M_{TS}) and the task feedback model (M_{TF}).

$$M_{\text{TS}} = \langle M_{\text{TI}}\langle M_{\text{BI}}, M_{\text{CI}}\rangle, M_{\text{TC}}, M_{\text{TD}}, M_{\text{TP}}\rangle, \tag{8}$$

where M_{TS} can be expressed as (8). There are four basic behavior models in the M_{TS}. Since the tasks generated by the model are used for task send, the M_{FI} is not included in the M_{TI}.

According to the M_{TS}, the specific tasks constructed in the form of JSON are shown in Fig. 3. The task is used to transfer the user program. The source field in the base_info part of the info part corresponds to the $\text{BI}_{\text{source}}$ in the M_{BI}, which is used to describe the ip of the sender of the task. The id field corresponds to the BI_{id} in the model, and the id of the current task is 2. The level field corresponds to the $\text{BI}_{\text{preference}}$ in the model, and the priority of the task is the normal level. The time field corresponds to BI_{time} in the model and is used to describe the time while the task is sent. The deadline field corresponds to the $\text{BI}_{\text{deadline}}$ field in the model, which can represent the lifetime of the task. The lifetime of the task is 60 s after the task is sent out. The estimated field in the constraint part corresponds to the $\text{CI}_{\text{estimated}}$ in the M_{CI}, which is used to describe the estimated execution time of the task. The estimated execution time of the task is 10 s. The latency field corresponds to the CI_{tmax} in the model, which is used to indicate the maximum delay that can be accepted while interacting with the task. The field of the current task is 0 s, which means that the current task has no interaction with the outside world. The cpu field corresponds to the CI_{cpu} in the model, the mem field corresponds to the CI_{mem} in the model, the storage field corresponds to the $\text{CI}_{\text{storuage}}$ in the model, and the devices field corresponds to the $\text{CI}_{\text{devices}}$ in the model. Their corresponding fields mean that CPU takes up 1.5% of the standard node, memory takes up 2% of the standard node, and does not take up extra storage space but requires FPGA devices. The id field in the program part corresponds to the P_{ID} in the M_{TP}, which is the unique identification of the user program. The id of the user program is 15. The addr field corresponds to P_{addr} in the model and is used to describe the storage address of the program FPGA. The num field corresponds to the P_{fpga} in the

```
{                                    command:
info:                                    {
        {                                    target:,
        base_info:                           id:,
                {                            name:,
                source: ip,                  args:,
                id: 2,                       ...
                level: n,
                time: xxxx,                  },
                deadline: 60,        data:
                ...
                }                            {
        constraint:                          type:,
                {                            content:,
                prediction: 10,              compression:,
                 max_latency: 0,             checkout:,
                cpu: 1.5,                    ...
                mem: 2,                      },
                storage: 0,          program:
                device: fpga,
                ...                          {
                }                            id: 15,
        },                                   addr: ip:port@file_name,
                                             fpga_num: 1,
                                             input: [2, 5, 9],
                                             output:,
                                             ...

                                             }
                                     }
```

Fig. 3.   JSON form of sending task.

model and is used to describe the FPGA number of the node used by the program. The input field corresponds to the P_{in} in the model. The value in the input field corresponds to the id of the user program in the node, indicating that the input of the current task comes from the corresponding user program. The content fields of the instruction part and data part in the figure are empty, indicating that the current task has no function of sending commands and data.

$$M_{\text{TF}} = \langle M_{\text{TI}} \langle M_{\text{BI}}, M_{\text{FI}} \rangle, M_{\text{TD}} \rangle, \tag{9}$$

where M_{TF} can be expressed as (9). In the T_{FM}, there are only two basic behavior models: T_{IM} and T_{DM}. The T_{IM} includes B_{IM} and F_{IM}. Because the transmission is the result of the task request, there is no need to set constraints for the current task execution, the M_{CI} is not included in the M_{TI}.

According to M_{TF}, the specific tasks created in the form of JSON are shown in Fig. 4. The task transfers the data generated by the node to the outside. The source field in the base_info part of the info part corresponds to the $\text{BI}_{\text{source}}$ in the M_{BI}, which is used to describe the ip address of the task sender. The id field corresponds to the BI_{ID} in the model, which is the unique identification of the task. The id of 4-1 in this task indicates that the task is the feedback task of task 4. The level field corresponds to $\text{BI}_{\text{preference}}$ in the model, which is used to describe the priority

```
{
info:
            {
            base_info:
                        {
                        source: ip,
                        id: 4-1,
                        level: n,
                        time: xxxx,
                        deadline: 10,
                        ...
                        }
            feedback_info:
                        {
                        type: program,
                        source: 2,
                        result: ok ,
                        ...
                        }
            },
    data:
            {
            type: stream,
            content: [12041, 12128, ...],
            compression:,
            checkout:,
            ...
            }
}
```

Fig. 4.   JSON form of the feedback task.

of the task. The priority of the task is normal. The time field corresponds to the BI_{time} in the model and describes the sending time of the task. The deadline field corresponds to the $BI_{deadline}$ in the model and is used to describe the lifetime of the task. The lifetime of the task is 10 s after the task is sent out. The type field in the task feedback part corresponds to the FI_{type} in the M_{FI}. The type in this task is a program, which means that the source of the task is the user program. The source field corresponds to FI_{source} in the model. The source field in this task is 2, which means that the feedback task comes from user program 2. The result field corresponds to the FI_{result} in the model. The result field in the task is OK, which means that the task feedback is normal. The type field in the data part corresponds to D_{type} in the M_{TD}. The type in this task is a stream, which means that the data to be sent is streaming. The content field corresponds to $D_{content}$ in the model, and the data in the task is filled in the content field in the form of an array. Since the data type in this task is streaming data, the compression field and checkout field are empty.

6. Simulation Experiments

Through the experiment of remotely reconfiguring the FPGA module of the edge node in the cloud, whether the specific task instantiated by the task model can be correctly parsed and used by the edge node is tested, thereby verifying the usability of the task model. Through the experiment of multi-node collaborative processing of data, the availability of the task-based cloud-edge collaboration method is verified.

The edge node used in the experiment of remotely reconfiguring the FPGA model of the edge node in the cloud is shown in Figs. 5 and 6. Figure 5 shows the

Fig. 5.   FPGA module and embedded module.

Fig. 6.   FPGA-based edge node.

two modules of the edge node, the left is the FPGA module, and the right is the Linux-based embedded system module. Figure 6 shows an FPGA-based edge node, which connects the FPGA module and the embedded system module through a card slot.

FPGA is commonly used for data filtering. Taking the remote reconfiguration of the FIR filter algorithm as an example, the remote reconfiguration of FPGA is carried out. In this experiment, by monitoring the interactive traffic between the cloud task host and the runtime host, and the edge node, it is verified that the cloud and the edge can usually parse the task and use the information exchange task. By monitoring the reconfiguration completion signal of the FPGA module, verify whether the edge node based on FPGA can use the task instantiated by the task model for remote reconfiguration to verify the availability of the task. The relationship between traffic and time is drawn by monitoring the traffic received and sent by the cloud, as shown in Fig. 7.

K1 and K2 are used for heartbeat connection to observe changes, the heartbeat interval is reduced and set to every 4 s. Edge nodes send heartbeat information regularly to maintain the connection status between the node and the cloud and report the currently available devices to the cloud. As can be seen from the figure, at time T1, the cloud sends the task of reconstructing the FPGA module of the edge node. Since the task carries the address of the reconfiguration program, the task size is small. The edge node receives the task quickly. By parsing the task information, the edge node does not find the file that the task depends on in the local environment and immediately requests the cloud for the required task-dependent file through the address of the task description. Therefore, the cloud sends the task-dependent file at D1. After the cloud sends the task-dependent file, the cloud receives information different from the heartbeat connection at F1. The information is the feedback of

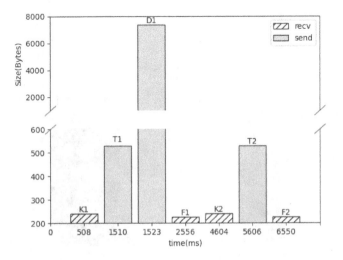

Fig. 7.   Using task configuration FPGA module.

the completion of the task execution of the edge node. The feedback marks the completion of the FPGA module reconfiguration of the edge node. At this time, the FPGA module also sends out a signal that the configuration is complete. This information indicates that the edge node successfully parses and executes the tasks sent by the cloud. In order to verify that the edge node can reduce the traffic pressure in the cloud by caching task-dependent files after the edge node completes the reconfiguration task, the cloud sends the same task again. At T2, the cloud sends the reconfiguration task again. The figure shows that the cloud does not send out extensive traffic data like D1, but at F2, the cloud receives feedback from the edge node task completion. The edge node saves the task-dependent files related to the task after the task is executed. Therefore, while the same task is performed again, the process of task-dependent file requests is reduced. Thus, the execution time of the second task is about 9.75% shorter than that of the first task. There is only one task-dependent file for the current experiment, and the task-dependent file is small in size. The effect is not too obvious. While the task is complex, the size of task-dependent files is larger, and the number of task-dependent files is powerful, the more pronounced the effect of reducing cloud traffic pressure by caching task-dependent files on edge nodes.

The way of multi-node collaborative processing data is shown in Fig. 8. Node 1 is a normal edge node for collecting device data, and node 2 is an FPGA-based edge node for data processing. The process of the experiment is as follows: first, the cloud sends the task of data transfer to node 1 and transfers the data collected by node 1 to node 2. Then the cloud sends the data processing task to node 2, in which the specified data comes from other nodes. Figure 9 is drawn by detecting the traffic interaction of the cloud, node 1, and node 2.

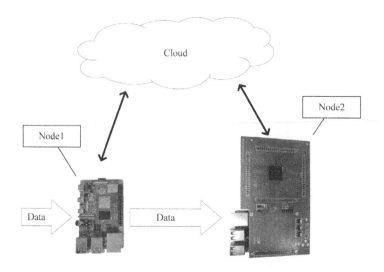

Fig. 8.   Multi-node collaborative processing structure.

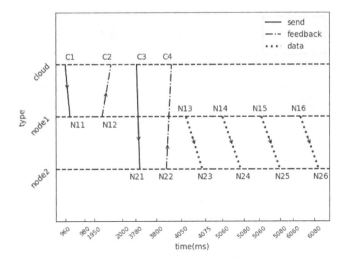

Fig. 9.   Multi-node collaborative processing data.

The abscissa of the figure is time, the unit is MS, and the ordinate is node type. In order to facilitate observation, the process of sending task-dependent files from the cloud is omitted. Node 1 collects data, and node 2 processes data. The cloud sends the task of device data collection and data transfer to node 1 at time C1. Node 1 receives the task at time N11, obtains the task-dependent file, and starts the task from N11 to N12. Send feedback on completion of task execution at time N12. The cloud receives feedback from the task at time C2. Then the cloud sends a data processing task to node 2 at time C3. This task states that the data comes from other nodes. Node 2 completed the task start during N21 to N22 and sent feedback information at time N22. The cloud receives feedback on task completion at time C4. At this point, node 1 and node 2 establish a collaborative relationship. While the data collected by node 1 reaches the data transfer threshold, node 1 actively sends data flow to node 2, corresponding to the N13–N23, N14–N24, N15–N25, N16–N26 processes in the figure. Node 2 passes the data from node 1 to the corresponding data processing program.

The experiment of remotely reconfiguring the FPGA module of the edge node through the cloud can prove that the cloud and the edge can correctly analyze the specific task instantiated by the task model, and the edge node can use the task model to create detailed feedback information after completing the task. The task-dependent files in the task are reusable. While the cloud sends the reconfiguration task again, the task's execution time is lower than the first time. In the multi-node collaborative processing of data experiment, the specific task instantiated by the task model demonstrated data transferability. The data can be placed on the node with more vital processing ability through the data transfer to meet the multi-node collaborative data processing. The use of data transfer can also achieve the purpose of saving the resources of edge nodes. Selecting some nodes for centralized data processing can avoid wasting resources caused by each node configuring the same data processing program.

The above experiments can prove the availability of the specific task instantiated by the task model. The multi-node collaboration experiments can prove the feasibility of the task-based collaboration method.

7. Conclusion

In order to meet the collaboration of edge nodes with cloud and other nodes, this paper designs a task-based collaboration method. The task consists of task information and task-dependent files. Task information contains all kinds of behaviors of tasks. Through the analysis of various behaviors of tasks, four basic behaviors are summarized. By analyzing the critical attributes of the four essential behaviors, the corresponding behavior models are built. Finally, according to the task initiation and feedback type, a M_{TS} and a M_{TF} are built. Experiments show that the specific task instantiated by the task model can be correctly parsed and used by cloud and edge nodes. The contributions of this paper are as follows:

- A task-based cloud-edge collaboration method is proposed, which meets the reuse of common parts of tasks.
- By analyzing the task, four basic behaviors of the task are summarized, and the corresponding behavior model is built by analyzing the critical attributes of each behavior.

The experiment shows that the FPGA reconfiguration task constructed by the task model can meet the FPGA reconfiguration of edge nodes. At present, the task of building the task model is relatively simple. In the next step, we continue this work and use the task model to create more complex tasks.

Acknowledgment

This work is supported by the National Key R&D Program of China (Grant No. 2018YFB1701600).

References

1. Al-Fuqaha A., Guizani M., Mohammadi M., Aledhari M., Ayyash M., Internet of things: A survey on enabling technologies, protocols, and applications, *IEEE Commun. Surv. Tutor.* **17**(4):2347–2376, 2015.
2. Reka S. S., Dragicevic T., Future effectual role of energy delivery: A comprehensive review of Internet of Things and smart grid, *Renew. Sust. Energ. Rev.* **91**:90–108, 2018.
3. Almusaylim Z. A., Zaman N., A review on smart home present state and challenges: Linked to context-awareness internet of things (IoT), *Wirel. Netw.* **25**(6):3193–3204, 2019.

4. Le D. N., Le Tuan L., Dang Tuan M. N., Smart-building management system: An Internet-of-Things (IoT) application business model in Vietnam, *Technol. Forecast. Soc. Change* **141**:22–35, 2019.

5. Singh S., Sharma P. K., Yoon B., Shojafar M., Cho G. H., Ra I. H., Convergence of blockchain and artificial intelligence in IoT network for the sustainable smart city, *Sustain. Cities Soc.* **63**:102364, 2020.

6. Chen S., Li Q., Zhang H., Zhu F., Xiong G., Tang Y., An IoT edge computing system architecture and its application, *2020 IEEE Int. Conf. Networking, Sensing and Control*, Nanjing, China, IEEE, pp. 1–7, 2020.

7. Liu Y., Fan P., Zhu J., Wen L., Fan X., High-efficient energy saving processing of big data of communication under mobile cloud computing, *Int. J. Model. Simul. Sci. Comput.* **10**(4): 1–11, 2019.

8. Varghese B., Reano C., Silla F., Accelerator virtualization in fog computing: Moving from the cloud to the edge, *IEEE Cloud Comput.* **5**(6):28–37, 2018.

9. Cao J., Zhang Q., Shi W., Challenges and opportunities in edge computing, in *Edge Computing: A Primer*, Springer Briefs Computer Science, Springer, Cham, pp. 59–70, 2018.

10. Porambage P., Okwuibe J., Liyanage M., Ylianttila M., Taleb T., Survey on multi-access edge computing for internet of things realization, *IEEE Commun. Surv. Tutor.* **20**(4):2961–2991, 2018.

11. Hu P., Dhelim S., Ning H., Qiu T., Survey on fog computing: Architecture, key technologies, applications and open issues, *J. Netw. Comput. Appl.* **98**:27–42, 2017.

12. Shirazi S. N., Gouglidis A., Farshad A., Hutchison D., The extended cloud: Review and analysis of mobile edge computing and fog from a security and resilience perspective, *IEEE J. Sel. Areas Commun.* **35**(11):2586–2595, 2017.

13. Morabito R., Beijar N., Enabling data processing at the network edge through lightweight virtualization technologies, *2016 IEEE Int. Conf. Sensing, Communication and Networking, SECON Workshops*, no. 607728, London, UK, IEEE, pp. 1–6, 2016.

14. Chen F., Deng P., Wan J., Zhang D., Vasilakos A. V., Rong X., Data mining for the internet of things: Literature review and challenges, *Int. J. Distrib. Sens. Netw.* **11**:431047, 2015.

15. Linthicum D., Architecture for the body, *Computer* **49**(10):72–75, 2016.

16. Wu S. *et al.*, When FPGA-Accelerator meets stream data processing in the edge, *Proc. Int. Conf. Distributed Computing Systems*, Dallas, TX, IEEE, pp. 1818–1829, 2019.

17. Ricco M., Manganiello P., Monmasson E., Petrone G., Spagnuolo G., FPGA-based implementation of dual Kalman filter for PV MPPT applications, *IEEE Trans. Ind. Inf.* **13**(1):176–185, 2017.

18. Zou X., Wang L., Tang Y., Liu Y., Zhan S., Tao F., Parallel design of intelligent optimization algorithm based on FPGA, *Int. J. Adv. Manuf. Technol.* **94**(9-12):3399–3412, 2018.

19. Chen F. *et al.*, Enabling FPGAs in the cloud, *Proc. 11th ACM Conf. Computing Frontiers*, Association for Computing Machinery, New York, NY, United States, Cagliari, Italy, pp. 1–10, 2014.

20. Yadav P. K., Singh M. P., Sharma K., Task allocation model for reliability and cost optimization in distributed computing system, *Int. J. Model. Simul. Sci. Comput.* **2**(2):131–149, 2011.

21. Man S., Yang R., Application of discrete artificial bee colony algorithm for cloud task optimization scheduling, *Int. J. Model. Simul. Sci. Comput.* **11**(4):1–11, 2020.
22. Yadav S. K., Kyatanvar D. N., Deshmukh S. R., Load balancing in cloud environs: Optimal task scheduling via hybrid algorithm, *Int. J. Model. Simul. Sci. Comput.* **12**(2):1–26, 2021.
23. Ullah A., Nawi N. M., Enhancing the dynamic load balancing technique for cloud computing using HBATAABC algorithm, *Int. J. Model. Simul. Sci. Comput.* **11**(5):1–20, 2020.
24. Deng S., Cao H., Shen J., Liu H., A model of task collaboration with simulation for IOT, *Proc. - 2011 IEEE Int. Conf. Computer Science and Automation Engineering*, Vol. 1, Shanghai, IEEE, pp. 331–335, 2011.
25. Tran M. Q., Nguyen D. T., Le V. A., Nguyen D. H., Pham T. V., Task placement on fog computing made efficient for IoT application provision, *Wirel. Commun. Mob. Comput.* **2019**:6215454, 2019.
26. Li C., Bai J., Tang J. H., Joint optimization of data placement and scheduling for improving user experience in edge computing, *J. Parallel Distrib. Comput.* **125**:93–105, 2019.
27. Ma J., Zhou H., Liu C., E M., Jiang Z., Wang Q., Study on edge-cloud collaborative production scheduling based on enterprises with multi-factory, *IEEE Access* **8**:30069–30080, 2020.
28. Fan J., Wei X., Wang T., Lan T., Subramaniam S., Deadline-aware task scheduling in a tiered IoT infrastructure, *China Commun.* **16**(8):162–175, 2019.
29. Sahni Y., Cao J., Yang L., Ji Y., Multi-hop multi-task partial computation offloading in collaborative edge computing, *IEEE Trans. Parallel Distrib. Syst.* **32**(5):1133–1145, 2021.
30. Vijayalakshmi R., Vasudevan V., Kadry S., Lakshmana Kumar R., Optimization of makespan and resource utilization in the fog computing environment through task scheduling algorithm, *Int. J. Wavelets Multiresolut. Inf. Process.* **18**(1):1–12, 2020.
31. Chuan X., Chun Z., Yue L., Lin Z., A FPGA-based cloud-edge collaboration platform in cloud, *Proc. ASME 2021 16th Int. Manufacturing Science and Engineering Conf.*, Virtual, Online, Vol. 2, ASME, 2021.

Chapter 11

Hybrid intelligent modeling approach for online predicting and simulating surface temperature of HVs

Ming Tie[*], Hong Fang[†], Jianlin Wang[‡] and Weihua Chen[§]

Science and Technology on Space Physics Laboratory
Beijing, 100076, P. R. China
[*]tming7611@sina.com
[†]fanghongfox@163.com
[‡]20051186@163.com
[§]veihua1984@163.com

Abstract

Online prediction as well as online simulation of surface temperature will play a significant role in flight safety of future near space hypersonic vehicles (HVs). But it still remains a classical scientific problem both in thermodynamics and aerospace science. In view of the complex HV structure and complex heat conduction procedure, three-dimensional numerical simulation is too inefficient for online prediction, while current rapid computation methods cannot meet the requirement of accuracy. Therefore, a hybrid intelligent dynamic modeling approach is proposed to estimate the surface temperature of HV with the combination of mechanism equations, test data and intelligent modeling technology. A simplified model based on a mechanism equation and experimental formulas is presented for predicting or simulating transient heat conduction procedure efficiently, while a case-based reasoning (CBR) algorithm is developed to estimate two uncertain coefficients in the simplified model. Furthermore, a support vector regression (SVR)-based model is developed to compensate the modeling error. With the data both from high-precision finite element computation and from real-world HV thermal protection experiments, a number of comparative simulations demonstrate the effectiveness of the proposed hybrid intelligent modeling approach.

1. Introduction

In the recent years, hypersonic vehicles (HVs) have attracted a lot of research attention for their military and civil potential, such as high speed up to flying anywhere on earth in 2 h in the near space, low launch cost, great payloads, much efficient propulsion and dynamic performance.[1,2] Different from many other aircrafts, large envelope flights of HVs usually fly in a wide range of velocity and flight height, which is so large that an envelope flight involves great challenge on thermal protection performance. Due to long time flying with such high velocity in near space, the intense compression and friction of the hypersonic air flow together with the

---

[*]Corresponding author.

retardation influence from gas viscosity can cause very high temperature on its surface. Moreover, continuous aerodynamic heating may impair the structure performance and lead to thermal ablation.[3] In the flight test of unmanned Falcon HTV-2 (Hypersonic Technology Vehicle 2) on 11 August 2011, shown as Fig. 1, the hypersonic vehicle lost control and result in self-destruction as a safety precaution during its Mach 20 glide flight. The vehicle's surface reached 3500 degrees Fahrenheit and controlled itself for 3 min before crashing, the speed and heat caused part of the skin to peel away from the aero-structure.[4]

On the other hand, future HV would require much longer flight range with much more maneuverability. Thus, the payload proportion must be as large as possible, which means the thermal protection structure should be as light as possible. However, the harsh aero heating in near space for HV is always the greatest danger. As shown in Fig. 1, the nose as well as the edge of wing and rudder meet extremely hot flow, which may cause high temperature on inner wall of vehicle through the heat conduction and damage control equipment. Therefore, online prediction of surface and inner wall temperature can be much helpful to the flight safety for HVs. Especially, the online prediction result for the rest trajectory or even the whole flight envelope may help HVs to find the optimal trajectory online.

In current aerospace engineering, the numerical simulation methods, such as finite difference methods (FDMs), finite element methods (FEMs), boundary element methods,[5] boundary face methods[6] and meshless methods,[7] are still the regular methods for the thermal protection design and computation. Nonetheless, FDM can only be applied to structured grid and is not appropriate to complicated area. Particularly, B-spline Interpolation Boundary Face Method has been successfully

Fig. 1.   Aero heating and ablation of HTV-2 in flight process.

applied to the computation of steady thermal conduction.[8] In addition, its time complexity can be lowered from $O(N_2)$ to $O(NlogN)$ with the adaptive cross approximation and hierarchy matrix algorithm. Nonetheless, transient thermal conduction prediction is much preferred in aerospace engineering, especially for some precise and efficient algorithms. Therefore, meshless methods are then developed and more commonly used for transient thermal field computation, since they can reduce the computation difficulty of mesh distortion as well as avoid the mesh generating procedure and integration procedure.[9] To meshless method, the setting of virtual boundary improves the convergence velocity of numerical computation as well as instability due to its randomness. In view of this, a boundary knot method improved the solving stability by replacing the singular fundamental solution with the general solution of nonsingular radius basis function (RBF).[10] To improve the efficiency and agility, the dual reciprocity boundary element method (DRBEM)[11] is applied to thermal conduction computation with a series of approximate particular solutions for partial differential equations.

Although the above meshless methods and DRBEM can be applied to thermal protection performance computation for hypersonic vehicles, the computation complexity of current numerical methods cannot afford online prediction or large-scale offline thermal conduction estimation. On the other hand, a large amount of historical data from high-cost physical tests and some time-consuming high-precision numerical computation is still unused in modeling, which means a huge waste of data resource. With the development and application of data-driven intelligent modeling approaches, how to model and reuse such considerable idle data resource may be a feasible way to overcome the inherent defects of the numerical simulation.

In this paper, instead of the time-consuming three-dimensional numerical simulation models, a simplified one-dimensional heat conduction model is proposed based on two-order partial difference equations with Crank–Nicolson solving method and an experimental formula for hot wall flux. In view of the problems of the proposed mechanism model, a hybrid intelligent modeling strategy is presented to improve its precision as well as computation efficiency. A case-based reasoning algorithm is developed to derive two thermal conduction coefficients of the simplified model which may vary with different boundary conditions. Additionally, a support vector regression-based model is employed to compensate the unknown parts which are not included in the mechanism model. Moreover, the proposed hybrid intelligent model is verified with data both from hypersonic thermal protection experiments and three-dimensional high-precision numerical simulation. Finally, general conclusions are presented.

2. Mechanism Model for Thermal Conduction of HV

As shown in Fig. 2, HV's wall and thermal protection structure include the heat shield layer by composite material, the thermal insulation layer and the metal

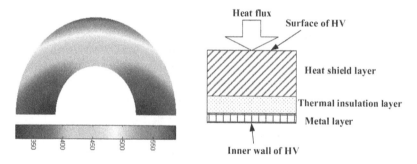

Fig. 2.   Heat conduction procedure for HV with thermal protection.

layer, which are all mechanically attached. During the hypersonic flight procedure, aerodynamic heating caused by the friction and resistance of air flow will result with much high temperature on the vehicle skin and even burning it through. On the other hand, high temperature on inner wall may damage the control system or other airborne equipment.

From the heat-transfer theory and energy conservation equations on the basis of finite element methods,[6] the three-dimensional unsteady heat-conduction equation for anisotropic structure can be

$$\rho c_p \frac{\partial \theta}{\partial t} = \frac{\partial}{\partial x}\left[\lambda_x(\theta)\frac{\partial \theta}{\partial x}\right] + \frac{\partial}{\partial y}\left[\lambda_y(\theta)\frac{\partial \theta}{\partial y}\right] + \frac{\partial}{\partial z}\left[\lambda_z(\theta)\frac{\partial \theta}{\partial z}\right] + Q_C(t) \qquad (1)$$

where c_p is specific heat capacity, ρ is medium density, θ is instantaneous temperature of position (x, y, z), Q_C denotes the cold wall thermal flux from aerodynamic heating, x denotes the value of radial direction, λ_x, λ_y and λ_z are thermal conductivity coefficients of medium for the three directions, respectively. Since it may take a missile-borne computer at least several hours to achieve precise numerical solution for Eq. (1), a much more simplified method must be derived for online prediction or online simulation. Therefore, we may assume that there is little temperature difference for different regions on HV's surface, which means every point with the same x value is isothermal. Thus, a one-dimensional thermal conductivity model can be derived as the following 2-order parabolic partial differential equation if only radial heat conduction is concerned:

$$\frac{\partial \theta}{\partial t} = \frac{\lambda}{\rho c_p}\frac{\partial^2 \theta}{\partial x^2} + Q_C(t) \qquad (2)$$

where λ is thermal conductivity coefficient of medium, $\lambda = \lambda_x$. In the numerical simulation, the Crank–Nicolson (CN) method based on the trapezoidal rule is unconditionally stable,[12] giving second-order convergence in time. Equation (1) can be solved with CN method as follows:

$$\frac{\theta_i^{n+1} - \theta_i^n}{\Delta t} = \frac{\lambda}{\rho c_p} \cdot \frac{\frac{\theta_{i+1}^{n+1}+\theta_{i+1}^n}{2} - 2\frac{\theta_i^{n+1}+\theta_i^n}{2} + \frac{\theta_{i-1}^{n+1}+\theta_{i-1}^n}{2}}{(\Delta x)^2} + Q_C \qquad (3)$$

In the FEM analysis for aerospace engineering, hot wall thermal flux is one of the thermal environment variables for the temperature computation, which denotes the unit of aerodynamic heating flux absorbed by the structure result with structural thermal response. An iteration computation equation for hot wall thermal flux is as follows:

$$Q_H(t+1) = Q_C(t)\left(1 - \frac{E_W}{E_R}\right) - \beta\gamma\theta^4(t), \tag{4}$$

where Q_H denotes hot wall thermal flux, β is Boltzmann constant $5.67 \times 10^{-8}\mathrm{W/m^2K^4}$, γ is the radiation coefficient of structure surface, E_R denotes the recovery enthalpy or the air flow enthalpy value at recovery temperature. E_W is the enthalpy value at surface temperature which can be calculated by

$$E_W = \begin{cases} 0.796329\theta^{1.041} & 170\,\mathrm{K} < \theta < 1748\,\mathrm{K} \\ 78.4187\exp\left[3.178\left(\dfrac{\theta}{1748}\right)^{\frac{1}{2.41+709.637(\ln P - \ln P_0)}}\right] & \theta \geq 1748\,K, \end{cases} \tag{5}$$

where P_0 is the standard atmosphere pressure and P is wall pressure.

The above one-dimensional thermal conductivity model can improve much impressive efficiency and is appropriate for missile-borne computation. But on the other hand, the specific heat capacity λ and the thermal conductivity coefficient c_p will vary with different temperatures and thermal boundary conditions. Additionally, heat conduction among different regions with the same thickness is overlooked in the presented assumption. Therefore, the precision of the one-dimensional thermal conductivity model is too low for the application of aerospace engineering.

3. Hybrid Intelligent Modeling Approach for Surface Temperature of HV

3.1. *Hybrid intelligent modeling strategy*

In view of the above problems of the proposed one-dimensional thermal conductivity model, a data-driven hybrid intelligent modeling approach is developed, as shown in Fig. 3. A case-based reasoning (CBR) algorithm for time-varying parameters is developed to quickly derive the appropriate thermal conductivity coefficient and specific heat capacity for different flight states and thermal conditions. In relative research, genetic algorithms (GA) have been developed to determine the coefficients of thermal conduction equations for different conditions, where the model precision can be improved a lot.[13,14] However, the coefficients optimization procedure with GA may cost the missile-borne computer more than 1 h, which cannot be employed online. With the CBR technique, the consumed time can be overlooked if the number of cases to be indexed is not too large. Moreover, CBR can be convenient in incorporating prior knowledge and has significant effectiveness in complex

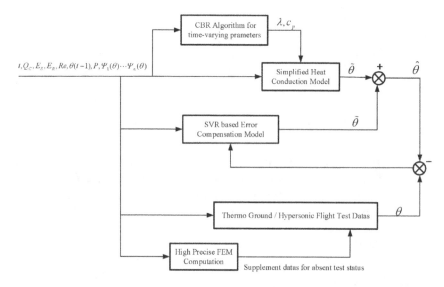

Fig. 3.   Hybrid intelligent modeling strategy for surface temperature of HV.

and unstructured decision making,[15] which means knowledge from thermodynamics and aerospace engineering experiences can be helpful to improve the prediction precision.

With the developed CBR algorithm, the thermal conductivity coefficient λ and specific heat capacity c_p can be online rectified, which can improve the prediction accuracy in various flight states. However, the accuracy loss from being reduced to radial heat conduction procedure would still be a problem. Thus, a compensation model based on support vector regression (SVR) is developed as a supervised learning technique. Compared with other methods, SVR shows rapid convergence[16] in function estimation problems due to its ability to detect correlations between output and input data.[17]

In general, hybrid intelligent modeling strategy for prediction can be described as follows:

$$y(t) = f_0(u_1, u_2, \ldots, \xi_1, \xi_2, \ldots) + f_1(u_1, u_2, \ldots, \xi_1, \xi_2, \ldots) \tag{6}$$

$$[\xi_1, \xi_2, \ldots]^T = f_2(x_1, x_2, \ldots) \tag{7}$$

where y denotes the prediction result, $u_1 \ldots$ denote the input variables, f_0 denotes a much simplified and efficient mechanic model, $\xi_1 \ldots$ denote the coefficients varying with different working conditions or boundary conditions, f_1 can be an intelligent model based on machine learning algorithms to estimate the modeling error of f_0, f_2 is another intelligent model for $\xi_1 \ldots$, and $x_1 \ldots$ denote the variables of boundary conditions. The intelligent models should have high computation efficiency and be trained with data samples from various working conditions, which are very important to the real-time and generalization ability of online prediction.

Due to the time-continuous variation of thermal field, aero heating in every previous moment may have effect on current temperature. Therefore, previous temperature $\theta(t-1)$ should be one of the model inputs, while a set of functions $\Psi_1(\theta) \sim \Psi_n(\theta)$ are defined as input variables to describe the feature of temperature variation procedure. The difference between the test data and prediction result will also be an input to train the SVR model.

3.2. *CBR algorithm for thermal conductivity coefficient and specific heat capacity*

Each case can be defined as CA = {Solution | $E_1, \ldots$}, where Solution consists of ω and c_p. The case feature set should include cold wall thermal flux Q_C which denotes the unit of aerodynamic heating flux without the consideration of vehicle structural thermal response, the static enthalpy E_S which denotes the air flow enthalpy value at surface temperature, the recovery enthalpy E_R, Reynolds number Re which denotes the ratio of inertia force to viscous force of air flow, the previous temperature $\theta(t-1)$, the wall pressure P. Thus $E_1, \ldots, E_6$ denote Q_C, E_S, E_R, $Re, \theta(t-1)$, P, respectively.

In information retrieval systems, the nearest neighbor cosine matching function has been extensively used as it is a direct numerical method for similarity assessment. Especially, the followed modified cosine matching function can be applied for cases lack of few features:

$$\text{SIM}(CA_j, CA_k) = \frac{\sum_{i=1}^{6} \omega_{i,j} \times \omega_{i,k} \times \text{sim}(E_{i,j}, E_{i,k})}{\sqrt{\sum_{i=1}^{6} (\omega_{i,j})^2 \times \sum_{i=1}^{6} (\omega_{i,k})^2}}, \tag{8}$$

$$\text{sim}(E_{i,j}, E_{i,k}) = 1 - \frac{|E_{i,j} - E_{i,k}|}{\text{Maximum}(E_{i,j}, E_{i,k})} \tag{9}$$

where CA_j represents the case of the input future flight condition, CA_k is the kth retrieved case, SIM is their similarity measuring function, $\omega_{i,j}$ and $\omega_{i,k}$ denote the weight value of feature E_i in the two cases respectively, and $\text{sim}(E_{i,i}, E_{i,k})$ is the similarity measuring function for E_i of the two cases. If any feature value in a retrieved case is absent, its weight value can be assumed to be zero in similarity computation.

Feature weighting is the method of assigning a proper weight value to each feature according to its relative importance in case retrieval. The feature weights can be assigned based on some prior knowledge or experiences, but it must be optimized to retrieve the cases accurately in a given domain. Feature weighting can reflect the relative importance with sophistication, and feature selection is only its special case. Consequently, the feature weighting optimization of the CBR system is always better than feature selection optimization.

Generally, decreasing gradient algorithm, the particle swarm optimization (PSO) algorithm and GA are all frequently used method for offline feature weighting of CBR. GA could be applied in a variety of optimization problems with discontinuous, nondifferentiable, stochastic, or highly nonlinear objective function, but it will consume too much time if data sample size is too large. With GA-based CBR weight value optimization algorithm as that in Tie's modeling method for rolling process,[16] the accuracy of case index and reuse can be improved.

The optimization algorithm is described in the following steps:

Select m cases to be input into an experiment case set, while all the others are input into the reference case set. Then the fitness function, which returns the evaluation results of each chromosome, can be defined as follows:

$$CR = \frac{1}{m} \sum_{i=1}^{m} CM_i, \tag{10}$$

$$CM_i = \begin{cases} 1, & \sqrt{\dfrac{\sum_{k=1}^{n} (\theta(k) - \hat{\theta}(k))^2}{\sum_{k=1}^{n} \theta(k)^2}} \le \varepsilon, \\[4mm] 0, & \sqrt{\dfrac{\sum_{k=1}^{n} (\theta(k) - \hat{\theta}(k))^2}{\sum_{k=1}^{n} \theta(k)^2}} > \varepsilon, \end{cases} \tag{11}$$

where CR denotes the retrieval precision of the experiment case set, CM_i represents the retrieval precision for ith experiment case and ε is an error threshold.

Step 1. Initiation

Assume $\omega_1 \ldots \omega_6$ as the weight values of six features, and are encode them with a real-coded chromosome GA, then provide n chromosomes $\Omega_1 \ldots \Omega_n$ as the initial population, and set the evolution limitation.

Step 2. Reasoning

For each chromosome of $\Omega_1 \ldots \Omega_n$, input each of the $m$experiment cases $CA_1 \ldots CA_m$ as a new problem and perform the above CBR process with the reference set, then get the solution W_{ik} $(k = 1 \ldots m, i = 1 \ldots n)$.

Step 3. Evaluation

Achieve state space models with W_{ik} $(k = 1 \ldots m, i = 1 \ldots n)$, then perform simulation with these hybrid models and compute $CR_1 \ldots CR_n$ with Eq. (10). If any of them satisfies the stopping criteria, then output its corresponding chromosome as the final result and complete the optimization process. Else, execute the following genetic operation and then return to step 2.

Step 4. Evolutionary Procedure

According to fitness values of the chromosomes, apply the following reproduce, crossover, mutation genetic operators to produce a new generation. For any chromosome $\Omega_i (i = 1 \ldots n, \Omega_i = [\omega_{i,1} \ldots \omega_{i,6}]^T)$ and its fitness value CR_i, the evolutionary rule can be defined as follows:

If $CR_i = \text{Max}\{CR_1 \ldots CR_n\}$.

Then Ω_i should be reproduced into offspring;

Else if $\dfrac{\mathrm{CR}_i}{\sum_{j=1}^{n-1} \mathrm{CR}_j} \leq 0.02$.

Then execute the mutation operation;

Else execute the crossover operation.

Return to step 2.

3.3. *SVR-based error compensation model*

As the precision of the proposed simplified heat conduction model may be much lower than the three-dimensional numerical simulation model, a compensation model must be developed to improve the accuracy as possible with little computation efficiency lost. Based on the analysis of thermal conduction mechanism,[19,20] $Q_C(t)$, $E_R(t)$, $\mathrm{Re}(t)$, $\theta(t)$ and $P(t)$ may have effect on temperature computation error $\tilde{\theta}(t+1)$. In addition, from Eq. (3), it can be assumed that the computation step size Δt should also be one input variable if it is varied. Thus, $\tilde{\theta}(t+1)$ can be computed as follows:

$$\tilde{\theta}(t+1) = f(\Delta t, P, E_R, Q_C, \mathrm{Re}, \theta(t), \Psi_1(\theta), \ldots, \Psi_n(\theta)) \tag{12}$$

where f denotes a nonlinear function, $\Psi_1(\theta)\Psi_n(\theta)$ represent n functions for temperature varying procedure. Here, ith order origin moment can provide information about the temperature variation procedure, but high-order origin moment may lead to great error fluctuation. Therefore, the function $\Psi_i(\theta)$ can be defined as ith root of ith order origin moment

$$\Psi_i(\theta) = \sqrt[i]{\dfrac{\int_{t_0}^t \theta(\tau)^i d\tau}{t - t_0}} \quad (i = 1 \ldots n). \tag{13}$$

To improve online prediction efficiency, the support vector prediction is presented to construct a linear regression function in high-dimensional space with training. SVR can avoid overfitting by compromising on the minimization of both the training error and generalization error.[17] For a given training sample set $[X(k), \tilde{\theta}(k)]$, $X(k) = [\Delta t(k), P(k), Q_C(k), E_R(k), \mathrm{Re}(k), \theta(k), \Psi_1(\theta(k)), \ldots, \Psi_n(\theta(k))]^T$, temperature error prediction regression function can be $f(X) = W^T \varphi(X) + b$, $\varphi(X)$ could map the input vector X into a high dimension space, and b is a constant bias. Constructing in high dimension space with support vector prediction for stagnation temperature, this problem can be transformed into the following optimization problem:

$$\dfrac{1}{2} W^T W + C \sum_{i=1}^n \varphi(\tilde{\theta}_i, f(X_i^T)),$$

$$\text{s.t. } \xi_i^* \leq \varphi(\tilde{\theta}_i, f(X_i^T)) = \|\tilde{\theta}_i - W^T \phi(X_i) - b\| - \eta \leq \xi_i \tag{14}$$

Here, the constant $C > 0$ is the penalty factor, which has an inverse relation with generalization ability, and $\xi_i, \xi_i^* \geq 0$ are two non-negative slack variables, η

is the error of insensitive loss function. An appropriate penalty factor value will avoid the problem of under-fitting and over-fitting, since a larger value may lead to much larger training error while a smaller one may lead to little limitation on the model structure complexity. SVR not only minimizes the training error by minimizing the sum of ξ_i, ξ_i^*, but also minimizes $\|w\|$ in order to increase the flatness of the function.[18] Equation (10) can be transformed into dual problem with the Lagrange multiplier method, and derived the following Karush–Kuhn–Tucker (KKT) conditions:

$$\begin{cases} \dfrac{\partial\varphi}{\partial\alpha_i} = \displaystyle\sum_{i,j=1}^{n} (\alpha_j - \alpha_j^*)\phi(X_i)\phi^T(X_j) + \eta - y_i + \xi - \delta_i + u_i = 0, \\[3mm] \dfrac{\partial\varphi}{\partial\alpha_i} = \displaystyle\sum_{i,j=1}^{n} (\alpha_j - \alpha_j^*)\phi(X_i)\phi^T(X_j) + \eta + y_i - \xi - \delta_i + u_i = 0, \\[3mm] \dfrac{\partial\varphi}{\partial b} = \displaystyle\sum_{i=1}^{n}(\alpha_j - \alpha_j^*)\phi(X_i) = 0, \end{cases} \tag{15}$$

where $\alpha_j - \alpha_j^*$ are regression coefficients for the kth training sample and can be achieved from Eq. (11). The points with $\alpha_j - \alpha_j^* \neq 0$ are support vectors.

Radial basis functions (RBFs) have played a most common role in the kernel function of SVR, while its sensitivity to parameters is always a problem to be solved. With Laplacian kernel, the sensitivity and dependency to parameters can be lowered. Therefore, the kernel function can be defined as follows:

$$\phi(X_i)\phi^T(X_j) = 0.5e^{-\frac{\|X_i - X_j\|^2}{2\sigma^2}} + 0.5e^{-\frac{\|X_i - X_j\|}{\sigma}}. \tag{16}$$

4. Experimental Verification

To verify the effects of the proposed modeling and virtual sensing approach, a dynamic hybrid intelligent model is developed with the data from both thermal protection tests and high precise three-dimensional FEM computation. Since the data from hypersonic flight tests and physical ground tests is not enough for intelligent modeling samples, high precise computation may be an effective supplement way.

The following relative root-mean-square error RRMSE(θ) and the relative mean error RME(θ) are defined as the evaluation standard:

$$\text{RRSME}(\theta) = 100\sqrt{\frac{\sum_{k=1}^{n}(\theta(k) - \hat{\theta}(k))^2}{\sum_{k=1}^{n}\theta(k)^2}}\%,$$

$$\text{RME}(\theta) = \frac{100}{n}\sum_{k=1}^{n}\left|\frac{\theta(k) - \hat{\theta}(k)}{\theta(k)}\right|\%. \tag{17}$$

The case weight of CBR model is optimized offline with data samples from historical flight tests, since it will be employed online without rectifying. The initial value is $[1\ 1\ 1\ 1\ 1\ 1]^T$, while the prediction errors of CBR algorithm are RRSME(θ) = 7.25% and RME(θ) = 8.14%.

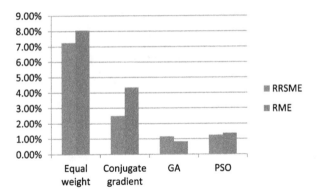

Fig. 4. Optimization result of CBR feature weight with different methods.

As shown in Fig. 4, the PSO and the GA can both be applied to achieve the global optimization solution, while the conjugate gradient method may not be capable. At the 115th generation of GA optimization, the computation error is reduced to RRSMN(θ) = 1.25%, RME(θ) = 1.14%, where it can be lowered little. The optimization result is shown in Table 1.

In our experiments, the length of flight time or hypersonic aero heating time is from 200 s to 1000 s. Therefore, the SVR-based model in Eq. (12) can achieve enough little training error when $n = 3$. The developed discretized SVR model is as follows:

$$\tilde{\theta}(k+1) = f\left(\Delta t, P, E_R, Q_C, Re, \theta(k), \frac{1}{k}\sum_{i=1}^{k}\theta(i),\right.$$
$$\left.\sqrt{\frac{1}{k}\sum_{i=1}^{k}\theta(i)^2}, \sqrt[3]{\frac{1}{k}\sum_{i=1}^{k}\theta(i)^3}\right) \tag{18}$$

The predicted results via different modeling methods are compared with the measured values and high precise three-dimensional FEM simulation result. The high precise three-dimensional FEM simulation is a very accurate and time-consuming method, which may cost computation time dozens of thousand times longer than the proposed hybrid intelligent model. Thus, it can only be used to generate modeling and test data set. The test results are shown in Figs. 5 and 6, where the horizontal axis represents the sampling time and the vertical axis represents the surface temperature of the hypersonic vehicles.

Table 1. Optimization result of feature weights.

Case feature	Q_C	E_S	E_R	Re	$\theta(t-1)$	P
Weight value	0.65	0.03	0.17	−0.26	1.14	0.19

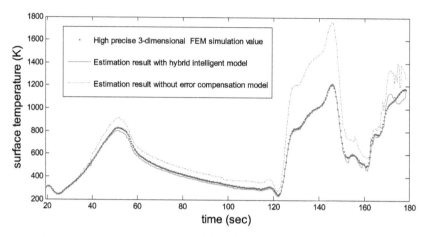

Fig. 5.   Contrast curves of estimation value with high precise three-dimensional FEM simulation value.

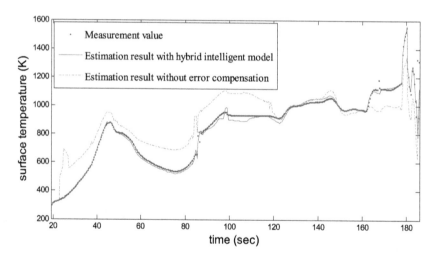

Fig. 6.   Contrast curves of estimation value with measurement value.

From Figs. 5 and 6, we can see that the estimation value trend of the mechanic model with CBR algorithm for the two parameters is almost the same as the real value, when there is no sharp variation of aero heating. These may indicate that both the mechanic model and the CBR algorithm are effective. In Fig. 5, the flight sideslip angle varies frequently in a large scale after 130 s, while the mechanic model with CBR algorithm cannot achieve the accurate value as well as its variation trend. That is because the heat conduction among different regions of the same thickness is too significant to be overlooked.

Comparing to mechanic model with rectification of thermal conductivity coefficient and specific heat capacity, the hybrid intelligent model with SVR-based residual compensation can get best performance. It is obvious that the prediction accuracy is improved after compensation which verifies the effectiveness of this proposed method. Moreover, at work conditions where the thermal environment and surface temperature is in significant variation, the proposed hybrid intelligent model can remain accurate on both estimation value and dynamic characteristics. On the other hand, the mechanics model without SVR compensation can only be accurate for the working conditions where the surface temperature varies smoothly and gently, although the thermal conductivity coefficient and specific heat capacity are identified and rectified every 50 s. Therefore, the presented hybrid intelligent modeling approach can be an appropriate virtual sensing method for surface temperature of HV in both precision and efficiency.

5. Conclusions

Online prediction of surface temperature will play a significant role in the flight safety of future hypersonic vehicles. Nonetheless, complex numerical simulation methods and inaccurate fast algorithms from experiences are still mainly concerned in current heat conduction modeling research on aerospace engineering. A hybrid intelligent modeling strategy with mechanism model, CBR algorithm for coefficients and SVR-based data-driven model is proposed in this paper. Its precision is proved in simulation experiments with data from both physical tests and three-dimensional high precise computation, while the one-dimensional heat conduction equation and intelligent algorithm have also advantages of high computation efficiency. The proposed modeling approach may be a feasible online prediction way which will not only provide a new solution for the classic problem in the aerospace science but also have great significance in the development of HV. To be a credible prediction approach in real-world hypersonic vehicle engineering, the modeling sample data from flight tests is not enough yet. Therefore, the future research should be how to derive more knowledge and achieve more data through high-performance computation for thermal field, which may probably be helpful for our hybrid intelligent model to be adaptive to more different operating conditions.

Acknowledgments

This research is funded by the National Key Research and Development Program of China (No. 2018YFB1701600) and the National Natural Science Foundation of China (No. 61773068).

References

1. Fiorentini L. *et al.*, Robust nonlinear sequential loop closure control design for an air-breathing hypersonic vehicle model, *American Control Conf.*, Washington, pp. 3458–3463, 2008.
2. Tao X., Li N., Li S., Multiple model predictive control for large envelope flight of hypersonic vehicle systems, *Inf. Sci.* **328**:115–126, 2016.

3. Cheng T., Li W., Heat transfer and failure mode analyses of ultrahigh-temperature ceramic thermal protection system of hypersonic vehicles, *Math. Probl. Eng.* **2014**:412718, 2014.

4. DARPA, Hypersonic vehicle advances technical knowledge, DARPA 11 August 2011, Archived from the original on 6 April 2014.

5. Zhang J., Qin X., A boundary face method for potential problems in three dimensions, *Int. J. Numer. Meth. Eng.* **80**:320–337, 2009.

6. Xie G., Zhang J., A direct traction boundary integral equation method for 3-dimension crack problems in infinite and finite domains, *Comput. Mech.* **53**:1–12, 2013.

7. Wang H., Qin Q., A meshless model for transient heat conduction in functionally graded materials, *Comput. Mech.* **38**:51–60, 2006.

8. Qin X., Zhang J., Steady-state heat conduction analysis of solids with small open-ended tubular holes by BFM, *Int. J. Heat Mass Transf.* **55**:6846–6853, 2012.

9. Fu Z., Chen W., Qin Q., Three boundary meshless methods for heat conduction analysis in nonlinear FGMs with Kirchoff and Laplace transformation, *Adv. Appl. Math. Mech.* **4**:519–542, 2012.

10. Chen W., Tanaka M., A meshless integration-free and boundary-only RBF technique, *Comput. Math. Appl.* **43**:379–391, 2002.

11. Qin X. Y. *et al.*, A finite element implementation of the boundary face method for potential problems in three dimensions, *Eng. Anal. Bound. Elem.* **34**:934–943, 2010.

12. Weng Z., Feng X., A new mixed finite element method based on Crank–Nicolson scheme for the parabolic problems, *Appl. Math. Model.* **36**:5068–5079, 2012.

13. Raudenský M., Woodbury K., Genetic Algorithm in solution of inverse heat conduction problems, *Numer. Heat Transf. Fundam.* **28**:293–306, 2012.

14. Stota D., Using genetic algorithms for the determination of an heat transfer coefficient in three-phase inverse Stefan problem, *Int. Commun. Heat Mass Transf.* **35**:149–156, 2008.

15. Begum S., Ahmed M., Case-based reasoning systems in the health sciences: A survey of recent trends and developments, *IEEE Trans. Syst. Man Cybern.* **41**:421–434, 2011.

16. Su H., Li X., Yang B., Wen Z., Wavelet support vector machine-based prediction model of dam deformation, *Mech. Syst. Signal Process.* **110**:412–427, 2018.

17. Balogun A., Rezaie F., Phamd Q., Spatial prediction of landslide susceptibility in western Serbia using hybrid support vector regression (SVR) with GWO, BAT and COA algorithms, *Geosci. Front.* **12**(3):101104, 2021.

18. Tie M., Bi J., Ding J. L., Hybrid intelligent modeling and simulation for cold tandem rolling process, *IET Control Theory Appl.* **10**:1420–1430, 2016.

19. Ervin C., Vladimir C., Adrijan B., A strategy for short-term load forecasting by support vector regression machines, *IEEE Trans. Power Syst.* **28**:4356–4364, 2013.

20. Huang G., Song S., Wu C., Robust support vector regression for uncertain input and output data, *IEEE Trans. Neural Netw.* **23**:1690–1700, 2012.

Chapter 12

Knowledge-driven material design platform based on the whole-process simulation and modeling

Gongzhuang Peng[*,**], Tie Li[†], Xiang Zhai[‡,§,¶],
Wenzheng Liu[‖] and Heming Zhang[‖]

[*]*National Engineering Research Center for Advanced Rolling Technology*
University of Science and Technology Beijing
Beijing 100083, P. R. China

[†]*Shanghai Electro-Mechanical Engineering Institute*
Shanghai 201109, P. R. China

[‡]*State Key Laboratory of Intelligent Manufacturing System Technology*
Beijing Institute of Electronic System Engineering
Beijing 100854, P. R. China

[§]*Beijing Complex Product Advanced Manufacturing Engineering Research Center*
Beijing Simulation Center, Beijing 100854, P. R. China

[¶]*Science and Technology on Space System Simulation Laboratory*
Beijing Simulation Center, Beijing 100854, P. R. China

[‖]*National CIMS Engineering Research Center, Tsinghua University*
Beijing 100084, P. R. China
[**]*gzpeng@ustb.edu.cn*

Abstract

In order to realize the agility, collaboration and visualization of alloy material development process, a product development platform based on simulation and modeling technologies is established in this study. In this platform, the whole-process simulation module builds multi-level simulation models based on metallurgical mechanisms from the production line level, the thermo-mechanical coupling field level and the microstructure evolution level. The design knowledge management module represents the multi-source heterogeneous material design knowledge through ontology model, including customers' requirement knowledge, material component knowledge, process design knowledge and quality inspection knowledge, and utilizes the case-based reasoning approach to reuse the knowledge. The data-driven modeling module applies machine learning algorithms to mine the relationships between product mechanical properties, material components, and process parameters from historical samples, and utilizes multi-objective optimization algorithms to find the optimal combination of process parameters. Application of the developed platform in actual steel mills shows that the proposed method helps to improve the efficiency of product design process.

1. Introduction

Material design refers to the process of determining the chemical compositions, process routes, and key parameters to meet the performance indicators required by the customer. It is a systematic project integrating customer requirements analysis, market investigation, design testing, batch production, and product tracking. The current new material development is trail-and-error mode, which needs repeated adjustments and iterations through small batch trial production.[1] The whole process is not only very time-consuming and costly, but also difficult for engineers to track due to various sub-processes. The complex physical and chemical reactions contained in each sub-process have significant nonlinearity, strong coupling and multi-parameter characteristics.[2] From the perspective of the market, customers' demand for diversification and individualization of steel products continues to increase, with the rapid development of automotive industries and household electric enterprises. Under this background, how to establish a product R&D platform to quickly adjust the composition and process design and realize the agility and visualization of the development process has become the key to enhancing the core competitiveness of the enterprise.

Computer simulation technology provides strong support for the design of complex electromechanical products to achieve improved efficiency in terms of both time and cost, by helping practitioners generate, verify, validate and optimize the design solutions.[3] Commonly used simulation tools include dynamic design software — ADAMS, hydraulic system design software — EASY5, control system design software — MATLAB and three-dimensional shape design software — CATIA. As the modern product design process becomes more and more distributed and multi-disciplinary, many new simulation technologies emerge and become popular, such as virtual prototype technology, co-simulation technology,[4,5] cloud simulation technology,[6] and digital twin technology.[7,8] In recent years, finite element modeling (FEM) tools have been widely used to simulate the macroscopic deformation and microstructure distribution of materials and finally develop the optimum process sequence and determine the optimum process parameters.[9,10] Nalawade *et al.*[10] applied FORGE software to study the deformation behavior and microstructural evolution of steel 38MnVS6 during the hot rolling process. The rolling load, torque, stress distribution and phase constitution of simulation results agreed very well with experiment results. Dai *et al.*[11] applied the numerical simulation to study the influences of gap, baffle length and purging air velocity on the lubricant during the steel sheet temper rolling process. The rapid development of high performance computing technology has further promoted the application of high-throughput simulations in establishing structure-property relationships of a variety of materials.[12,13]

Although high-fidelity simulations can improve the efficiency of product development, it also has some shortcomings. On the one hand, the large-scale material simulation has heavy computing burden, which often takes dozens of hours. On the other hand, the simulation is highly dependent on the mechanism model. The mechanism model can accurately describe the thermal behavior and microstructure evolution of the material. Chen *et al.*[14] created an oxide growth model to predict the oxide thickness on metals under high temperature solid-particle erosion. But sometimes it is difficult to establish an accurate mechanism model. Big data and machine learning methods are boosting the intelligent design of advanced materials by mining the relationships between chemical compositions, process parameters, organizational structures, and mechanical properties.[15,16] Especially with the development of advanced sensing and communication technologies, the industrial Internet of things (IIoT) has become widely used in enterprises. Multi-source heterogeneous data including market orders, production processes, quality monitoring, product sales and user feedback are collected in the enterprise data platform, enabling data modeling methods to help companies in various aspects of design, manufacturing, operation and maintenance. Mohanty *et al.*[17] developed an artificial neural network (ANN)-based model with 22 input variables to predict the yield strength (YS), ultimate tensile strength (UTS) and percentage elongation (EL) of the interstitial free (IF) steel strip. The mechanical properties' prediction model has been one of the most important data-driven models in the material design process.[18,19] Paul *et al.*[18] applied the ANN model to predict the fracture toughness of low alloy steel under different alloy compositions.

As a knowledge-intensive and complex process, new product design contains a wide variety of knowledge during the entire development cycle.[20,21] However, most of the domain knowledge exists in the minds of experts and cannot be coded or managed, causing the difficulty in knowledge reusing. Due to the lack of a collaboration mechanism, effective knowledge sharing cannot be formed among members in a development team either within an organization or across several organizations. Furthermore, massive and multi-source design knowledge has heterogeneity in format and semantics, which increases the difficulty for designers to obtain knowledge and further reduces the efficiency of knowledge reuse.[22] Peng *et al.*[20,21] developed several knowledge representation models such as issue-based model and ontology-based model to store and reuse the multi-faceted design knowledge.

In this work, a new material development platform is developed, which integrates whole-process simulation, data-driven modeling and design knowledge management. The simulation module combines the mechanism model and numerical simulation to establish a simulation model of the whole process including steelmaking, continuous casting, heating, rolling and cooling. Through the digital characterization of multi-level physical phenomena from microview and macroview, the influence of composition and process parameters on the evolution of microstructure can be analyzed rapidly, which provides theoretical guidance for composition and process design. The modeling module collects actual production data and applies machine learning algorithms to mine the relationship between key input parameters and mechanical properties, in view of the multi-variable and strong coupling characteristics of metallurgical production processes. The data-driven models can achieve quick and accurate prediction of product performance. The knowledge management module extracts domain knowledge related to material design through natural language processing technology to reuse existing design cases and expert experience. The developed material R&D platform will not only shorten the product delivery cycle and improves production efficiency, but also save the R&D cost by reducing the number of tests and experiments.

The rest of this paper is organized as follows. Section 2 introduces the multi-scale simulation of the whole hot rolling process. The framework of material design knowledge representation and reuse are described in Sec. 3. Then in Sec. 4, data-driven models used in the product development process are analyzed. System implementation and case study are presented in Sec. 5. Finally conclusions are drawn in Sec. 6, together with some discussion of potential future work.

2. Multi-Scale Simulation of the Whole Hot Rolling Process

In this study, we take the 1580 mm Compact Strip Production (CSP) line as the simulation object. The layout of the production line is shown in Fig. 1, which includes two reheating furnaces, one rough descaling machine, one vertical-roller roughing mill, one flying shear, one fine descaling machine, seven-stand finishing rolling, laminar cooling equipment and two coiling machines. The production processes are as follows: the continuous casting slabs enter the reheating furnace as the raw material, and go through roughing mill after descaling; after being rolled by the reversible rough rolling, the irregular shape of the head and tail of the rolling piece is cut by the flying shear; after removing the surface oxide scale, it enters the finishing rolling mill, and then it is cooled by laminar flow and coiled by a coiler to become a hot rolled coil product. Due to the coupling of deformation and structure evolution in the metal hot forming process, the precise forming of the product and the control of the structure and performance are more complicated. In order to simulate the forming process of metal materials more realistically, this research simulates the production process from different levels, including the simulation of the production line, the simulation of the temperature field and the deformation field, and the simulation of the evolution of the microstructure.

2.1. Production line simulation

Production line simulation models the workpiece, the production equipment and the production process in CSP line by visual models. In workpiece simulation the

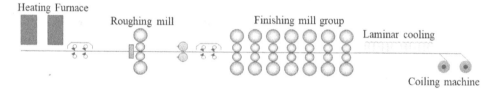

Fig. 1.   Layout of the CSP hot rolling line.

position and shape indices such as length, width, thickness and crown of the rolling piece synchronize with the real-time production site. The production process simulation takes the form of production rhythm to ensure that the production time and running speed of equipment (such as rolling mills, roller tables, etc.) correspond to the production site. The simulation of production equipment is mainly the automatic control models of various equipment, such as hydraulic loop and tension simulation, plate thickness simulation, flying shear control process simulation. Figure 2 illustrates the three-dimensional visual simulation models of the laminar cooling process. At the same time, the production line 3D simulation system also provides abundant data interfaces, such as industrial Ethernet communication and OPC protocol, which can realize real-time interaction with external data and build a production line cyber physical system.

2.2. *Thermo-mechanical and microstructure simulation*

The metal hot forming is a complex process with multi-physical field coupling, multi-parameter influence. Temperature field, stress field and microstructure are coupled and interact with each other. Traditional macroscopic finite element simulation is difficult to accurately describe the deformation and microstructure evolution behavior of components under complex thermal-mechanical coupling. Therefore, this study establishes a multi-scale simulation model of thermal-mechanical coupling field and microstructure distribution, as shown in Fig. 3, and concentrates on the three key processes in CSP, namely reheating, rolling and cooling.

Fig. 2.   3D Visual simulation models of the laminar cooling.

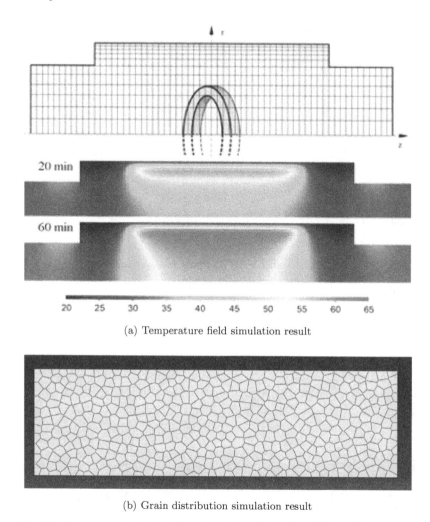

(a) Temperature field simulation result

(b) Grain distribution simulation result

Fig. 3.   Thermo-mechanical and microstructure simulation of the rolling process.

During the heating process, the austenite grains gradually grow up with the change of heating temperature and holding time, which can be characterized by the grain growth model. During the rolling process, under the influence of rolling temperature, rolling speed, and rolling load distribution, austenite crystals are deformed and refined in the recrystallization temperature zone to form a uniform recrystallization structure. The dynamic recrystallization and static recrystallization models are utilized to represent the process. During the cooling process, with the different cooling rate, austenite transforms into ferrite, pearlite and bainite in different distributions, and finally forms a stable microstructure distribution. The final YS, tensile strength and EL of the material are related to the size and distribution of microstructure grains. Thermo-Calc and TC-Prisma software can be

Table 1. Microstructure prediction models used for rolling simulations.

Model name	Formulations	Parameters
Grain growth model	$d_r^n - d_0^n = [A\exp(-Q_g/RT)]t$	d_r^n — Grain size after reheating, d_0^n — Grain size before reheating, t — Reheating time, n, Q_g, A — Parameters related to steel grade
Dynamic recrystallization model	$X_d = 1 - \exp[-k((\varepsilon - a_3\varepsilon_c)/\varepsilon_p)^n]$ $d_{drx} = aZ^b$ $Z = \varepsilon \exp(Q_1/RT_{drx})$	X_d — Dynamic recrystallization fraction ε — Single-pass strain d_{drx} — Recrystallized grain size Z — Zener–Hollomon parameter
Static recrystallization model	$X_{Srex} = 1 - \exp[-0.693(t_{Srex}/t_{0.5})^{n_1}]$ $t_{0.5} = Bd_r^m \Delta\varepsilon^p \varepsilon^q \exp(Q_{srex}/RT_{srex})$ $d_{Sdrx} = A_1 d_r^{a_4} \Delta\varepsilon^{a_5} \varepsilon^{a_6} \exp(Q_{srex}/RT_{srex})$	X_{Srex} — Static recrystallization fraction $t_{0.5}$ — Time for 50% recrystallization d_{Sdrx} — Recrystallized grain size $\Delta\varepsilon$ — Cumulative strain after dynamic recrystallization
Phase transition model	$X_f = \sum_{i=0}^{n} \left(1 - \frac{k_f \Delta t_i^{n_f}}{d_a^m}\right)$ $\ln d_f = -0.47[ln(\frac{2.24}{d_a} + 0.114 \times \Delta\varepsilon_{jn}^2) +$ $0.0057ln(1 + 4 \times \Delta\varepsilon_{jn}) + 0.13\ln X_f - 2.217]$	X_f — Ferrite volume fraction d_f — Transformed ferrite grain size d_a — Grain size after finishing rolling $\Delta\varepsilon_{jn}$ — Cumulative strain after finishing rolling

used to simulate the phase field distribution and phase evolution, while Abaqus and Deform 3D are applied to model the recrystallization process. The models used in the microstructure simulation are summarized in Table 1.

3. Material Design Knowledge Management

As mentioned above, the product design process relies heavily on the experience and knowledge accumulated by R&D engineers. With the development of information technologies, on the one hand, big data technology can be used to crawl and collect metallurgical specifications and general standards disclosed in the network, patents, documents, etc., and on the other hand, natural language processing and semantic representation techniques can be used to extract knowledge from historical design cases and generate the enterprise-specific knowledge base. In this study a material design knowledge management platform is established, which involves knowledge of customer demand analysis, material chemical composition, process design, design experiment, quality inspection, and product improvement analysis. Figure 4 shows the framework of material design knowledge management. Through the extraction and integration of massive irregular data and text, structured design information

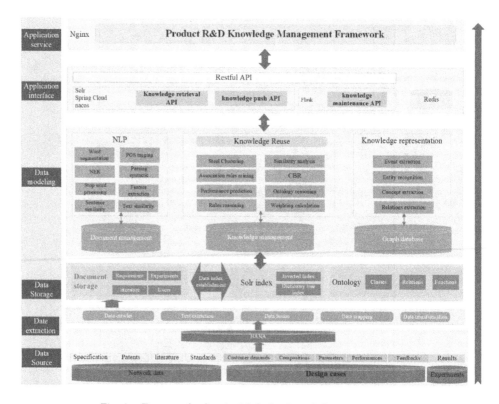

Fig. 4.   Framework of material design knowledge management.

is generated, and then the design knowledge base is formed through the link and representation of the knowledge unit. The reuse of design knowledge can assist designers in decision-making and reasoning in new material development process.

The data collection layer gathers structured and unstructured data from the manufacturing execution system, quality control system, and inspection and testing system. Data source contains market analysis, user requirements, quality design, production process parameters, inspection and testing processes, process changes, product delivery, and user tracking. At the same time, we also use crawlers to grab metallurgical specifications, general standards and other data disclosed in the Internet, patents, and literature. At the data extraction layer, word segmentation service improves the accuracy of full-text retrieval by optimizing Solr keyword retrieval; knowledge graph establishes a data basis for search association; log feedback provides users with annotations on search accuracy; spark data processing engine completes basic data cleaning and associating; the knowledge map extracts entities, relationships and attributes of the data, and completes the establishment of the graph database. The data storage layer mainly includes relational data storage, Solr index storage, professional word segmentation thesaurus and graph database storage.

Due to the wide variety of material design data, the requirements for automatic data extraction and integration are relatively high. In this study we use D2RQ semantic mapping technology to transform structured data into Resource Description Framework (RDF) data for ontology retrieval and reasoning services. Odoo Web Library (OWL)-based ontology modeling technique is then utilized to represent the product design knowledge. In addition to inheriting RDF, OWL also adopts the ontology reasoning layer Ontology Inference Layer (OIL) to facilitate rule-based reasoning. The constituent elements such as classes, attributes, and individuals in OWL are defined as RDF resources and identified by URIs. We first formulate the D2RQ mapping rules and formalize the corresponding rules template according to the established ontology model, then call the D2RQ mapping engine on the development platform, load the ontology model and mapping templates, and establish the connection between the ontology model and the data source, so as to finally transform the actual production into design ontology. Figure 5 shows the material design ontology model constructed by the platform.

The data calculation layer performs data cleaning, data transformation, content analysis, keyword extraction, and data reduction on the collected data according to the data template to complete the classification and association of the data and the weighting of the lexicon. The data calculation also includes steel grades merging, product similarity analysis, association rule mining of process routes, and similar case reasoning, which will be introduced in detail in Sec. 4. The data service layer performs index processing on the calculated data, provides search and intelligent semantic analysis for the data application layer, and realizes intelligent search and push services of product design knowledge. The data application layer provides corresponding data call interface services and data application interface services.

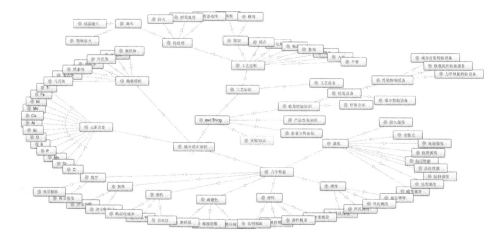

Fig. 5.   Material design ontology model.

4. Data-Driven Models in New Material Development

Figure 6 shows the main data-driven models used in the product development process, including steel grade merging model, performance prediction model, and parameter optimization model. The specific functions of each model are as follows:

4.1. *Steel grade merging model*

For different steel grades and specifications, there exists large difference between the relationships of their mechanical properties, process parameters, and chemical

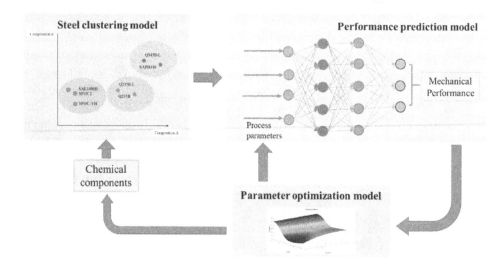

Fig. 6.   The flow of data-driven models in the development process.

composition, which drives a need to establish their own prediction models for different steel grades. However, a large steel mill usually produces hundreds of steel grades. Moreover, the sample of each steel grade is extremely unbalanced, and some steel grades have only dozens of samples. In order to solve the problem, we use clustering algorithms (e.g., K-means, DBSCAN) to analyze the chemical composition of different grades of steel, find the similarity and specificity of the raw material compositions, and automatically merge the grades with the same or similar raw material composition into sub-clusters. In this way, the establishment of steel grade clusters according to the composition range will help establish a more accurate prediction model and improve the efficiency of new product development. At the same time, the number of steel-making grades can be reduced under the condition of meeting product performance requirements, so as to realize the full use of surplus slabs. It can also effectively help enterprises realize flexible rolling with multiple varieties and small batches.

4.2. *Performance prediction model*

The performance prediction model is to predict the mechanical properties of products based on the microstructure changes during the steel production or the known raw material composition and process parameters. Due to the complexity of the manufacturing process, the mechanical properties of hot-rolled products are often affected by material parameters and high-dimensional process parameters in the production process, and the relationship between the parameters is nonlinear. Based on massive, high-dimensional process quality datasets, this study uses the machine learning algorithms (e.g., BPNN, ELM, SVM) combined with metallurgical mechanisms to establish a data-driven statistical model for hot-rolled product performance prediction. The performance prediction model can help researchers to establish a quality monitoring system in the production process, adjust process parameters in time, and improve the quality and performance of the final product. The experiment number can also be cut down during the development of new products, which reduces the test time and shortens the test period greatly.

4.3. *Parameter optimization model*

The parameter optimization model is based on the performance prediction model to find the optimal combination of process parameters and chemical composition according to the mechanical properties required by the users. Grid search cross-validation can be used to select the optimal parameters, which traverses all permutations and combinations of incoming parameters, and returns the prediction performance under all parameter combinations in a cross-validation manner. Due to the wide variety of material chemical compositions and process parameters, we also choose evolutionary algorithms (e.g., GA, PSO, ABC) to solve the approximate optimal solution of the model. Meanwhile, since there are multiple conflicting goals in the product design process, such as between different performances, and between performances and chemical composition costs, the platform also integrates multi-objective optimization algorithms to solve the Pareto optimal solution. The parameter optimization model helps to form the rapid design of the global hot rolling and cold rolling process, and the coordination and matching of multiple processes also contribute to improving the stability of product quality and production efficiency.

5. System Implementation and Case Study

The proposed material design platform is implemented in large steel mills, which includes the whole process simulation module, product design knowledge management module, process design optimization and quality tracking module. The following takes the development of a steel grade as an example to introduce the application process of the platform. The requirements for the mechanical properties of new steel grade are: RP0.2 (stress at 0.2 of the specified extensometer gauge length) ≥ 345 MPa, Rm (tensile strength) ≥ 485 MPa, A200 (EL percentage) ≥18%. We first use the case-based reasoning method to form the preliminary plan of product components and process routes, and select the case with the highest degree of similarity to the demand performance from the product design knowledge base. The performance attributes of materials are generally in the form of intervals, and we define the similarity of the two attributes $[a1, a2]$ and $[b1, b2]$ as follows:

$$\text{sim}([a_1, a_2], [b_1, b_2]) = 1 - \left[\frac{1}{2}[|b_2 - a_2|^r + |b_1 - a_1|^r]\right]^{\frac{1}{r}}. \tag{1}$$

when r is taken as 1, sim is the Hamming distance of two attributes, and when r is taken as 2, sim is the Euclidean distance. The material compositions corresponding to the top three cases retrieved from the knowledge base is shown in the following Table 2.

After the material composition is determined, the key process parameters can be configured with reference to the process knowledge base. Then the system determines the new product process and its processing parameters in each sub-process according to the manufacturing standards, process route rules, and material deformation rule. The simulation module performs simulation analysis based on the generated process parameters. At the same time, the platform predicts the final mechanical properties of the product based on the chemical compositions, process parameters and the microstructures obtained by the simulation results. Figure 7

Table 2.   The retrieved similarity grades from the knowledge base.

Steel grade	C	Si	Mn	P	S
50CrV	0.46–0.54	0.17–0.37	0.5–0.8	≤0.02	≤0.015
40Cr4Mo3	0.35–0.45	0.1–0.35	0.5–0.8	≤0.035	≤0.035
1522H	0.17–0.25	0.15–0.35	1.0–1.5	≤0.03	≤0.05

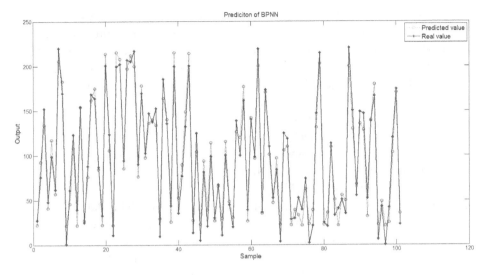

Fig. 7.   Prediction error of the YS.

Fig. 8.   GUIs of the developed platform.

illustrates the prediction results of the YS based on the BPNN model, which shows that the accuracy of the 10 error interval exceeds 95, and the accuracy of the 5 error interval is about 90.

Figure 8 shows some Graphical User Interface (GUI) of the developed product development platform actually used in steel mills. The left one is the process parameter matching GUI, and the right is the process parameter optimization GUI.

6. Conclusion

The traditional trial-and-error alloy product development mode is not only time-consuming and costly, but also lacks multi-disciplinary collaboration and the reuse of design knowledge. In this study an alloy material development platform is established, including the full-process simulation, design knowledge management and data-driven modeling. The full-process simulation module quantitatively characterizes the evolution of the microstructures in the full rolling process from different levels, based on the principle of physical metallurgy and advanced simulation techniques. The design knowledge management module divides the materials design into requirements analysis knowledge, composition design knowledge, process design knowledge, experimental knowledge, quality inspection knowledge and product improvement analysis knowledge. These knowledge units are organized and linked through ontology technology to form a graphical networked design knowledge model. Through knowledge matching and reuse, the knowledge model assists designers in decision-making and reasoning. The data-driven modeling module mines the mapping relationships between material properties, chemical composition, and process parameters from historical samples through big data technology, and determines key process parameters through multi-optimization technology. The proposed platform has been practically applied in a large steel plant. It indicates that the platform can effectively manage the material development process and design knowledge, and is helpful to engineers in making scientific decisions during the product development process, thus improving the development efficiency.

Acknowledgments

This research is supported by the National Key R&D Program of China under the Grant No. 2018YFB1701602, the National Natural Science Foundation of China under the Grant No. 61903031, and the Fundamental Research Funds for the Central Universities under the Grant No. FRF-TP-20-050A2.

References

1. Ma B., Wu Y., Hua M., Uusitalo J., DeArdo A. J., The development and characterization of ultra high GIGA-strength ferritic hot band steels, *Mater. Sci. Eng. A.* **796**:140048, 2020.
2. Zhang K., Peng K., Zhao S., Chen Z., A novel common and specific features extraction-based process monitoring approach with application to a hot rolling mill process, *Control Eng. Pract.* **104**:104628, 2020.
3. Zhang H., Wang H., Chen D., Zacharewicz G., A model-driven approach to multidisciplinary collaborative simulation for virtual product development, *Adv. Eng. Informatics.* **24**:167–179, 2010.
4. Tang S., Xiao T., Fan W., A collaborative platform for complex product design with an extended HLA integration architecture, *Simul. Model. Pract. Theory.* **18**:1048–1068, 2010.
5. Wang H., Zhang H., Using collaborative computing technologies to enable the sharing and integration of simulation services for product design, *Simul. Model. Pract. Theory.* **27**:47–64, 2012.
6. Wu D., Rosen D. W., Wang L., Schaefer D., Computer-aided design cloud-based design and manufacturing: A new paradigm in digital manufacturing and design innovation, *Comput. Des.* **59**:1–14, 2015.
7. Tao F., Sui F., Liu A., Qi Q., Zhang M., Song B., Guo Z., Lu S. C. Y., Nee A. Y. C., Digital twin-driven product design framework, *Int. J. Prod. Res.* **57**:3935, 2019.

8. Havard V., Jeanne B., Lacomblez M., Baudry D., Digital twin and virtual reality: A co-simulation environment for design and assessment of industrial workstations, *Prod. Manuf. Res.* **7**:472–489, 2019.

9. Wang X., Li F., Yang Q., He A., FEM analysis for residual stress prediction in hot rolled steel strip during the run-out table cooling, *Appl. Math. Model.* **37**:586–609, 2013.

10. Nalawade R. S., Puranik A. J., Balachandran G., Mahadik K. N., Balasubramanian V., Simulation of hot rolling deformation at intermediate passes and its industrial validity, *Int. J. Mech. Sci.* **77**:8–16, 2013.

11. Dai, S., Kang, Y., Zhu, G., Zheng, X., Wen, Y., Numerical simulation of air purging conditions during steel sheet temper rolling process, *Int. J. Mod. Simulat. Sci. Comput.* **8**(1):1750007, 2017.

12. Saal J. E., Kirklin S., Aykol M., Meredig B., Wolverton C., Materials design and discovery with high-throughput density functional theory: The open quantum materials database (OQMD), *JOM* **2013**:1501–1509, 2013.

13. Yang X., Wang Z., Zhao X., Song J., Zhang M., Liu H., MatCloud: A high-throughput computational infrastructure for integrated management of materials simulation, data and resources, *Comput. Mater. Sci.* **146**:319–333, 2018.

14. Chen J., Chen K., Liu R., Liang M., Analytical modeling of oxide thickness variation of metals under high temperature solid-particle erosion, *Int. J. Mod. Simulat. Sci. Comput.* **5**(3):1450002, 2014.

15. Lu S., Zhou Q., Ouyang Y., Guo Y., Li Q., Wang J., Accelerated discovery of stable lead-free hybrid organic–inorganic perovskites via machine learning, *Nat. Commun.* **9**:1–8, 2018.

16. Liu Y., Zhao T., Ju W., Shi S., Shi S., Materials discovery and design using machine learning, *J. Mater.* **3**:159–177, 2017.

17. Mohanty I., Sarkar S., Jha B., Das S., Kumar R., Online mechanical property prediction system for hot rolled if steel, *Ironmak. Steelmak.* **41**:618–627, 2014.

18. Paul S., Bhattacharjee S., Modeling and computation by artificial neural network of fracture toughness of low alloy steel to study the effect of alloy composition, *Int. J. Mod. Simulat. Sci. Comput.* **9**(6):1850051, 2018.

19. Bui T. Q., Tran A. V., Shah A. A., Improved knowledge-based neural network (KBNN) model for predicting spring-back angles in metal sheet bending, *Int. J. Mod. Simulat. Sci. Comput.* **5**(2):1350026, 2014.

20. Peng G., Wang H., Zhang H., Huang K., A hypernetwork-based approach to collaborative retrieval and reasoning of engineering design knowledge, *Adv. Eng. Informatics.* **42**:100956, 2019.

21. Peng G., Wang H., Zhang H., Zhao Y., Johnson A. L., A collaborative system for capturing and reusing in-context design knowledge with an integrated representation model, *Adv. Eng. Informatics.* **33**:314–329, 2017.

22. Zhang Y., Luo X., Zhao Y., Zhang H., An ontology-based knowledge framework for engineering material selection, *Adv. Eng. Informatics.* **29**:985–1000, 2015.

Chapter 13

A model validation method based on the orthogonal polynomial transformation and area metric

Huan Zhang, Wei Li, Ping Ma and Ming Yang*

Control and Simulation Center
Harbin Institute of Technology
Harbin, P. R. China
*myang_hitcsc@163.com

Abstract

Modeling and Simulation Technology has become an important means to study various complex systems with its extensive application. Thus, the accuracy of the simulation models becomes a critical problem and needs to be assessed by employing an appropriate model validation method. The simulation models often have multivariate dynamic responses with uncertainty, while most of the existing validation methods concentrate on the validation of the static responses. Hence, a new validation method is proposed in this paper to validate the dynamic responses of the simulation models over the time domain at a single validation site and multiple validation sites through introducing the discrete Chebyshev polynomials and area metric. For each time series, the orthogonal expansion coefficients are extracted primarily by representing the time series with the discrete orthogonal polynomials. Then, the area metric and the u-pooling metric are employed to validate all the uncorrelated coefficients at a single validation site and multiple validation sites, respectively, and the final validation result is obtained by summarizing the metric values. The feasibility and effectiveness of the proposed model validation method are illustrated through the example of the terminal guidance stage of the flight vehicle.

1. Introduction

As the third important means for recognizing and rebuilding the objective world, Modeling and Simulation (M&S) Technology provides means, tools, and technologies to understand, analyze, predict, and evaluate complex systems.[1,2] Therefore, M&S Technology has become the most important method for studying various complex systems and the focusing point gradually.[3,4] Since simulation is a model-based activity, the credibility of the simulation model has become a significant problem and needs to be assessed.[5,6]

Model validation is the process of determining the degree to which a model is an accurate representation of the real world from the perspective of the intended uses of the model.[7,8] Model validation can be viewed as two steps based on the work by the ASME Standards Committee on Verification and Validation in Computational

Solid Mechanics.[9] The first step is to quantitatively compare the computational and experimental results through a validation metric and the second step is to determine whether the model meets the acceptable agreement. An appropriate validation method is the basis of the model validation and various model validation methods have been investigated in recent years. To measure the deterministic computational and experimental results, the root mean squared error and the Minkowski distance are used which is easy to interpret physical meanings. Furthermore, considering the uncertainty of the computational and experimental results, various model validation methods can be classified into four main categories, namely, classical hypothesis testing, Bayes factor, frequentist's metric, and area metric.[10] Classical hypothesis testing and Bayes factor can only give the result whether the model is accurate enough to represent the actual system, not the specific value to quantify the accuracy of the model. Frequentist's metric can quantitatively validate the accuracy of the model by measuring the distance between the mean of the predictions and the estimated mean of the physical observations. However, frequentist's metric concentrates on the central tendencies and other summary statistics of the model predictions and the physical observations rather than the entire distribution.[11] Considering the distribution, the area metric proposed by Ferson *et al.*[12,13] measures the mismatch between the cumulative distribution of the model predictions and the empirical cumulative distribution of the physical observations to assess the accuracy of the model. As area metric only compares the marginal distributions of the model predictions and the physical observations, it is more suitable for the univariate or uncorrelated multivariate scenarios.

Due to the characteristics of complex composition relationship, model complexity, unstructured output, complex interaction relationships among subsystems, etc., the simulation models of the complex simulation systems generally have dynamic responses which may be multivariate, correlated, and uncertain. Time-dependent models need to be validated in the input space and the time domain, which makes the validation of the models more challenging. The aforementioned model validation methods are mainly used for static data and cannot be applied to validate dynamic responses directly. Therefore, dynamic model validation technology needs to be utilized to assess the accuracy of the simulation models of complex simulation systems. Dynamic model validation methods are sparse and several methods have been studied in recent years. The wavelet-based model validation method[14,15] was developed to objectively assess the validity of the computational model with dynamic output through extracting the wavelet coefficients and performing the statistical test in the time/frequency domain. Laili *et al.*[16] performed the pattern-based metric based on an overall perspective and this metric also applies to the inconsistent size of the reference data and that of the simulation results or the insufficient reference data for a specific input configuration. For validating dynamic models at multiple validation sites, Wang *et al.*[17] proposed the area-based validation metric that combined the truncated Karhunen–Loève expansion, probability integral transform (PIT), and area metric to validate the dynamic model over both the time domain and the model input space at multiple validation sites. Xi *et al.*[18] extended the *u*-pooling metric for dynamic responses and enhanced the computational efficiency of the proposed metric by transforming the dynamic correlation responses into a few uncorrelated principal components using principal component analysis (PCA). Considering multivariate correlation and uncertainty quantification and propagation, the Bayesian confidence-based validation metric and the enhanced Bayesian model validation method proposed by Zhan *et al.*[19,20] utilized the probabilistic PCA to extract critical features and then quantitatively assess the quality of the multivariate dynamic model by using Bayesian interval hypothesis testing. The aforementioned feature-based model validation methods have several disadvantages, such as the ambiguous physical meaning of the time-independent

Table 1.   Comparison of several dynamic model validation methods. In the second column, √ and × denotes whether the model validation method can validate the responses under uncertainty or not, as does the third column. In the fourth column, ○ that the model validation method can assess the accuracy of the simulation models at one single validation site and similarly, ⊙ denotes at one single validation site and multiple validation sites.

Model validation method name	Uncertainty	Feature-based	Validation site	Validation result	Time/frequency domain
WANOVA validation method	×	√	○	Qualitative	Time/frequency domain
Wavelet spectral analysis-based model validation method	×	√	○	Qualitative	Time/frequency domain
Pattern-based metric	√	√	○	Quantitative	Time domain
Area-based validation metric	√	√	⊙	Quantitative	Time domain
Validation metric based on PCA and shape deviation	√	√	○	Quantitative	Time domain
Bayesian confidence-based validation metric	√	√	○	Quantitative	Time domain
An enhanced Bayesian-based model validation method	√	√	○	Quantitative	Time domain
Instantaneous reliability metric	√	×	⊙	Quantitative	Time domain
First-passage reliability metric	√	×	⊙	Quantitative	Time domain
Accumulated reliability metric	√	×	⊙	Quantitative	Time domain

features which makes the meaning of the metric unexplainable, only providing an overall assessment, etc. In order to overcome these drawbacks, instantaneous reliability, first-passage reliability, and accumulated reliability directly working in the time domain are proposed by Ao et al.[21] and have clear physical and probability interpretations. All of the dynamic model validation methods discussed above are summarized in Table 1.

In summary, assessing the accuracy of the dynamic models faces the challenges in extracting features with the definite physical meaning, validating at both a single validation site and multiple validation sites, etc. Considering the uncertainty and the aforementioned challenges, a new model validation method utilizing the discrete orthogonal polynomials and area metric is developed to validate the dynamic responses of the simulation models in this paper. The remainder of this paper is organized as follows. Section 2 presents the detailed content of the model validation method based on the discrete orthogonal polynomials and area metric. In Sec. 3, the usage and the effectiveness of the validation method are illustrated by an example of the terminal guidance stage of the flight vehicle. Section 4 is the summary and conclusions of the paper.

2. Validation Method Based on Orthogonal Polynomials and Area Metric

In this section, a new model validation method is proposed to assess the accuracy of the simulation models with time series responses. The technology background, including extracting coefficients through the discrete orthogonal polynomials, the area metric, and the u-pooling metric, is briefly introduced in Sec. 2.1 and the details of the proposed model validation method are described in Sec. 2.2.

2.1. *Technology background*

2.1.1. *Extract coefficients through the discrete orthogonal polynomials*

Suppose a time series $Y = \{y_i\}$ is the real value of the observations in time t_i with $i = 1, 2, \ldots, N$ and Y is not required to be linear or equidistant in time. $Y = \{y_i\}$ can be approximately represented by a polynomial $y(t)$ of degree K, which is a linear combination of $K + 1$ basis functions p_k

$$y(t) = \sum_{k=0}^{K} \omega_k p_k(t). \tag{1}$$

The basis functions p_k must have the following properties:

① They must have different ascending degrees $0, \ldots, K$.
② They must have a leading coefficient 1.

③ Each pair of p_i and p_j, $i \neq j$, $0 \leq i, j \leq K$, must be orthogonal with respect to the inner product, i.e.,

$$\langle p_i | p_j \rangle = \sum_{t=0}^{T} p_i(t) p_j(t) = 0. \tag{2}$$

According to the properties of the orthogonal polynomials, it is known that the orthogonal polynomials fulfill the following three-term recurrence relation:

$$\begin{aligned} p_{-1}(x) &= 0, \\ p_0(x) &= 1, \\ p_{k+1}(x) &= (x - a_k) p_k(x) - b_k p_{k-1}(x), \end{aligned} \tag{3}$$

where the coefficients $a_k = \frac{\langle n p_k | p_k \rangle}{\langle p_k | p_k \rangle}$ and $b_k = \frac{\langle p_k | p_k \rangle}{\langle p_{k-1} | p_{k-1} \rangle}$, n is the identity in the vector space.

The discrete Chebyshev polynomials, which is an example of the discrete orthogonal polynomials used for the approximation, fulfill the three-term recurrence relation with $a_k = \frac{N}{2}, b_k = \frac{k^2(N+1)^2 - k^4}{16k^2 - 4}$. Thus, the discrete Chebyshev polynomials with the degree up to 4 are

$$p_0(x) = 1,$$

$$p_1(x) = x - \frac{N}{2},$$

$$p_2(x) = x^2 - Nx + \frac{N^2 - N}{6},$$

$$p_3(x) = x^3 - \frac{3N}{2}x^2 + \frac{6N^2 - 3N + 2}{10}x - \frac{N^3 - 3N^2 + 2N}{20}, \tag{4}$$

$$p_4(x) = x^4 - 2Nx^3 + \frac{9N^2 - 3N + 5}{7}x^2 - \frac{2N^3 - 3N^2 + 5N}{7}x,$$

$$+ \frac{N^4 - 6N^3 + 11N^2 - 6N}{70}.$$

The orthogonal expansion of the approximating polynomial p is

$$p(t) = \sum_{k=1}^{K} \frac{\alpha_k}{|p_k|^2} p_k(t), \tag{5}$$

where the squared norm of p_k is $\|p_k\|^2 = \frac{(k!)^4}{(2k)!(2k+1)!} \prod_{i=-k}^{k} (T + i + 1)$, $k = 0, 1, \ldots, T$ and $\frac{\alpha_k}{\|p_k\|^2}$ is equal to w_k. Then, the approximation problem "find a polynomial p of degree K which minimizes $\sum_{i=0}^{N} (p(i) - y_i)^2$" can be solved using the orthogonal expansion with the basis polynomials p_k and $w_k = \frac{1}{\|p_k\|^2} \sum_{i=0}^{N} y(i) p_k(i)$. More details of this orthogonal polynomial approximation can be found in Refs. 22 and 23. w_k is called orthogonal expansion coefficients, which has the following properties:

① The coefficients are independent.[24,25]
② The orthogonal polynomials extract the multidimensional shape features of time
  series. The coefficients can represent the average, slope, curve, and other characteristics of time series.

The dynamic response of the simulation models can be represented by the discrete Chebyshev polynomials and different time series usually has different orthogonal expansion coefficients. Figure 1 shows an example of utilizing the discrete
Chebyshev polynomial to approximate the time series and the original time series
is the line of sight angle of the flight vehicle obtained from the terminal guidance
stage of flight vehicle simulation. In Fig. 1(a), the curves of the approximating
polynomial $p1$, $p2$, and $p3$ denote the approximated values obtained by fitting the
original data with the orthogonal polynomial of degree 0, 1, and 2, respectively,
and we notice that the original time series can be almost perfectly represented by
the orthogonal polynomial of degree 2. Meanwhile, Fig. 1(b) shows the orthogonal
basis polynomials of degrees 0, 1, and 2 approximating the original time series.
When the approximating orthogonal polynomials are used to represent the time
series, the approximation becomes more accurate with the increase of the degree of
the orthogonal polynomials in theory. Nevertheless, due to the increase of time and
the higher degree polynomials, the approximate value calculated by the discrete
polynomials can be larger, which results in the over-fitting phenomenon. Therefore,
one of the principles to choose the degree of the orthogonal polynomials is to avoid
the over-fitting phenomenon. Besides, the choice of the degree of the orthogonal
polynomials is also affected by several factors such as approximate accuracy, the
physical meaning of the time series and calculation efficiency, etc.

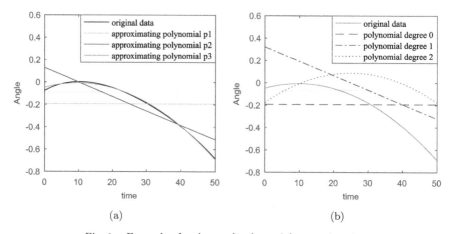

(a)   (b)

Fig. 1.   Example of orthogonal polynomial approximation.

2.1.2. *Area metric and u-pooling metric*

Area metric proposed by Ferson *et al.*[12,26] measures the area discrepancy of the predictions from a simulation model and relevant experiment data expressed as probability distributions. The model predictions are expressed by Y and the cumulative distribution function (CDF) of Y is F_Y. Similarly, R and F_R represent the experiment data and its empirical CDF (ECDF), respectively. At a single validation site, the disagreement between the model predictions and the experiment data is the area between F_Y and F_R, i.e.,

$$d(Y,R) = \int_{-\infty}^{+\infty} |F_Y - F_R| dx. \tag{6}$$

When the model predictions are collected at different validation sites, the experimental data are compared against different prediction distributions. Accordingly, the area metric cannot be directly used unless the predicted distribution happens to be identical at different validation sites. u-pooling metric proposed by Ferson *et al.*[12] could pool the overall disagreement between the model predictions and the experiment data at multiple validation sites. u-pooling metric transforms every experiment datum r_i to u-values which range on the unit interval [0,1] according to its corresponding prediction distribution F_{Y_m} at the same validation site, i.e.,

$$u_i = F_{Y_m}(r_i). \tag{7}$$

Through the PIT theorem[27] in statistics, we can know that the random variable $Y = F(X)$ has the distribution of $U(0,1)$ when the real-valued random variable X has the CDF $F(\cdot)$. Then, u_i will obey the uniform distribution on $[0,1]$ if r_i exactly has the same distribution of the model predictions. Therefore, the difference between the model predictions and the experiment data is the area between the ECDF $F(u)$ of u-values and the uniform distribution $U(0,1)$, i.e.,

$$d(U, F(u)) = \int_0^1 |u - F(u)| du. \tag{8}$$

The value of d ranges from 0 to 0.5. A smaller u-pooling metric value indicates less difference between the model predictions and the experiment data at the multiple validation sites, that is, the more accurate the computational model is over the prediction domain.

Area metric and u-pooling metric could detect any discrepancy between the model predictions and the experiment data despite having the same average, variance or both. Moreover, the area metric is applicable even when the predictions are sparse. However, the value of the area metric may be totally different due to different x-axis units although the shapes are the same, which makes the metric values in different scales not comparable. Besides, the area metric value is between 0 and ∞ and the u-pooling metric value is between 0 and 0.5. With these considerations, the following normalization transformation is utilized in this paper to obtain the consistency between the model predictions and the experiment data. For area metric d_a, the consistency result $c = \frac{s - d_a}{s}$, where $s = \max(\int_{x_{\min}}^{x_{\max}} F_Y dx, (x_{\max} - x_{\min}) - \int_{x_{\min}}^{x_{\max}} F_Y dx)$ and $x_{\max}$ and $x_{\min}$ are the maximum and minimum of the predictions and the experiment data. For the u-pooling metric d_u, the consistency result $c = 1 - 2 * d_u$. The consistency results range from 0 to 1, with 1 representing a perfect match between the simulation model and the actual system and 0 denoting the worst match. The area metric and the u-pooling metric only compare the difference of the marginal distributions of model predictions and physical observations. Hence, the area metric and the u-pooling metric can only deal with irrelevant responses and static model validation issues.

2.2. *Validation method for dynamic response*

In this section, we propose a model validation method is to assess the predictive capability of the simulation models with uncertainties and time series responses. The proposed validation method measures the difference between the dynamic responses of the simulation model and the physical observations over the time domain. Considering the uncertain parameters, two sets of time series responses are obtained from the simulation model and the actual physical system, respectively. The dynamic response of the simulation model is denoted as $Y = \{y_i\}$, $i = 1, 2, \ldots, M$, where M represents the number of sampling time nodes. Similarly, the physical observations are expressed as $R = \{r_i\}$, $i = 1, 2, \ldots, M$. Here, Y and R represent the time-dependent data obtained by running the system once.

At a single validation site, the consistency between the dynamic simulation responses and the physical observations can be calculated through the following validation method. Figure 2 shows the validation process of the proposed model validation method for a single validation site and the detailed steps are as follows:

Step 1. Dynamic simulation responses $Y_l = \{y_i\}_l$ $(l = 1, 2, \ldots, N_s)$ and physical observations $R_k = \{r_i\}_k$ $(k = 1, 2, \ldots, N_r)$ are obtained from the simulation model and the actual physical system at a specified validation site. N_s and N_r are the sampling number of the uncertain parameters.

Step 2. The orthogonal expansion coefficients of Y_l and R_k are extracted through employing the discrete Chebyshev polynomials to approximate each time series and denote as $\{a_{sl}\}_q$ and $\{a_{rk}\}_q$, $q = 1, \ldots, Q$, where Q means the number of the orthogonal expansion coefficients of the response. Then, the CDFs $F_{sq}(\alpha)$ of $\{a_{sl}\}_q$ and the ECDFs $F_{rq}(\alpha)$ of $\{a_{rk}\}_q$ are estimated.

Step 3. The area discrepancy between $F_{sq}(\alpha)$ and $F_{rq}(\alpha)$ is measured based on the area metric operator $d_q(S, R) = \int_{-\infty}^{+\infty} |F_{sq} - F_{rq}| d\alpha$. Next, $\{d_q\}$ are transformed into consistent results $\{c_q\}$ according to the aforementioned transformation.

Step 4. The model validation result C of the simulation model is obtained by summarizing the consistency results c_q, i.e., $C = \sum_{q=1}^{Q} w_q c_q$ where w_q is the weight of the coefficient and $\sum_{q=1}^{Q} w_q = 1$.

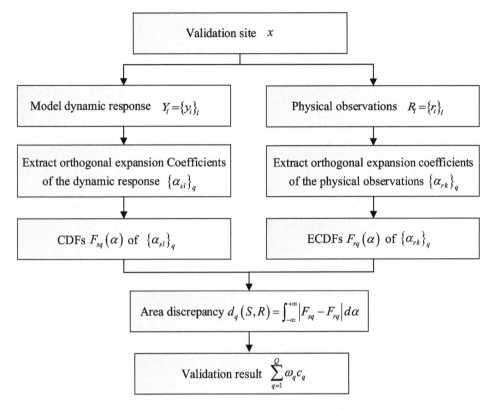

Fig. 2.   Flowchart of the proposed validation method for a single validation site.

As the above method cannot be used to validate the accuracy of the simulation model at multiple validation sites, a transformation-based area metric is proposed to pool all physical observations over the validation domain into a single measure and assess the overall accuracy of the simulation model. The dynamic simulation responses and experiment observations collected at different validation sites are denoted as $Y_l^j = \{y_i\}_l^j$ and $R_k^j = \{r_i\}_k^j$, $i = 1, 2, \ldots, M$, $j = 1, 2, \ldots, P$, $l = 1, 2, \ldots, N_s$, $k = 1, 2, \ldots, N_r$, where P is the number of the validation sites. The flowchart of the proposed model validation method for multiple validation sites is illustrated in Fig. 3. The detailed steps are as follows:

Step 1. Dynamic simulation responses $\{y_i\}_l^j$ and physical observations $\{r_i\}_k^j$ are collected from running the simulation model of the complex simulation system and physical experiments with the given input sites $\{x_1, x_2, \ldots, x_P\}$.

Step 2. The orthogonal expansion coefficients $\{\alpha_{sl}^j\}_q$ and $\{\alpha_{rk}^j\}_q$, $q = 1, \ldots, Q$, are also extracted by applying the discrete Chebyshev polynomials, which is the same as the above.

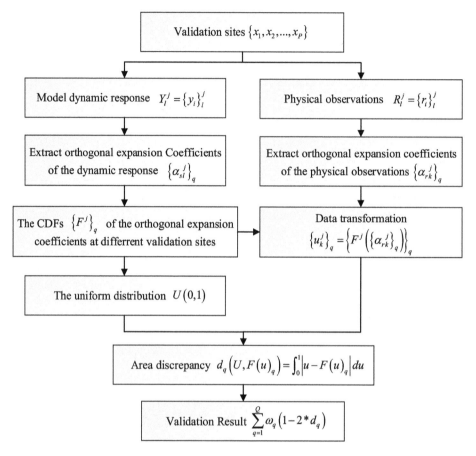

Fig. 3.   Flowchart of the proposed validation method for multiple validation sites.

Step 3. The CDFs $\{F^j(\alpha)\}_q$ of the orthogonal expansion coefficients $\{\alpha_{sl}^j\}_q$ are estimated and then $\{F^j(\alpha)\}_q$ of each coefficient are transformed into the uniform distribution $U(0,1)$ through the PIT. Meanwhile, the orthogonal expansion coefficients $\{\alpha_{rk}^j\}_q$ are transformed into a set of u-values by the corresponding CDFs $\{F^j(\cdot)\}_q$, i.e., $\{u_k^j\}_q = \{F^j(\{\alpha_{rk}^j\}_q)\}_q$.

Step 4. The area between the u-values $\{u_k^j\}_q$ and the uniform distribution $U(0,1)$, is measured by the u-pooling metric. That is, the discrepancy of each coefficient is $d_q(U, F(u)_q) = \int_0^1 |u - F(u)_q| du$, where the ECDF $F(u)_q$ is estimated based on $\{u_k^j\}_q$. After that, the consistency result c_q of each coefficient can be obtained and $c_q = 1 - 2 * d_q$.

Step 5. Finally, all of the consistency results $\{c_q\}$ are merged by the weighted comprehensive method and the final model validation result $C = \sum_{q=1}^Q \omega_q c_q$, where ω_q is the weight of each coefficient and $\sum_{q=1}^Q \omega_q = 1$.

The model validation result is between 0 and 1 and a larger validation result indicates the more accurate simulation model. Furthermore, it is worth noting that in order to ensure the validity and credibility of the validation result, the discrete Chebyshev polynomials employed to approximate the time series of the same dynamic response which obtained from the simulations and the corresponding experiments must be consistent. In other words, each of the time series responses has equal numbers of the extracted orthogonal expansion coefficients. The degree of the discrete Chebyshev polynomials utilized to approximate different responses may be different, so the degree of the discrete Chebyshev polynomials needs to be determined first. Additionally, both of the above validation methods are more applicable to the univariate or uncorrelated multivariate.

3. Example

In this section, an example of the terminal guidance stage of the flight vehicle[28] is used to demonstrate the effectiveness of the proposed model validation methods by comparing the validation results with those from the area-based validation metric. This terminal guidance process is often complicated with a variety of uncertain parameters and dynamic outputs. Figure 4 shows the geometry relationship of the relative motion between the fight vehicle and target.

Assume that the flight vehicle is flying without power and its heading is aligned with the target. Neglecting the rotation of the earth, the motion equation of the centroid of the flight vehicle with time as the independent variable is defined as follows:

$$\dot{v} = -\frac{D}{M} - g\sin\theta,$$

$$\dot{\theta} = \frac{L}{Mv} - \frac{g\cos\theta}{v},$$

$$\dot{h} = v\sin\theta,$$

$$\dot{d} = v\cos\theta,$$

(9)

where v and θ are the velocity and the velocity angle of the flight vehicle, respectively, h is the height of the flight vehicle, M denotes the mass of the flight vehicle and d represents the horizontal distance between the flight vehicle and the target. The gravity acceleration $g = g_0[R_0/(R_0 + h)]^2$, where $g_0 = 9.806665\,\text{m/s}^2$ and $R_0 = 6{,}371{,}000\,\text{m}$. $D = 0.5\rho v^2 S C_{DC} C_D(\text{Ma}, \alpha)$ and $L = 0.5\rho v^2 S C_{LC} C_L(\text{Ma}, \alpha)$ denote the drag and lift of the flight vehicle, respectively. C_D and C_L are the drag coefficient and lift coefficient, respectively. C_{DC} and C_{LC} represent the uncertain disturbance of C_D and C_L, respectively. α is the stack angle, $\text{Ma} = v/v_s$ is the Mach number, and S is the reference area. ρ and v_s are calculated according to the standard atmosphere environment.

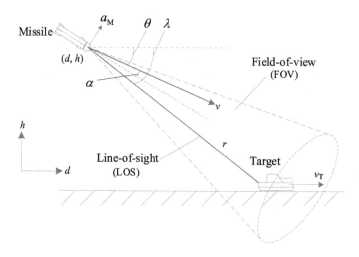

Fig. 4.   Planar missile–target engagement geometry.

Ignoring the acceleration of the target, the variance ratio of the line of sight angle is

$$\ddot{\lambda} = -\frac{2\dot{r}}{r}\dot{\lambda} - \frac{1}{r}a_{\mathrm{M}},$$

$$a_{\mathrm{M}} = \frac{D\sin(\lambda - \theta) + L\cos(\lambda - \theta)}{M} - g\cos\lambda. \tag{10}$$

Using v to represent $\ddot{\lambda}$, Eq. (10) can be rewritten into the equation of state form as

$$\dot{\mathbf{x}}(t) = \mathbf{A}x(t) + \mathbf{B}v(t),$$

$$\mathbf{x} = \begin{bmatrix} \lambda - \lambda^* \\ \dot{\lambda} \end{bmatrix}, \quad \mathbf{A} = \begin{bmatrix} 0 & 1 \\ 0 & 0 \end{bmatrix}, \quad \mathbf{B} = \begin{bmatrix} 0 \\ 1 \end{bmatrix}, \tag{11}$$

where t is the time variable, $\mathbf{x}$ is the state vector, the constant λ^* represents the expected falling angle, and v is the control variable which is defined as

$$v = -\frac{D\sin(\lambda - \theta) + L\cos(\lambda - \theta)}{Mr} + \frac{g\cos\lambda}{r} - \frac{2\dot{r}\dot{\lambda}}{r}. \tag{12}$$

From the above equations, the model inputs are initial line of sight angle and initial flight path angle and the model uncertain parameters are initial mass, atmosphere density, lift coefficient, drag coefficient, etc. The unit and the actual probability distribution of the uncertain parameters in the terminal guidance process of flight vehicle are shown in Table 2. For demonstrating the effectiveness of the proposed validation methods, the candidate simulation models which just have different initial mass are given in Table 3. Theoretically, the initial mass of the flight vehicle is 750 kg. Two sample sets, which contain 100 samples and 1000 samples, respectively, and are subsequently used as model or system parameters to generate simulation

Table 2. Uncertain parameters in the terminal guidance process of the flight vehicle.

Variable	Unit	Probability distribution
initial mass m	kg	750
Atmosphere density C_ρ	N/A	$N(0, 0.033)$
Lift coefficient C_D	N/A[a]	$N(0, 0.05)$
Drag coefficient C_L	N/A[a]	$N(0, 0.033)$

Table 3. Value of the initial mass of the candidate simulation models.

Test	Model ID	Initial mass
At a single validation site	1	750
	2	730
	3	710
At multiple validation sites	1	$N(750, 5)$
	2	$N(750, 40)$
	3	$N(750, 80)$

responses and observations, are obtained according to the probability distribution of the uncertain parameters.

Line of sight angle λ is one of the dynamic responses that we are interested in and the consistency between simulation responses and physical observations of the line of sight angle is validated in this example. At first, the degree of the discrete Chebyshev polynomials for the dynamic responses needs to be determined. The average, slope, and curvature of the line of sight angle all have specific physical meanings and the error of using 2-degree discrete Chebyshev polynomials to approximate the time series of line of sight angle is small. Therefore, line of sight angle λ can use 2-degree discrete Chebyshev polynomials to approximate.

At a single validation site, as shown in the upper part of Table 3, model 1 has a correct initial mass parameter which is the same as the theoretical value. Models 2 and 3 have the incorrect initial mass parameter. Therefore, model 1 should be the most accurate simulation model, followed by models 2 and 3 is the worst in theory. To assess the accuracy of these simulation models, 100 groups of physical observations and 1000 groups of simulation responses are collected from actual physical system and each simulation model, respectively, considering the uncertain parameters when the model inputs are $[0, 0]$. Then, each time series is represented by a linear combination of the corresponding degree discrete Chebyshev polynomials, respectively, and three orthogonal expansion coefficients can be obtained. The area discrepancies of three orthogonal expansion coefficients for the line of sight angle λ are shown in Fig. 5 and their quantitative results are $[545.75, 1,192,274.38, 2,319,263,547.95]$, $[2298.39, 6,364,265.38, 5,847,431,599.39]$, and $[4551.26, 12,559,857.79, 11,401,297,573.40]$. Meanwhile, the aggregated

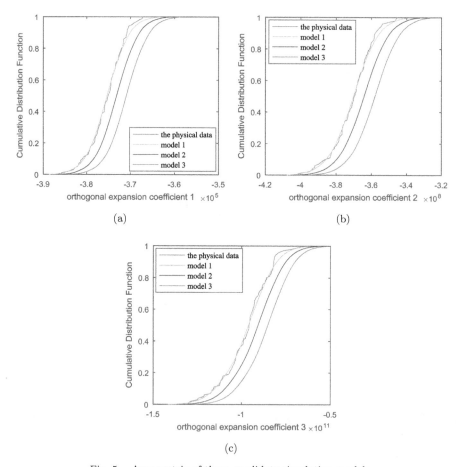

Fig. 5.   Area metric of three candidate simulation models.

validation results by the proposed method and the area-based validation metric are shown in the upper part of Table 3. The area-based validation metric results suggest that model 1 is the most accurate simulation model and model 3 is more accurate than model 2. However, the proposed validation method results suggest that the accuracy of the models is model 1 > model 2 > model 3 which conforms to the actual situation. The comparison between the area-based validation metric and the proposed validation method shows that the area-based validation metric is not suitable for assessing the simulation models at a single validation site and the proposed validation method can distinguish the candidate simulation models well.

Since the initial mass of the flight vehicle has the measurement deviation in practice, we assume that the initial mass with uncertainty follows the Gaussian distribution. As shown in the lower part of Table 3, all three candidate simulation models have the incorrect initial mass with the theoretical value of the initial mass being 750 kg, and similarly, model 1 should be the most accurate simulation model, followed by models 2 and 3 in theory. As the initial line of sight angle and the initial flight path angle are obtained in the early stage of the terminal guidance process, it can be inferred that they both follow Gaussian distribution $N(0,3)$ on the interval $[-9,9]$. To assess the simulation models in the validation domain, the simulation models are validated at 50 validation sites. Then, 100 groups of physical observations and 1000 groups of dynamic simulation responses are collected at each corresponding validation site in this case. 50 sets of each orthogonal expansion coefficient are obtained by employing the proposed validation method for multiple validation sites and each set contains 100 points transformed from observations and 1000 points transformed from the dynamic simulation responses. The comparisons between the ECDFs of the transformed observations and the standard uniform distribution $U(0,1)$ are demonstrated in Fig. 6, while the u-pooling metric values of three orthogonal expansion coefficients for the line of sight angle

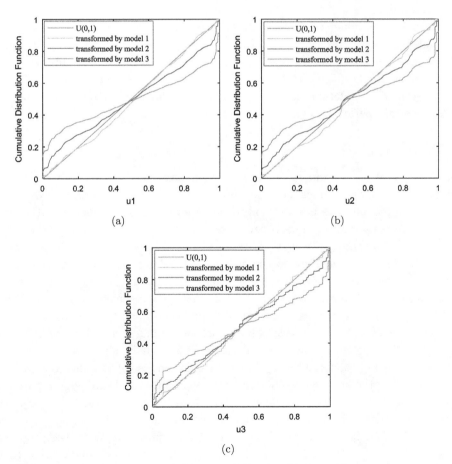

Fig. 6. u-pooling metric of three candidate models.

Table 4.   Model validation results by the proposed method and the area-based validation metric for different candidate simulation models.

Validation sites	Methods/models	Model 1	Model 2	Model 3
Single validation site	Proposed method	0.9636	0.8633	0.7485
	Area-based validation metric	0.9617	0.7138	0.7870
Multiple validation sites	Proposed method	0.9614	0.8799	0.7604
	Area-based validation metric	0.9794	0.9392	0.9211

λ are $[0.0222, 0.0201, 0.0156]$, $[0.0679, 0.0623, 0.0499]$, and $[0.1328, 0.1256, 0.1010]$, respectively. As shown in the lower part of Table 4, both the area-based validation metric results and the proposed validation method results indicate that the accuracy of the three simulation models is model 1 > model 2 > model 3, which is consistent with the theoretical situation. Additionally, the area-based validation metric results suggest that model 2 is slightly more accurate than model 3. Therefore, the proposed validation method can better differentiate the accuracy of the simulation models.

Besides, it is noted that the validation results at a single validation site and multiple validation sites are not equal to 1. The reason is that the sampling values of the residual uncertain parameters are not completely consistent and all the values in the range of the uncertain parameters cannot be exhausted. In summary, the proposed model validation method is effective for validating the simulation models with uncertain parameters and dynamic responses.

4. Conclusion

As the application of complex simulation systems more and more widely, the validity of the simulation models becomes more and more important and needs to be assessed. In this paper, a new method to validate the simulation model with uncertainty and time series responses is developed. The time series responses of the simulation model and the actual physical system can be obtained at each validation site. Then, the discrete Chebyshev polynomials are carried out to identify the significant orthogonal expansion coefficients of each time series. In this way, all time series are transformed into two sets of uncorrelated orthogonal expansion coefficients. Next, the area metric or the u-pooling metric is applied to quantify the consistency of the simulations and the observations for each orthogonal expansion coefficient at a single validation site or multiple validation sites. Finally, all consistency results are synthesized to calculate the final model validation result. The effectiveness and applicability of the proposed validation method are illustrated through the terminal guidance stage of the flight vehicle case. The validation results and the anticipated effect of the proposed validation method are consistent.

Compared with the existing dynamic model validation methods, the proposed model validation method has several advantages. The proposed validation method introduces the discrete Chebyshev polynomials to transform time series into several static uncorrelated coefficients which reduces calculation amount to a certain extent. It is worth mentioning that this transformation does not require that these time series must be equidistant in time and the physical meanings of the coefficients are unequivocal which makes the meaning of the validation results easy to express. In addition, the proposed validation method can assess the simulation models not only at a single validation site but also in the validation domain, which indicates the proposed method is capable of assessing the overall performance of the simulation model. Besides, the engineering example indicates that the proposed validation method can differentiate the simulation models with uncertain parameters well. In a word, the proposed validation method is suitable for validating the simulation models with uncertain and dynamic responses.

For future work, there are several issues that need to be explored such as how the simulation model with multiple correlated responses can be validated. Also, employing the validation method proposed in this paper to more engineering examples will be investigated in future work.

Acknowledgments

The research is supported by National Key R&D Program of China (Grant No. 2018YFB1701600).

References

1. Li B. *et al.*, Some focusing points in development of modern modeling and simulation technology, *J. Syst. Simul.* **16**(9):1871–1878, 2004.
2. Fujimoto R., Bock C., Chen W., Page E., Panchal J. H., *Research Challenges in Modeling and Simulation for Engineering Complex Systems*, Springer, Cham, 2017.
3. Zhang L., Liu Y., Laili Y., Zhang W., Model maturity towards modeling and simulation: Concepts, index system framework and evaluation method, *Int. J. Model. Simul. Sci. Comput.* **11**(3):2040001, 2020.
4. Wang R., Li X., Zhang Z., Ma H., Modeling and simulation methods of sea clutter based on measured data, *Int. J. Model. Simul. Sci. Comput.* **12**(1):2050068, 2021.
5. Sargent R. G., Verification and validation of simulation models, *Proc. Winter Simulation Conf.*, Washington, DC, USA, IEEE, pp. 124–137, 2007.
6. Wang Z., Zhang B., Yang M., Verification, validation and accreditation (VV&A) for simulation system: Current status and future, *J. Syst. Simul.* **11**(5):321–325, 1999.
7. AIAA, *Guide for the Verification and Validation of Computational Fluid Dynamics Simulations*, American Institute of Aeronautics and Astronautics, 1998, AIAA-G-077-1998.
8. ASME, *Guide for Verification and Validation in Computational Solid Mechanics*, American Society of Mechanical Engineers, 2006, ASME Standard V&V 10-2006.
9. ASME, Council on Codes and Standards, Board of Performance Test Codes: Committee on Verification and Validation in Computational Solid Mechanics, American Society of Mechanical Engineers, 2003.
10. Liu Y., Chen W., Arendt P., Huang H. Z., Toward a better understanding of model validation metrics, *J. Mech. Des.* **133**:071005, 2011.

11. Li L., Lu Z., A new method for model validation with multivariate output, *Reliab. Eng. Syst. Saf.* **169**:579–592, 2018.
12. Ferson S., Oberkampf W. L., Ginzburg L., Model validation and predictive capability for the thermal challenge problem, *Comput. Methods Appl. Mech. Eng.* **197**(29):2408–2430, 2007.
13. Li W., Lin S., Zhou Y., Ma P., Yang M., Research progress on credibility assessment of a complex simulation system (in Chinese), *Sci. Sin. Inf.* **48**:767–782, 2018.
14. Atkinson A. D., Hill R. R., Pignatiello Jr. J. J., Vining G. G., White E. D., Chicken E., Wavelet ANOVA approach to model validation, *Simul. Modelling Pract. Theory* **78**:18–27, 2017.
15. Jiang X., Mahadevan S., Wavelet spectrum analysis approach to model validation of dynamic systems, *Mech. Syst. Signal Process.* **25**(2):575–590, 2010.
16. Laili Y., Zhang L., Luo Y., Pattern-based validation metric for simulation models, *Sci. China Inf. Sci.* **63**(5):159203, 2020.
17. Wang Z., Fu Y., Yang R. J., Barbat S., Chen W., Validating dynamic engineering models under uncertainty, *J. Mech. Des.* **138**(11):111402, 2016.
18. Xi Z., Pan H., Fu Y., Yang R., Validation metric for dynamic system responses under uncertainty, *SAE Int. J. Mater. Manuf.* **8**(2):309–314, 2015.
19. Zhan Z. *et al.*, Research on validation metrics for multiple dynamic response comparison under uncertainty, *SAE Int. J. Mater. Manuf.* **8**(2):300–308, 2015.
20. Zhan Z., Fu Y., Yang R., Peng Y., An enhanced Bayesian based model validation method for dynamic systems, *J. Mech. Des.* **133**(4):041005, 2011.
21. Ao D., Hu Z., Mahadevan S., Dynamics model validation using time-domain metrics, *J Verif. Valid. Uncertain. Quantif.* **2**(1):011004, 2017.
22. Fuchs E., Gruber T., Nitschke J., Sick B., Online segmentation of time series based on polynomial least-squares approximation, *IEEE Trans. Pattern Anal. Mach. Intell.* **32**(12):2232–2245, 2010.
23. Fuchs E., Gruber T., Pree H., Sick B., Temporal data mining using shape space representations of time series, *Neurocomputing* **74**(1–3):379–393, 2010.
24. Liu H., Motoda H., *Feature Selection for Knowledge Discovery and Data Mining*, Kluwer Academic Publishers, Boston, 1998.
25. Liu H., Motoda H. (eds.), *Feature Extraction, Construction, and Selection:A Data Mining Perspective*, Kluwer Academic Publishers, Boston, 1998.
26. Ferson S., Oberkampf W. L., Validation of imprecise probability models, *Int. J. Reliab. Saf.* **3**(1–3):3–22, 2009.
27. Angus J. E., The probability integral transform and related results, *SIAM Rev.* **36**(4):652–654, 1994.
28. Li W., Lin S., Qian X., Ma P., Yang M., An evidence theory-based validation method for models with multivariate outputs and uncertainty, *Simulation* **97**(12):821–834, 2021.

Chapter 14

A mixed reality simulation evaluation method for complex system

Lijun Wang*, Yang Xue, Yi Lv, Yufen Wu, Dawei Wang and Shuhong Xu

Beijing Aircraft Technology Research Institute
Comac, Beijing 102211, P. R. China
*wanglijun1@comac.cc

Abstract

In order to analyze the proposed method, this paper takes the cockpit as the complex system, since the traditional cockpit design evaluation method can set up an actual engineering prototype. Although this method can realize the accurate evaluation of the internal structure layout, control devices, and interface display of the cockpit, it is difficult to make modifications once the production is completed, which is not suitable for multi-scheme comparison and rapid iteration in the early stage of civil aircraft design. In this regard, this paper establishes the civil aircraft cockpit physical environment and the corresponding virtual cockpit environment based on the virtual-real matching technology, then proposes a mixed reality simulation evaluation method so as to realize the real-time ergonomic evaluation of the digital human body followed by a real person. Experimental results show that this mixed reality simulation evaluation method can effectively improve the evaluation accuracy of cockpit design, ensure the efficiency of multi-scheme comparison and optimization iteration in the early stage of cockpit design.

1. Introduction

As one of the most complex systems, the civil aircraft cockpit is the central part of the plane, flight information, flight control, and stores detection devices of all kinds of an interactive interface, which has various complexes and compact space. It not only considers the realization of the function of the plane technology, but also the feasible pilot operation, efficiency, safety, and reliability. Once there is a mistake or omission in the design of the cockpit, it will seriously affect the development progress of the aircraft and increase the development cost. Modern civil aircraft cockpit design emphasizes the "people-oriented" design principle, requiring the crew to participate in the whole cockpit design to ensure that the design meets the needs and potential needs of the crew as much as possible.[1-3] The closest existing cockpit person-in-loop simulation systems are flight simulators and flight trainers, which are carried out in aircraft manufacturing to test phase, after the detailed design for the pilot training. If any design flaws are found, then the design changes can greatly extend the development cycle with a huge cost. Moreover, airworthiness has strict classification and manufacturing requirements. Generally, it uses simulation parts that meet airworthiness certification, and some parts even require real aircraft parts, which are expensive.[4] The aircraft design phase will manufacture a kind of engineering prototype for evaluation of cockpit design, hence the principle of engineering prototype with the flight simulator is roughly the same without high fidelity, it mainly sets the accurate simulation cockpit internal structure, layout, control device, interface display, and airborne systems based on the different stages of design. The complexity of engineering prototypes with different assessment requirements can be adjusted. For example, the Nanjing University of Aeronautics and Astronautics has developed an aircraft cockpit simulation system oriented to the ergonomic study of display interface so as to carry out the simulation of the whole flight process, modify and record the attributes of display interface elements in real time, and complete the ergonomic study of display interface.[5-7] However, it is difficult to modify the engineering prototype after completion, which is not suitable for the comparison of multiple schemes under rapid optimization and iteration in the initial design stage. The close combination of virtual reality technology and simulation has become a new idea for simulation evaluation of civil aircraft design, which has important practical significance for reducing physical modeling and experiments, identifying problems as early as possible and reducing rework. Different from pure system simulation, the simulation process and results are more intuitive and realistic. Different simulation models and data can be displayed which can be interactive more realistically with virtual reality, thus bringing the design evaluation to the early stage and deepening the understanding of simulation results.[8-11] The application of immersive virtual reality technology makes the human-in-loop design evaluation more convenient, then designers and pilots can enter the three-dimensional, full-size display of the virtual cockpit "immersive." Pure "empty", however, can display the interaction (e.g., through the data glove or force feedback device with a touch), but it is difficult to provide the pilot interaction with a sense of reality, not only the weak degree of simulation, and the virtual reality peripheral is easy for the feeling of the user "pull out" from the virtual cockpit, thus affecting the accuracy of the cockpit design review. Mixed reality cockpit design simulation is evaluated with the method of nakedness "fusion," which can not only make the cockpit design result "look like reality", but also "operate like a true cockpit," thus effectively enhancing the accuracy of the cockpit design review, ensuring early cockpit design scheme comparison and optimization of the efficiency of iteration. The flight simulator trainer for rotorcraft pilots based on mixed reality obtained the first virtual reality system certification from European EASA,[9-15] which also expands the ideas for the application of mixed reality technology in aircraft development.

2. Construction of Mixed Reality Cockpit Simulation Scene

The mixed reality simulation scene mainly includes three parts: virtual cockpit scene, physical simulation scene including seats, side rods, throttle pads, pedals, and typical operation buttons and flight logic. The schematic diagram is shown in Fig. 1.

The cockpit virtual scene is based on its engineering model, including indoor, and outdoor parts. As the model is lightweight,[16–21] it is imported into the rendering engine. In order to ensure that independent interactive behaviors can be realized, the parts that need interactive operation are rendered in real form according to the independent models. The rendering effect close to the real cockpit can be achieved mainly by defining the material of each part in the cockpit, adjusting the material strength and 3D attributes, as shown in Fig. 2.

The physical simulation scene adopts a modular design, mainly including seat module, side rod module, throttle platform module, rudder module, and button module. The position, size, and shape of each module are independent and can be adjusted and replaced according to the design requirements, thus achieving rapid iteration of the design scheme, as shown in Fig. 3.

Cockpit virtual scene and the physical simulation scenario space state synchronization can be realized by using the actual fusion technology updates, or any physical parts in the original position after the replacement can be automated in the digital simulation interface to update the corresponding simulation, physical motion state data can also be updated to the virtual parts through the embedded sensor module with recognition and detection of various physical motions.

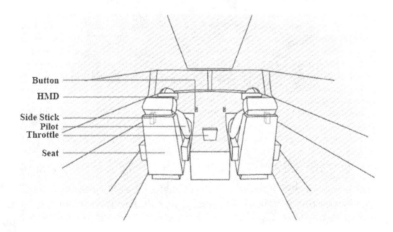

Fig. 1.   Mixed reality cockpit simulation architecture diagram.

Fig. 2.   Rendering schematic diagram of the cockpit virtual scene.

Fig. 3.   Schematic diagram of cockpit physical simulation scenario.

The logic of flight simulation is based on the actual takeoff, climbing, cruising, falling, landing, and other data, while the cockpit simulation scenario, instrument display, and the cockpit part such as visual, physical simulation, and dynamic interaction can be presented through the development of engine and the simulation of the cockpit flight dynamic visual display interface along with flight instrument interface, and real-time video streaming transmission. The human–machine interaction in virtual and real scenarios can be realized to achieve the objective of simulation evaluation of cockpit design.

3. Mixed Reality Simulation Evaluation Method

The cockpit is the space of pilot activities, hence the focus of the design evaluation is based on the cockpit design requirements and seaworthiness requirements, the mixed reality environment for cockpit efficiency assessment, namely, with the pilot digital dynamic 3D modeling for accurate space position, attitude, and action, it collects human posture and action data, clear pilot attitude, behavior and feeling of different subjective and objective parameters of cockpit optimization design quantitative relationship through action capture system.

Because there are a large number of complex situations and multiple factors in the cockpit evaluation process, and there are also a series of problems like the ambiguity of evaluation criteria and the difficulty to quantify qualitative indicators, in this paper, the relatively mature fuzzy comprehensive evaluation method is selected to fulfill the evaluation.[8–10] First, it determines what the evaluated object is. Second, it explores the set of factors and evaluation levels, establishes the evaluation matrix, and then determines the weight of each factor and their membership vector. Finally, the fuzzy evaluation matrix and the factor weight vector are operated and normalized so as to obtain the fuzzy comprehensive evaluation results. The implementation step is shown in Fig. 4.

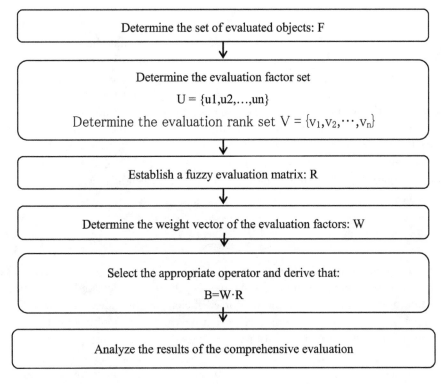

Fig. 4. Fuzzy comprehensive evaluation process.

(1) Determine the set of evaluated objects: F

The collection of evaluated objects refers to the evaluation content and objectives. For example, the collection of evaluated objects in the cockpit control panel can be determined according to the cockpit operation area, F = {top control panel, main dashboard, central console}.

The evaluation factor set U is the evaluation index, indicating from which aspects the evaluation describes the evaluation object. Evaluation grade V is the set of the evaluation results of the evaluated objects. For example, for the evaluated object F = {top control panel, main dashboard, central console}, can set U = {definition of character definition, character definition, character size, character location rationality}, V = {very bad (1), bad (2), medium (3), good (4), and excellent (5)}.

After establishing the fuzzy matrix R, determine the evaluation level set, and the membership of each evaluation factor object to each level fuzzy subset, then treat the evaluated object from each factor ui $(i = 1, 2, 3 \ldots, m)$ to obtain the fuzzy relation matrix:

$$R = \begin{bmatrix} r_{11} & r_{12} & \cdots & r_{1n} \\ r_{21} & r_{22} & \cdots & r_{2n} \\ \ddots & \ddots & \vdots & \ddots \\ r_{m1} & r_{m2} & \cdots & r_{mn} \end{bmatrix}.$$

In the above, $r_{ij}(i = 1, 2, \ldots, m, j = 1, 2 \ldots, n)$ indicates that the evaluated object is from the ith evaluation factor ui, and jth evaluation rating of v_j, membership of the fuzzy subset. When determining the affiliation relationship, experts and professionals related to the evaluation problem usually score the evaluation objects according to the evaluation level, and the statistical score results can obtain r_{ij}.

Determining the weight of the evaluation factor W is a very important indicator of the fuzzy comprehensive evaluation method. According to the importance of each evaluation factor, the fuzzy set W is composed of the weight allocation of the evaluation factor U, the ith evaluation factor u_i. The weight is w_i, $i = 1, 2, \ldots, m$, w_i satisfies

$$\begin{cases} w_i \leq 0 \\ \sum w_i = 1 \end{cases}.$$

A more common method to determine the weight of evaluation factors is the order relationship analysis method,[11] that is, the knowledge and experience of experts are used to determine the weight coefficient of the index, and the experts' judgment itself comes from long-term practice with strong objective basis. The specific steps of the sequence relationship method are shown in Fig. 5.

First, a series of evaluation factors $U = \{u_1, u_2, \ldots, u_n\}$ can sort u from high to importance $u_1 > u_2 > \cdots > u_n$, r_k represents the relative importance between neighboring factors, W_{k-1} takes part in W_k which represents the weights of k-1th

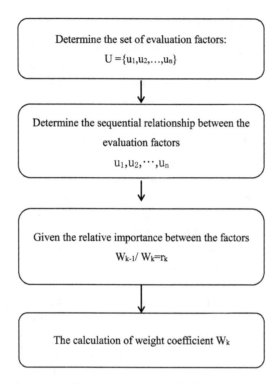

Fig. 5. Process of weight coefficient determination by the sequence relationship method.

and kth evaluation factors, $r_k = W_{K-1}/W_K$. With the help of experts, the weight coefficient W_k can be calculated.

Results B of the fuzzy comprehensive evaluation can be obtained by determining the appropriate weight operator W,

$$B = W \cdot R = (w_1, w_2, \ldots, w_m) \begin{bmatrix} r_{11} & r_{12} & \cdots & r_{1n} \\ r_{21} & r_{22} & \cdots & r_{2n} \\ \vdots & \vdots & \ddots & \vdots \\ r_{m1} & r_{m2} & \cdots & r_{mn} \end{bmatrix} = (b_1, b_2, \ldots, b_n).$$

Results $B = \{b_1, b_2, \ldots\}$. Analysis is performed for the $b_n\}$, $b_j (j = 1, 2, \ldots, n)$ as obtained from the j-column operation of the weight A and the evaluation matrix R, which represents the membership degree of the evaluated object to the V_j grade fuzzy subset as a whole.

To sum up, with the sequence relationship method and constructing a comprehensive evaluation model of cockpit human factor engineering based on engineering efficiency parameters through fuzzy mathematical theory, it can optimize the guidance in the early stage of cockpit design so as to realize the "design-analysis-and-improve" closed-loop iteration based on the mixed reality cockpit.

4. Simulation Evaluation Test

The test is mainly divided into three parts: Virtual and real scene fusion accuracy test, virtual and real fusion interaction accuracy test, and human factor simulation function test, which will complete the simulation evaluation of the accessibility and visibility of the cockpit simulation system.

4.1. Accuracy test of virtual and real scene fusion

It builds standard cubes, make marking points in the center, determines the position and angle information in the optical capture system as markers marking the real physical environment coordinates, and builds the same size virtual cube as the virtual scene, as shown in Fig. 6, the optical tracking system can reach 0 mm to meet the requirements of human factor engineering analysis accuracy. The relative location relationship between the devices in the real physical environment is consistent with the virtual cube and the virtual environment.

Taking handwheel as an example, the marker can be placed above the handwheel, overlapping the center and handwheel center rotation axis, with cube long side parallel and the handwheel arc tangent, the marker in the real physical scene and virtual scene relative position relationship is shown in Fig. 7, it can find out the virtual cube and handwheel position relationship in the consistent real cube and handwheel position relationship, therefore, the virtual scene and real physical scene device position relationship is completely consistent.

4.2. Accuracy test of virtual fusion interaction

Human factor engineering analysis not only requires the accurate match of the static position and size of the virtual scene and the real physical scene, but also the accurate match of the manipulation device in the cockpit, and the interaction between the human and the manipulation device. The control device takes the side rod as an example, and the maximum movement range of the side rod along the

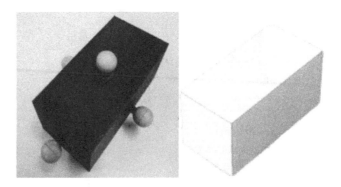

Fig. 6.   For equal size markers.

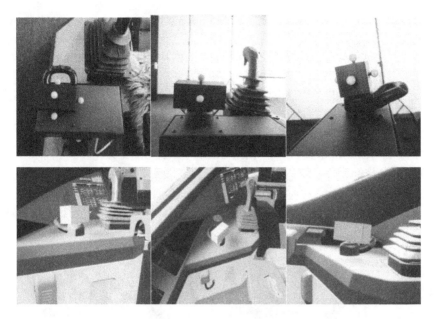

Fig. 7.　Accuracy test of virtual and real scene fusion.

Fig. 8.　Motion accurate matching test of the control device.

vertical is divided into five gears, which respectively record the position of the side rod moving in the virtual scene and the real physical scene. As shown in Fig. 8, the control dynamic position of the side bar in the virtual scene is consistent with the real physical scene.

The virtual scene can build a virtual human model according to the tester in real physical scene operation real physical device through an action capture device, the tester action can map the virtual scene, focus on the relative position relationship between hand and device, tester operation will select throttle and side rod, while handwheel is commonly used in manipulation device, virtual scene and real physical scene, as shown in Fig. 9, and can reach interaction match with manipulation device.

4.3. *Three human causes of simulation function test*

The two most direct types of simulation in the cockpit human simulation are visibility simulation and accessibility simulation. This paper analyzes visibility and accessibility by two methods: Desktop simulation and M R cockpit human-in-loop simulation.

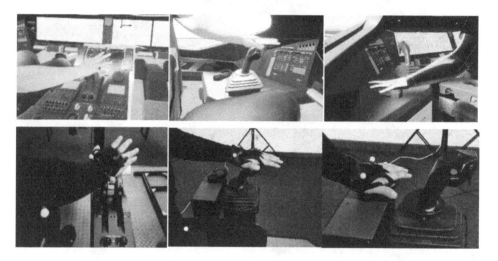

Fig. 9.   Exact match test of interaction with human and control device.

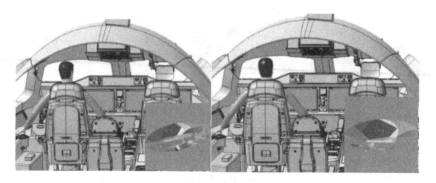

Fig. 10.   Schematic diagram of the desktop visibility simulation results.

The cockpit control panel can be used for visibility evaluation, since visibility simulation usually adopts the internal cut cone verification method with the principle of spatial geometry to generate the internal cut cone of physiological vision, which have different cone top angles. Depending on whether the visual accessibility

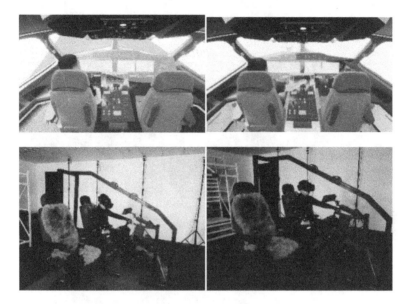

Fig. 11. Schematic diagram of the mixed reality visibility simulation results.

Table 1. Evaluation grade.

Poor	Bad	Medium	Good	Excellent
1	2	3	4	5

Table 2. Desktop simulation evaluation of cabin control panel.

	Assessment area factor of evaluation	Character meaning	Character clarity	Character dimension	Character position
1	Head Control Panel	4.75	4.75	4.5	4.5
2	Main Instrument Panel	4.75	4.5	4.25	4.5
3	Central Control Console	4.75	4.25	4.25	4.5

Table 3. Evaluation of mixed reality simulation of cabin control panel.

	Assessment area factor of evaluation	Character meaning	Character clarity	Character dimension	Character position
1	Head Control Panel	4.75	3.25	4	4.5
2	Main Instrument Panel	4.75	2.75	4	4.5
3	Central Control Console	4.75	3	4	4.5

of the internal cutting cone can contain the device object that the pilot will operate, the desktop simulation is shown in Fig. 10.

As shown in the ring simulation in Fig. 11, the transparent purple area is the virtual human cone range generated according to the real human field of vision, and the field of vision can be dynamically updated in real time with the movement of the real person.

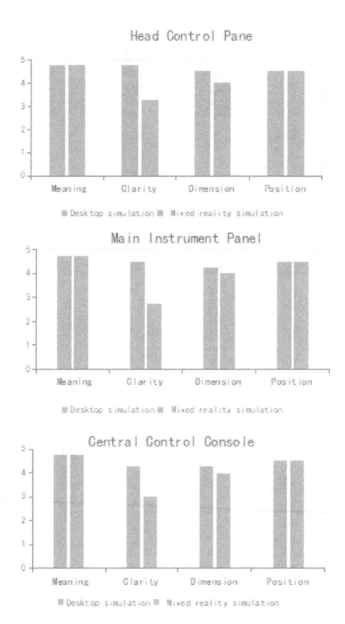

Fig. 12.   Evaluation of the visibility of the cockpit control panel.

The evaluation rating is shown in Table 1.

The results of visual desktop simulation and mixed reality simulation are shown in Tables 2 and 3, respectively,

The results are analyzed as shown in Fig. 12.

Desktop simulation and mixed reality simulation in character definition and character position in the two evaluation factors are basically the same, but in character definition and character size, mixed reality simulation is lower than desktop simulation score, it's vital to wear 3D stereo display equipment in the mixed reality simulation environment, clarity is affected by display equipment, and being a deviation from the actual driving environment, cockpit electronic display information clarity can be a mixed reality simulation, believing that with the improvement of display equipment performance and resolution, this problem can be solved.

The accessibility analysis of the cockpit human interface control devices with the desktop simulation and mixed reality simulation can operate the Head control panel, Central control console, Glareshield, Main instrument panel, Sidelever, Traction Bar, Steering handwheel to evaluate the accessibility of each main panel and control devices. Figure 13 shows the experimental comparison of the desktop simulation and MR cockpit simulation, and the transparent color part is the accessible area in the seat of the left hand and right hand in the flight standard sitting position.

The results of the accessibility simulation evaluation of the cockpit HCI control devices are shown in Table 4.

The results are analyzed as shown in Fig. 14.

In terms of the accessibility of cockpit control devices, pilots score different devices in different tasks. In general, for large manipulation devices, such as side rod, thrust rod, and turning wheel, the accessibility of mixed reality simulation and desktop simulation is not different, even slightly better than the desktop; and for small switch keys, such as various lamp switches, the accessibility of mixed reality is slightly worse than the desktop. According to the subjective description after the

Fig. 13. Schematic diagram of the accessibility simulation.

Table 4.   Accessibility simulation evaluation results of human–machine interface control devices in the cockpit.

	Assess Object Factor of Evaluation	Head Control Panel	Central Control Console	Glareshield	Main Instrument Panel	Side Lever	Traction Bar	Steering Hand Wheel
1	Desktop Simulation	4.5	4.5	4.8	4.5	4.25	4.75	4
2	Mixed Reality Simulation	4.25	4.5	4.55	4.25	4.75	4.75	4.6

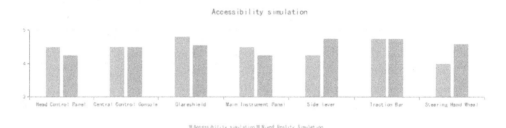

Fig. 14.   Results of the accessibility simulation evaluation of the human–machine interface control device in the cockpit.

pilot task, the virtual switch touch is not precise or the touch is a mismatch or difficult to touch, which is the main reason for the variability in scoring.

5. Conclusion

Based on virtual simulation scenario, real physical simulation scenario, flight logic, and flight instrument simulation environment, this paper proposes the mixed reality cockpit simulation evaluation method. It realizes the fusion accuracy of the virtual and real scene, the virtual and real fusion interaction accuracy test, and the human factor function test. The experimental results show that the cockpit components can be changed quickly in this system. Due to the simulation analysis of the visual accessibility, the method can be effectively introduced in loop evaluation, the subjective feelings of the pilot driving are fully considered early in the design so as to improve the comprehensiveness of the cockpit design assessment content, thus ensuring the early multi-scheme comparison and optimization and iteration efficiency of the cockpit design.

References

1. Shan F., *Cockpit Design Principles of Human Factors for Civil Transportation Aircraft*, Shanghai Jiao Tong University Press, 2013.
2. Fang W., Zheng L., He B., Wang Q., Automatic 3D model acquisition for unknown objects based on hybrid vision technology, *Int. J. Precis. Eng. Manuf.* 18(3):275–284, 2017.

3. Lima J. *et al.*, Markerless tracking system for augmented reality in the automotive industry, *Expert Syst. Appl.* **82**:100–114, 2017.
4. Makris S. *et al.*, Assembly support using AR technology based on automatic sequence generation, *CIRP Ann. Manuf. Technol.* **62**(1):9–12, 2013.
5. Jiang S., Ong S. K., Nee A. Y. C., An AR-based hybrid approach for facility layout planning and evaluation for existing shop floors, *Int. J. Adv. Manuf. Technol.* **72**(1):457– 473, 2012.
6. Ufkes A., Fiala M., Markerless augmented reality system for mobile devices, *Int. Conf. Computer and Robot Vision*, Sydney, Australia, pp. 226–233, 2013.
7. Engel J., Koltun V., Cremers D., Direct sparse odometry, *IEEE Trans. Pattern Anal. Mach. Intell.* **40**(3):611–625, 2018.
8. Rules for the Identification and Use of Flight Simulator Equipment CCAR-60, Civil Aviation Administration of PRC, 2005, P30.
9. Wei T., Youchao S., An aircraft cockpit simulation system for the study of display interface ergonomics, *Comput. Syst. Appl.* **25**(8):41–47, 2016.
10. Fang W., Zheng L., Distortion correction modeling method for zoom lens cameras with bundle adjustment, *J. Opt. Soc. Korea* **20**(1):140–149, 2016.
11. Durst P. J., Historical review of the development of verification and validation theories for simulation models, *Int. J. Model. Simul. Sci. Comput.* **8**(2): 1730001 (24 pages), 2017.
12. Kaminski-Morrow D., EASA approves virtual-reality simulation for R22 training, 27 April 2021, https://www.flightglobal.com/helicopters/easa-approves-virtual-reality-simulation-for-r22-training/143459.article.
13. Lyu W., Wu W., Laplacian-based 3D mesh simplification with feature preservation, *Int. J. Model. Simul. Sci. Comput.*, **10**(02): 1950002 (19 pages).
14. Wang X., Decoding pilot behavior consciousness of EEG, ECG, eye movements via an SVM machine learning model, *Int. J. Model. Simul. Sci. Comput.*, **11**(04): 2050028 (19 pages), 2020.
15. Silveira G., Malis E., Rives P., Efficient direct approach to visual SLAM, *IEEE Trans. Robot.* **24**(5):969–979, 2008.
16. Usenko V. *et al.*, Direct visual-inertial odometry with stereo cameras, *IEEE Int. Conf. Robotics and Automation*, Stockholm, Sweden, pp. 1885–1892, 2016.
17. Liu Y. *et al.*, Stereo visual-inertial odometry with multiple Kalman filters ensemble, *IEEE Trans. Ind. Electron.* **63**(10):6205–6216, 2016.
18. Gui J., Gu D., Direct Visual-inertial sensor fusion approach in multi-state constraint Kalman filter, *The 34th Chinese Control Conf.*, Hangzhou, China, pp. 6105–6110, 2015.
19. Rosten E., Drummond T., Machine learning for highspeed corner detection, *Eur. Conf. Computer Vision*, Graz, Austria, pp. 430–443, 2006.
20. Mustaniemi J. *et al.*, Inertial-based scale estimation for structure from motion on mobile devices, *IEEE Int. Conf. Intelligent Robots and Systems*, Vancouver, BC, Canada, pp. 4394–4401, 2017.
21. Tomazic S., Ckrjanc I., Fusion of visual odometry and inertial navigation system on smartphone, *Comput. Ind.* **74**:119–134, 2015.

Index

CPSIA information can be obtained
at www.ICGtesting.com
Printed in the USA
JSHW061951270223
37820JS00007B/9